SLEEP, DEATH, AND REBIRTH

MYSTICAL PRACTICES OF LURIANIC KABBALAH

New Perspectives in Post-Rabbinic Judaism

Series Editor
Shaul Magid (Dartmouth College)

SLEEP, DEATH, AND REBIRTH

MYSTICAL PRACTICES OF LURIANIC KABBALAH

ZVI ISH-SHALOM

BOSTON
2021

Library of Congress Cataloging-in-Publication Data

Names: Ish-Shalom, Zvi, author.
Title: Sleep, death, and rebirth: mystical practices of Lurianic Kabbalah / Zvi Ish-Shalom.
Description: Boston: Academic Studies Press, 2021. | Series: New perspectives in post-Rabbinic Judaism | Includes bibliographical references and index.
Identifiers: LCCN 2021011431 (print) | LCCN 2021011432 (ebook) | ISBN 9781644696286 (hardback) | ISBN 9781644696293 (adobe pdf) | ISBN 9781644696309 (epub)
Subjects: LCSH: Luria, Isaac ben Solomon, 1534-1572--Teachings. | Cabala--History. | Mysticism--Judaism. | Transmigration--Judaism. | Soul--Judaism. | Tsefat (Israel)--Religion--16th century.
Classification: LCC BM525.L835 I84 2021 (print) | LCC BM525.L835 (ebook) | DDC 296.1/6--dc23
LC record available at https://lccn.loc.gov/2021011431
LC ebook record available at https://lccn.loc.gov/2021011432

ISBN 9781644696286 (hardback)
ISBN 9781644696293 (adobe pdf)
ISBN 9781644696309 (epub)

Book design by Phi Business Solutions.
Cover design by Ivan Grave.

Published by Academic Studies Press.
1577 Beacon Street
Brookline, MA 02446, USA
press@academicstudiespress.com
www.academicstudiespress.com

For Shaul

Contents

Acknowledgments

I wish to thank Professors Eitan Fishbane and Ariel Mayse for their careful reading of the manuscript and thoughtful feedback and suggestions; the team at Academic Studies Press—especially Alessandra Anzani, Ilya Nikolaev, and Kira Nemirovsky—who, with professionalism and kindness, shepherded this project along and made the entire process smooth and enjoyable; Ben Notis and Stuart Allen, who helped prepare the book for submission, and for their astute editorial suggestions; Professors Arthur Green and Rachel Elior for their teaching, guidance, and care; and Rabbis Meshullem Fayish Segal-Lavi (of blessed memory) and Zalman Schachter-Shalomi (of blessed memory) for encouraging my study of Kabbalah and for seeing that which is yet to be born.

Finally, I wish to express my gratitude to Professor Shaul Magid, without whom this book would not have been written. When I met Shaul in the summer of 1995 at Camp Ramah, I was a twenty-year-old yeshiva dropout seeking to reconcile the depth of the tradition in which I was raised with the changing reality maps before me. I instantly recognized him as a brother, friend, mentor, and role model. Shaul introduced me to my first text in the Lurianic tradition—*Pitchei She'arim* by R. Yitzchak Isaac Chaver. We spent nearly every day that summer studying this text, singing *niggunim*, building things in the woodworking shop, and discussing all things hidden and revealed. With him, I could seamlessly shift between the *beis medrash* and the academy, between the *tischn* of Boro Park and the *satsangs* of Boulder. A scholar and musician extraordinaire, gifted with a fecund mind, a prolific hand, and a depth of heart, Shaul inspired and encouraged me to complete my doctorate and publish my research in the form of this book. This volume therefore represents the fruition of an academic and personal journey that began twenty-six years ago at Camp Ramah, where I sat with him in the woods beside a river, being eaten alive by mosquitoes to the point that blood was dripping down my face, deeply absorbed in the wondrous world of Lurianic Kabbalah. Shaul opened up the gates for me, invited me into the garden, and then nudged me back out to share its fruits with the world.

Preface

In *Sleep, Death, and Rebirth,* Zvi Ish-Shalom offers us an intricately researched, expansively theorized, and elegantly constructed study of Lurianic cosmology and its interface with the praxis of contemplative practice focusing on death and re-birth as spiritual exercises toward human perfection.

The Lurianic corpus, constructed by his students over the course of decades following the untimely death of Isaac Luria in 1572, is arguably the most complex exemplar of kabbalistic metaphysics in the history of Jewish thought. Basing itself on the zoharic corpus but moving considerably beyond it, the Lurianic system – if we can call it that – combines a panoply of metaphysical templates with detailed instructions for their application in the performance of mitzvot and specifically the act of prayer. Never before in Jewish thought has mystical metaphysics so intimately been coupled with physical praxis and contemplation such that the very gnosis it promises is embedded in acts performed, envisioned through the nexus of human effort and agency, and subsequent divine effluence.

In many ways Lurianism defies what we normally call "mysticism." The term, itself highly contested, is often thought to apply to a unitive experience of oneness, access to a transcendence that reaches beyond the fragmentary nature of our world. In fact, the Lurianic system is quite the opposite; the more one reaches beyond material existence, the more fragmentary, more detailed, and more complex the cosmos become. Depending on the recension of the Lurianic system one engages, it can be more cacophonous than harmonious. Contemplation is not achieved through the emptying of self to experience the utter simplicity of transcendence, but rather the entrance into a dizzying hall of cosmic mirrors. Infinitude is presented as infinite regress rather the quiescence of repose. The cosmos, in Luria's system, is a noisy and busy place. This may be one reason why many Hasidic masters whose focus was an experience of *devekut,* or boundedness with the divine, often did not focus on the intricacies of Luria's system but accepted its basic premises and utilized them for their own purposes. And yet Ish-Shalom argues that in fact, the non-dualism sought in many Hasidic texts is already at play dialectically in the Lurianic system itself, albeit concealed through the paradox of its opposite. This observation is not a *novum* but the way Ish-Shalom develops this through the praxis of death and re-birth sheds new light on that assumption, giving it a new series of refractions.

Ish-Shalom's book focuses on the relationship between cosmology and praxis, integral to the Lurianic schema, focusing specifically on two aspects of Lurianic contemplation, death and re-birth. This is all framed by the process of metempsychosis or reincarnation (*gilgul neshamot*) as a prism through which we can view the detailed daily fragmentation, and disembodiment, then reconstruction and embodiment, of the human soul by imaging and performing death as a spiritual praxis in the devotional life of the illuminati. Death, though, is not just imagined but is experienced through embodiment in the death of the body that is then enlivened through sex as an act one could liken to a kind of resurrection. Of the many contemplative practices available, Ish-Shalom focuses on two in particular, the bedtime Shma – the recitation of the Shma before sleep – and the supplicant prayers known as *tahanun*, recited immediately after the silent prayer morning and afternoon. *Tahanun* also known as *nefilat apayim* (falling on the face), is rendered kabbalistically as a performative enactment of death whereby the soul of the practitioner descends into a near-death experience only to rise up renewed.

Ish-Shalom brilliantly dissects these practices through the prism of their metaphysical foundations to explore what he calls the "integral monism" of the Lurianic system. That is, he argues that Lurianic Kabbala exhibits an "ontological dualism" and "epistemological non-dualism" simultaneously that permeates the entire system. The tension between dualism and non-dualism is for Ish-Shalom the theater of Lurianic practice. Ish-Shalom offers a new way of viewing the function and structure of the Lurianic system through the tension of dual and non-dual that is enhanced by his use of tantric and other practices that help contextualize the Lurianic corpus. Other scholars have utilized Hindu, Buddhist, and other systems and practices in studies in Jewish mysticism but Ish-Shalom does so with a practitioner's mentality, not in any apologetic sense, but rather with eyes to the way the embodiment of praxis brings to life the metaphysical insights therein.

In some way, the crux of this book is best expressed by Ish-Shalom in his conclusion:

> Here the most paradoxical and excessive expressions of Lurianic mysticism come to fruition; it is ultimately through the fragmentation of the

human soul and the death of the physical body that the cosmos can draw procreative life, while it is through the revivification of the human anatomy that the cosmos is erased of all hierarchical rank. This dialectical interplay reveals that Lurianic Kabbalah embraces a paradoxical mystical vision of total inclusivity that ultimately seeks to erase all hierarchical dualism while simultaneously upholding the reality of an ontological dualism. That is, distinct forms of manifested existence remain (ontological dualism) even while they are realized through the transformed gaze of the contemplative as equalized and neutralized of all hierarchical rank (hierarchical nondualism).

In some way there have been at least four genres of work being done in Lurianic Kabbalah. The first is the classical academic enterprise of deciphering, historicizing, and analyzing Luria's labyrinthine system and its aftermath. The second is the traditional exegetical enterprise of commentaries and annotated editions of Lurianic texts. The third comprises more popular studies meant for a non-academic audience of seekers and practitioners who want exposure to this cosmology as part of their spiritual toolkit. And the fourth comprises works of a comparative nature, looking at Lurianic teaching in relation to other traditions. Many studies combine two of these four genres. *Sleep, Death, and Rebirth* in some sense utilizes all four. The scholarship on primary and secondary literature is fully in conversation with the academic approach and a traditional reader will find Ish-Shalom's insights useful, if also provocative. Yet Ish-Shalom is attentive to the non-scholarly reader as well, and "translates" the intricate details in an accessible way.

Creating bridges between the purely academic (historical, contextual, analytic) and the more applied presentation of kabbalistic materials is no easy task. Ish-Shalom has been working in that area for some time, specifically in his *The Kadumah Experience: The Primordial Torah. Sleep, Death and Rebirth* is a more formally academic work but even here one senses Ish-Shalom's larger integrative project and his sensitivity to issues that lie outside the halls of academe.

Shaul Magid
Thetford, Vermont

Introduction

The doctrine of *gilgul* (the transmigration of the soul) has long been an important element of Jewish esoteric lore. From the very first kabbalistic literary expressions that appeared late in the twelfth century, the belief that human souls returned after death to inhabit new bodies was taken for granted. This idea developed in a number of different directions in the thirteenth and fourteenth centuries and, although kabbalists differed widely with regard to its details, it eventually became one of the central and most widely accepted doctrines of the Kabbalah.[1]

It was not until the sixteenth century, however, that this doctrine received its most articulate and comprehensive treatment. The esoteric school that formed in the Galilean town of Safed around the famous Kabbalah master Isaac Luria was particularly interested in the concept of metempsychosis, a topic that constitutes a major part of Lurianic teaching.[2] Luria not only significantly

---

1 Gershom Scholem, "Gilgul: The Transmigration of Souls," in *On the Mystical Shape of the Godhead* (New York: Schocken, 1991), 197–228 and Lawrence Fine, *Physician of the Soul, Healer of the Cosmos: Isaac Luria and His Kabbalistic Fellowship* (Stanford: Stanford University Press), 304–305.

2 For sources that deal with the history and development of the concept of *gilgul* in sixteenth-century Kabbalah, and in Lurianic Kabbalah in particular, see Scholem, "Gilgul," 228 and idem, *Origins of the Kabbalah*, 188–198, 457–460; idem, *Major Trends in Jewish Mysticism*, 3rd rev. ed. (Jerusalem: Schocken Publishing House, 1941), 278–284 (henceforth *MTJM*); Lawrence Fine, "The Art of Metoposcopy: A Study in Isaac Luria's Charismatic Knowledge," in *Essential Papers on Kabbalah*, ed. Lawrence Fine (New York: NYU Press, 1995), 331 and 337n51; idem, *Physician of the Soul*, 304–305; Rachel Elior, "The Doctrine of Transmigration in *Galya Raza*," in Fine, *Essential Papers on Kabbalah*, 243; Yehudah Liebes, "Perakim be-Milon Shere ha-Zohar" (PhD diss., Israeli Academy of Arts and Sciences, 1982), 291–327; R. J. Z. Werblowsky, *Joseph Karo: Lawyer and Mystic* (Oxford: Oxford University Press, 1962), 234–256; Shaul Magid, *From Metaphysics to Midrash: Myth, History, and the Interpretation of Scripture in Lurianic Kabbalah* (Bloomington: Indian University Press, 2008), 53–74; Alexander Altmann, "Eternality of Punishment: A Theological Controversy within the Amsterdam Rabbinate in the Thirties of the Seventeenth Century," in Fine, *Essential Papers on Kabbalah*, 270–287; Moshe Hallamish, *An Introduction to the Kabbalah* (Albany: State University of New York Press, 1999), 281–309; Pinhas Giller, *Reading the*

developed the theoretical aspects of the doctrine of *gilgul* by integrating it into his own intricate and innovative mythical system, but he also outlined practical meditative techniques to help shorten the duration of the transmigration process.

These specialized mystical techniques, which are to be performed when going to sleep at night and in the contemplative encounter with death, are designed to intentionally fragment the practitioner's soul into multiple parts. If performed properly, these practices not only grant the practitioner the possibility of total liberation in a single lifetime, but they also set the stage for the successful resurrection of the physical body, an event that marks the final stage in Luria's teleological goal of *tiqun*, the rectification of the cosmos.

The possibility of freeing oneself from reincarnation through intentionally fragmenting the soul has, to my knowledge, never been explored by scholars, despite the fact that it "appeals very strongly to the individual consciousness," as Scholem put it.[3] Since *gilgul* is a central component of the greater Lurianic project of cosmic redemption, the meditation practices designed to hasten this process are also essential to fully understand his metaphysical system.

In this book, I will make these provocative esoteric practices accessible to the public for the very first time. I will translate and explicate these meditations as they are articulated in the writings of Hayyim Vital, the foremost disciple and chief archivist of the oral teachings of Isaac Luria. In the process of unpacking the soul-splitting mechanics of these esoteric practices, I will also demonstrate how the soul's fragmentation in the process of transmigration and its ultimate reintegration in the reconstitution of the physical body at resurrection reveals a radical mystical view at the heart of Lurianic Kabbalah—one that sees the total dissolution of hierarchical division between body, soul, and cosmos.

This nonhierarchical view—itself a radical display of mystical monism—presents itself even more paradoxically in its simultaneous acknowledgment of the ontological reality of the distinct parts that make up the tapestry of existence. This integral expression of monism is marked by the inclusion of both

Zohar: The Sacred Text of the Kabbalah (New York: Oxford University Press 2001), 37–42; Dina Ripsman Elyon, *Reincarnation in Jewish Mysticism and Gnosticism* (Lewiston: Edwin Meller, 2003); Yigal Arikha, *Reincarnation: Reality That Exceeds All Imagination* [Hebrew] (Kefar Saba, Israel: Aryeh Nir, 2001); Rami Shekalim, *Torat ha-Nefesh ve-ha-Gilgul b'reshit ha-Kabbala* (Tel Aviv: Rubin Moss, 1998); Avraham Amos, *Be-gilgul Hozer: Gilgul in Kabbalah and Other Sources* [Hebrew] (Ashkelon: Pe'er Ha-Kodesh, 1997); Dov Ber Pinson, *Reincarnation and Judaism: The Journey of the Soul* (Northvale: Jason Aronson, 1999).
3 Scholem, *MTJM*, 283.

dual and nondual elements that fundamentally coexist.[4] Through this exploration, we will also come to appreciate how the metaphysical implications of
these practices challenge long-held assumptions in the academic field of Jewish
mysticism that view Lurianic Kabbalah as drawing sharp dualistic distinctions
between the physical and spiritual dimensions of reality.

Two sets of contemplative practices will be examined in this book: the first
derives from the *kavvanot* (intentional practices) for the *shema* prayer recited
at bedtime and the second from the morning prayer called *nefilat apayim*. The
remainder of this introduction will aim to provide the reader with an orientation to the various *problematica* associated with Lurianic texts and an overview
of the methodology I will be employing in this study. In order to properly sit-
uate this book within the broader context of the academic study of Kabbalah,
I will also provide a review of past and current scholarship on Lurianic
Kabbalah in general and on Lurianic conceptions of the soul and reincarnation
in particular. Finally, in order to establish the metaphysical background necessary to understand these esoteric practices, I will conclude this introduction
with an overview of Lurianic metaphysics and categories of soul, with the aim
of formulating a synopsis that is both academically rigorous as well as accessible
to the general reader.

The remainder of this book will demonstrate how each of these aforementioned *kavvanot* serve to consciously dismember the practitioner's soul
into dislocated parts in order to expedite the journey of rebirth. More poignantly, I will explore the implications of the soul's fragmentation and ultimate
re-integration in the reconstitution of the physical body at the resurrection of
the dead, emphasizing the paradoxical dialectic between dualism and nondualism implicit in Lurianic metaphysics and practice.

My central argument in this book is that Lurianic Kabbalah articulates a
radical form of mysticism that includes within its purview both an ontological dualism and an epistemological nondualism that fundamentally coexist.
I will demonstrate how this underlying metaphysical perspective of "integral
monism" expresses itself in contemplative practices that seek to erase the
boundaries separating life and death, body and soul, and human and cosmos.
The tendency towards the fragmentation of the soul on the one hand, and the

---

4 Mark S. G. Dyczkowski coins the term "integral monism" to describe the metaphysical view
   of Kashmiri Shaivism, which includes both dual and nondual features that simultaneously
   coexist. See his book *The Doctrine of Vibration: An Analysis of Doctrines and Practices of Kashmir Shaivism* (Albany: SUNY Press, 1987), 33–57. Also, see my comparative discussion of
   Kashmir Shaivism and Lurianic Kabbalah below on pages 64 and 144ff.

unification of the anatomical structure of the physical body on the other, will be explored in conjunction with the paradoxical interplay between these processes on the human plane and their parallel correspondences in the cosmic realms. Commensurate with the transgression of the limits of the physical body (through the intentional death of the practitioner) and the re-membering of the anatomical structure (in the resurrection of the dead), all hierarchical rank in the entire cosmos is simultaneously erased. This dialectical process of mystical deconstruction/reconstruction will be explored as the central underlying tension in Lurianic Kabbalah.

The specific contemplative exercises examined in this study provide us with an appropriate lens through which to examine this underlying tension between dualism and nondualism in Lurianic Kabbalah because they underscore in radical ways the tendency in Lurianic mysticism towards a dualistic metaphysics on the one hand, and a unitive vision of existence on the other. This dialectical tension has never been adequately addressed by scholars even though it represents the very heart of Lurianic mysticism. By examining how these two opposite poles of the spectrum express themselves in a specific set of practices, this study will further illuminate and clarify broader questions in our understanding of mysticism in general, and of Lurianic Kabbalah in particular.

PROBLEMATICA AND METHODOLOGY

The contemplative practices taught by Isaac Luria are performative expressions of what is widely recognized as the most intricate and complex cosmology in all of Jewish literature.[5] Indeed, Luria's architectonic framework is so metaphysically elaborate and technically daunting that only a few scholars have ventured beyond a restating of what Scholem outlined in his cursory synopsis of Lurianic metaphysics articulated in his classic work *Major Trends in Jewish Mysticism*.[6] It is curious that despite being universally recognized as one the most significant

---

5 See, e.g., Lawrence Fine's statement: "The cosmological myth Isaac Luria taught is without doubt the most elaborate such story in all of Jewish tradition" (*Physician of the Soul*, 124). Also see Elliot Wolfson's comment positioning Lurianic Kabbalah as "unquestionably the most complex body of Jewish mystical literature" (published on the back cover of Magid, *Metaphysics*).

6 Scholem wrote very little on Lurianic metaphysics beyond his seminal chapter on the topic in *MTJM*. For a review of scholars who have addressed substantive issues in the study of Lurianic Kabbalah, see my discussion below on page 14ff.

and consequential kabbalistic system of all time, still very little has been published detailing its metaphysical perspective or performative features.

When we consider the unique character of Lurianic literature, such omissions make sense. Lurianic texts—particularly those penned by Vital—are organized such that any single pericope lacks a complete or thorough exposition of any one topic. Partial segments of teachings are dispersed across a vast collection of texts and treatises in a manner that excludes the possibility of pointing to any single source as authoritative or exhaustive. This compositional format demands that the scholar take into account not only a vast amount of information on any given topic, but also that they make sense of the fragmentary nature of each textual variant, synthesizing each passage with an enormous associative network of interrelated texts, many of which seem at first blush to contradict each other.

This situation presents the student with several significant challenges. The first challenge is that any exposition of his metaphysical system cannot be limited to one particular text or passage. Not only is there not a single introductory text in all of Lurianic literature—nor is there any text that provides an overview of his system—there is no single treatment of *any* topic that is comprehensive or exhaustive. The student of this system is thus compelled to study *all* of it in order to make sense out of even *some* of it.

A second challenge is that any attempt at explicating a particular facet of Lurianic metaphysics requires an intertextual approach that ties together associative threads from diverse and scattered textual segments. In other words, developing a thesis by plucking statements out of context—and out of its intertextual matrix of associated textual references—can be misleading and unfaithful to the integrated purview of the Lurianic textual tradition. It also means that no particular feature of Luria's system can be properly understood if it is dissociated both from the totality of his metaphysical system as well as from the constellation of texts that interconnect to form the foundation of its literary expression.

A third challenge pertains to the self-enclosed nature of Lurianic metaphysical and performative symbolism and terminology. The way that Luria conceptualized and articulated his myths of cosmogenesis through the categories of withdrawal, rupture and reparation (*tzimtzum, shevirat ha-kelim* and *tiqun*) are unparalleled in the intellectual history of Judaism. This much has already been adequately demonstrated by Scholem's limited synopsis in *MTJM*. But the rub lies in Luria's unprecedented and unsurpassed stratification, classification, and categorization of the multidimensional cosmic dynamics that account for the textured fabric of both the ontological makeup of reality as well as its phenomenological and epistemological manifestations in the human soul, primarily through the performance of the *kavvanot* of prayer. These speculations constitute the majority of the literary formulations penned by Vital, and also represent a completely encapsulated metaphysical system in its own right, neither sprouting as an outcropping of earlier mystical ruminations on the one hand, nor synthesizing various strands of esoteric transmissions on the other.

If we take these three challenges to heart, we can better understand the primary unaccounted for oddity in the history of the academic study of Jewish mysticism: the lack of scholarly attention granted to Lurianic Kabbalah compared to other Jewish mystical schools. This makes sense when we appreciate the challenge of piecing together details of a completely self-enclosed metaphysical system. The scholar can thus be left with the sense that she cannot say *anything* about Lurianic metaphysics without saying *everything* about it, and it is difficult to say *everything* about it without getting lost in the seemingly endless minutiae that constitute the bulk of Vital's literary expressions.

To say it another way, the Lurianic literary corpus is a complex maze that is not conducive to explication or interpretation in any symbolic language other than its own. Therefore, when the scholar attempts to translate this system through the prism of another symbolic medium or methodology—such as that of the Western academic tradition—the nuances of this esoteric lore are easily lost or displaced from their conceptual ground. Conversely, when the details of its system *are* furnished and unpacked for the uninitiated reader, they can present themselves as a bewildering and unwieldy display of unrelated confabulations, irrelevant to the contemporary mindset, or to any conventional mindset whatsoever.

This dynamic is even more pronounced when we consider the contemplative and performative dimensions of Lurianic practice. While few scholars have grappled with Lurianic metaphysics in any detailed or comprehensive way, even fewer have ventured into an explication of the Lurianic practices of the *kavvanot* of prayer. In fact, only Menachem Kallus has attempted a comprehensive study of this facet of Lurianic lore in his doctoral dissertation dedicated to the topic.[7] However, only someone already thoroughly saturated in the particular

---

7 Menachem Kallus, "The Theurgy of Prayer in Lurianic Kabbalah" (PhD diss., Hebrew University, 2003). Kallus's dissertation, henceforth cited as "Theurgy," will be discussed in more detail below. Lawrence Fine also discusses the *kavvanot* of prayer in chapter seven of his important biographical study of Isaac Luria (see *Physician of the Soul*, 220–258), but

conceptual universe of Vital will understand Kallus's intertextual methodology, which is more an expression of that self-enclosed reality than it is of the hermeneutic tools of Western academia.

In light of these challenges, in this book I will aim to integrate the intertextual sensitivity of Kallus's approach while at the same time rendering the material more accessible and relevant for scholars and students of Kabbalah and of mysticism more broadly. To this end, the methodology I will employ in this study will seek to bridge the gap between the esoteric labyrinth of Lurianic texts on the one hand, and some of the current trends in the academic field of religious studies on the other.

This approach is perhaps best articulated as an hybridization of a classical model of phenomenological exegesis on the one hand, and an application of postmodern philosophical tools of interpretation on the other. The phenomenological aspect of this approach is reflected in my attempt to understand the esoteric meaning of Lurianic metaphysics and its contemplative practices through an in-depth analysis of primary texts, interpreted through its own intertextual and metaphysical frame of reference.

This phenomenological methodology is based on models of study articulated by scholars such as Chantepie de la Saussaye and William Brede Kristensen, who emphasized that religious thought is best understood by taking into account both the theoretical perspective and religious practices of the practitioners themselves. The essence of this approach is succinctly stated by Kristensen, who defines his methodology as investigating "what religion meant for them (i.e. the practitioners). It is *their* religion that we want to understand, and not our own" (emphasis his).[8] The fundamentals of this approach, although developed in different directions by figures such as Gerardus Van der Leeuw and Mircea Eliade, nevertheless remain consistent and very influential in the academic study of religion to this day.[9]

---

explicates them in considerably less detail than does Kallus. Fine's book will also be discussed at greater length below.

8 W. Brede Kristensen, *The Meaning of Religion: Lectures in the Phenomenology of Religion*, trans. John B. Carman (The Haugue: Martinus Nijhoff, 1960), 13. On Kristensen's methodology in general, see George James, *Interpreting Religion: The Phenomenological Approaches of Pierre Daniël Chantepie de la Saussaye, W. Brede Kristensen, and Gerardus van der Leeuw* (Washington: Catholic University of America Press, 1995), especially 98ff.

9 See, e.g., Gerardus Van der Leeuw, *Religion in Essence and Manifestation: A Study in Phenomenology*, 2 vols., trans. J. E. Turner (New York: Harper & Row, 1963); on Van de Leeuw in general, see Jacques Waardenburg, *Reflections on the Study of Religion: Including an Essay on the Work of Gerardus van der Leeuw* (The Hague: Mouton Publishers, 1978). While much has

This orientation is reflected in my attention to situating Lurianic contemplative practice within his larger metaphysical framework and in my inclusion of extensive cross-references (in the footnotes) to the multivalent associations implicit in the Lurianic literature. The heuristic objective of such extensive reference material is not exclusively academic; it is also designed to mirror in a contemporary work of scholarship a similar frame of mind that the subject of our investigation (i.e. Lurianic texts) itself assumes. Approaching it in this way allows the reader the opportunity to grasp more intuitively the interrelated constellations of concepts that inform and constitute the consciousness of the Lurianic practitioner.

This method can be best summed up as an embodied neo-narrative application of Wilhelm Dilthey and Max Weber's model of *Verstehen*, which (in my adaptation of this method) uses the structure, format, and writing style of the book itself as devices to help place the reader more squarely inside the shoes of the Lurianic practitioner.[10] This method, which I will term "embodied *Verstehen*," is reflected throughout this book in the anatomical structure of the document itself, in my extensive use of footnotes to highlight the intertextual matrix of the literature under investigation, and in my literary style. In this manner, I seek to embody in the text of this study the flesh and bones of Lurianic literature, even as I seek to simultaneously deconstruct the tradition through the prism of a postmodern hermeneutic.

This postmodern hermeneutic reflects a second facet of my methodological approach, which superimposes a deconstructive interpretive lens over the classical phenomenological model of textual analysis. That is to say that while attempting to appreciate Lurianic practice and metaphysics on its own terms, I am also simultaneously suggesting a radical revisioning, or resurrection, of

---

been written by and about Mircea Eliade, one of his most important formulations of methodology is to be found in Mircea Eliade, *The Sacred and the Profane: The Nature of Religion*, trans. Willard R. Trask (San Diego: Harcourt Brace Jovanovich, Inc., 1987).

10 The essential objective of the interpretive model of *Verstehen* is to provide a means for the scholar to enter more squarely into the conceptual and experiential context of the society, person, text, or phenomenon under investigation. On Wilhelm Dilthey's use of the method of *Verstehen*, see Michael Ermarth, *Wilhelm Dilthey: The Critique of Historical Reason* (Chicago: University of Chicago Press, 1978), 241–321 and Theodore Plantinga, *Historical Understanding in the Thought of Wilhelm Dilthey* (New York: Edwin Mellen Press, 1992) and especially 6–7 where he distinguishes between Dilthey's use of the term in his earlier and later writings and suggests a similarity with Eliade's methodological approach. On Weber's method of *Verstehen*, and how it differs from that of Dilthey, see Max Weber, *Collected Methodological Writings*, ed. Hans Henrik Bruun and Sam Whimster, trans. Hans Henrik Bruun (New York: Routledge, 2012), xxvii–xxviii.

the material for the contemporary, nontraditional, reader. To be sure, I am using the term "postmodern" in this context in its broadest sense: appreciation of difference, fragmentation, paradox, complexity, excess, the transgression of boundaries and limits, nonhierarchy, and the inclusion of opposites in literary and philosophical criticism.[11]

This orientation is reflected in my reading of Lurianic texts as expressions of a radical and excessive mysticism that seeks to fragment the self while simultaneously erasing the perception of hierarchical categories within the cosmic order of existence. This predilection towards pneumatic fracture as the means of achieving nondual teleological goals of the unity of self/cosmos reflects all of the central themes of paradoxical interpretation mentioned above that define the postmodern bias.

Moreover, my writing style also seeks to more subtly reflect two other categories of interpretation that have yet to become mainstream avenues of scholarly approaches to the study of Jewish mysticism. The first is reading Lurianic texts as literary fiction, a notion first articulated by Shaul Magid in his suggestion to expand the possibilities of reading kabbalistic texts beyond the traditional scholarly assumptions of myth and symbol. In this regard, Magid explains:

> I use fiction as opposed to myth because I suggest the former has a weaker connection to the real, although I argue below that fiction can indeed be viewed by the reader as *true*. This weaker connection allows a more skeptical modern reader—my sole interest here—the ability to stand inside the narrative and outside it simultaneously.[12]

In positing a method of reading Lurianic texts as fiction, Magid is responding to the particular situation in which contemporary, nontraditional, students of Kabbalah find themselves. While categories such as "myth" and "symbol" require more doctrinal investment on the part of the classical reader (that is, for the traditional kabbalist, these myths and symbols were *real* representations of ontological existence), orienting to these texts as fiction allows the reader to relate to the narrative not as ontologically accurate reflections of reality but

---

11 For a general overview of postmodernism and its application as a methodology in the academic study of religion, see Carl Olson, *Theory and Method in the Study of Religion* (Belmont: Thompson Wadsworth, 2003), 548–592.

12 Shaul Magid, "Lurianic Kabbalah and Its Literary Form: Myth, Fiction, History," *Prooftexts* 29, no. 3 (2009): 367.

as evocative expressions of sympathetic *truth* (to the degree that the reader is empathically stirred by the text).

This approach, which attempts to provide a more relevant method of orienting to Lurianic Kabbalah for the contemporary scholar and student, is reflected stylistically in this book in my use of language that positions the Lurianic divine personas as "actors" in the cosmic "theater," and relates to Lurianic myth as a "story" that we, the readers, also participate in through our engaged process of interpretation. My use of such language also gestures towards reading Lurianic literature as a mystical genre of "metafiction," explained by Shaul Magid in the following way:

> Proponents of metafiction argue that the separation between "fictional texts and their critical readings" is deconstructed to expose a more monistic and complex web intertwining the fictive and the real, language and metalanguage, and art and life. The reader becomes, by definition, part of the story that unfolds in light of the participatory act of reading and interpreting. The blurring of these boundaries, indicative of postmodern critiques of fiction, seems fundamental to Lurianic authors.[13]

Orienting to Lurianic texts as metafiction thus provides the contemporary scholar and interested reader with a more meaningful avenue of engagement with these obscure texts. In classic postmodern fashion, it is ultimately through the "participatory act of reading and interpreting" that the student embodies the unitive vision to which these very texts allude.

In this book I will argue that Lurianic mysticism, which seeks to deconstruct the soul (through the specialized *kavvanot* examined in this study) even as it seeks to reconstruct the body (through the act of resurrection also examined in this study), embraces the premise of such a metafictive "monistic and complex web" that interweaves what is ontologically real with what is epistemologically imagined (that is, between what is "real" and "fictive").

To take this "metafiction" approach even further, I suggest that this book, as a participant in the interpretive life of Lurianic Kabbalah, can *itself* be seen as a primary expression of this tradition. That is to say that by textually embodying some of the narrative features of Lurianic texts, this study serves as an extension of the paradoxical literary articulation of Lurianic mysticism. My suggestion of textual primacy thus further establishes the method of "embodied *Verstehen*"

---

13 Ibid.: 375–376.

even as it erases the boundaries between the body of the text and its reader. This dialectical method of embodied deconstruction is appropriate for the contemporary investigation of this material because its theoretical perspective is implicit in both Lurianic mysticism as well as in postmodern critical theory.

Thus, in reconstructing Lurianic literature in this manner, I am also embodying the ultimate nonhierarchical vision that this very mysticism claims. That is, reading this literature (which claims nonhierarchy as the ultimate nature of ontological existence) as "metafiction" (which claims a nonhierarchy of textual authority) allows for the more radical claim of textual *primacy* in a scholarly/literary work of this nature. Or, to say it more precisely, the project of resurrecting these esoteric texts (which embody monistic visions of nonhierarchy), entails the nullification of the secondary status of the scholar's work, and achieves the radical equalization of primary and secondary literature in the scholarly process of mystical interpretation.

Thus, this book may be engaged as a work of scholarship in the tradition of Western academia and/or as a literal/literary extension of the mystical tradition of Isaac Luria. Such a dialectical stance further embodies the principle of integral monism implied in Lurianic mysticism; a principle that simultaneously includes within its purview both dual and nondual truths. In this case, this mystical view is reflected in my subversion of traditional hierarchies of textual authority, while simultaneously allowing the hierarchical principles of traditional scholarship to maintain their structural validity.

The second category of embodied *Verstehen* reflected in my use of language is that of anatomy, particularly in its sexual expressions. By utilizing technical anatomical language I am attempting to embody in the act of writing the Lurianic claim of fundamental unity of body and soul. This mimics the Lurianic preference for articulating its metaphysical perspective in terms of anatomical structure and physiological dynamics. In this sense, language literally constructs the "body" of the text, a notion that underlies the project of Kabbalah in general, and Lurianic Kabbalah in particular.[14] Thus, the art of writing in this manner also acts as an interpretive gesture of "embodied *Verstehen*" that seeks to underscore the centrality of the body as a literal/literary trope in Lurianic Kabbalah.

By implementing a methodology that includes two seemingly opposing perspectives—classical phenomenological hermeneutics on the one hand and

---

14 On this topic, see Elliot Wolfson's study "The Body in the Text: A Kabbalistic Theory of Embodiment," *JQR* 95, no. 3 (2005): 479–500.

postmodern criticism on the other—I am (ironically) seeking to embody the very paradoxical dialectic that is displayed in Lurianic texts. That is to say that my use of a paradoxical methodology both in structural format and hermeneutical expression is an appropriate strategy to further establish a form of embodied *Verstehen* in the academic study of the very kind of paradoxical mysticism that Lurianic Kabbalah posits.

In addition to the orienting postures mentioned above, at several junctures in this book I will attempt to deepen the orienting posture of embodied *Verstehen* by comparing and contrasting these Lurianic teachings and practices with a select array of other mystical systems. This way, the contemporary student of mysticism and religion can make meaningful connections with related concepts and practices across a spectrum of traditions. My hope is that by integrating these comparative reflections into the main body of the text, the reader can glean deeper insights into both the mechanics of Lurianic mystical methodology and the structural principles of these related wisdom streams.

To be sure, since the priority of this study is a deeper understanding of specific theoretical issues in the study of mysticism, I will not be addressing questions of historical or cultural context as it pertains to Luria, Vital, or to their fellowship of practitioners in sixteenth-century Safed. Some of these important historical and contextual issues have already been explored by other scholars, and while further research in this direction remains a *desideratum*, it is not the focus of this study.[15]

Before we dive into the subject matter of this book, a final word on some of the technical difficulties involved in the explication of Lurianic literature, and a review of the sources that I will be utilizing in this study. Firstly, Luria

---

15 On the historical and cultural context of Lurianic Kabbalah in general, see Fine, *Physician of the Soul*, 19–55. The more nuanced suggestions by Magid (in his book *From Metaphysics to Midrash*) regarding the influence of the cultural context of sixteenth-century Safed on Lurianic biblical exegesis will be reviewed below. On the general demographic and economic history of this region in the sixteenth-century, see Abraham David, "Demographic Changes in the Safed Jewish Community in the Sixteenth Century," in *Occident and Orient: A Tribute to the Memory of A. Sheiber*, ed. R. Dan (Leiden: E. J. Brill, 1988); A. David, *To Come to the Land: Immigration and Settlement in Sixteenth-Century Eretz Yisrael*, trans. Dena Ordan (Tuscaloosa: University of Alabama Press, 1999); Abraham David, "Safed as a Center for the Re-Settlement of Anusim" [Hebrew], in *Proceedings for the Second International Congress for Research of the Sephardi and Oriental Heritage 1984*, ed. Abraham Haim (Jerusalem: Misgav Yerushalayim, 1991); Abraham David, "The Spanish Exiles in the Holy Land," in *Moreshet Sepharad: The Sephardi Legacy*, ed. Haim Beinart (Jerusalem: Magnes, 1992).

failed to organize or significantly edit what little he himself wrote.[16] Secondly, the bulk of Luria's legacy was communicated orally and recorded by his disciples, especially Hayyim Vital, the author of nearly all the major works that constitute the Lurianic corpus. That the task of editing and recording Luria's teachings was left to his students makes it difficult to distinguish authentic Lurianic teaching from the modifications of his disciples. Thirdly, even among the works of Luria's disciples there are thousands of manuscripts and dozens of printed editions, many of them contradicting each other on crucial doctrinal points.[17]

These difficulties aside, it is still possible to reconstruct a basic history of the texts I utilize in this study, so that we have a clearer sense of how they developed into their present form. During the last year of Luria's life in 1571, and immediately upon his death in 1572, Vital began to record his teacher's discourses. Shortly following Luria's death, Vital completed his most important and comprehensive work, *Sefer Etz Chaim* (henceforth referred to as *EH*). This work, which Vital tried to hide from the eyes of the other disciples, eventually made its way into the hands of his son, Shmuel, who, from 1649–1654, rearranged its contents into the *Shemona She'arim*. This work, which reorganized *Sefer Etz Chaim* topically, contains eight "gates": 1) *Sha'ar ha-Hakdamot (ShHk)*; 2) *Sha'ar Mamarei Rashbi (ShMR)*; 3) *Sha'ar Mamarei Razal (ShMRzl)*; 4) *Sha'ar ha-Pesukim (ShP)*; 5) *Sha'ar ha-Kavanot (ShK)*; 6) *Sha'ar ha-Mitzvot (ShM)*; 7) *Sha'ar Ruah ha-Kodesh (ShRhK)*; and 8) *Sha'ar ha-Gilgulim (ShG)*.

Each of these eight gates are themselves full-size books consisting of hundreds of pages each, with *Sha'ar ha-Kavvanot*, one of the main sources for this study, comprised of two complete volumes. Additional works redacted by Shmuel Vital that I have utilized in this book include *Pri Etz Chayyim (PEH)*, which explicates the performative details of the kavvanot and *Sefer ha-Hezynot*

---

16 The authentic writings of Luria that we have in our possession include a commentary on the *Sifra de-Tseniuta* [Book of Concealment] that constitutes one of the most esoteric sections of the Zohar; a number of other commentaries on various passages of the Zohar; and three mystical poems that correspond to the three Sabbath meals. See Yosef Avivi, *Binyan Ariel* (Jerusalem: Misgav Yerushalayim, 1987), 19; Scholem, *MTJM*, 254. Further passages possibly written by Luria himself are documented by Kallus in his dissertation, the most important of which I will analyze below. See page 96 note 6.

17 For a detailed history and analysis of the writings of Isaac Luria and his disciples, see Avivi's *Binyan Ariel*. For a more general survey, see Scholem, *MTJM*, 253–256. Also see Kallus, "Theurgy," 158–159 on the analysis of the various recensions of the *Shemonah She'arim* and in particular the early provenance of *Sefer Derashot* and *Sha'ar ha-Hakdamot*.

(*SHez*), which contains autobiographical material and descriptions of Hayyim Vital's dreams and visions. In addition to *Sha'ar ha-Kavvanot* and *Pri Etz Chayyim*, of particular relevance for this study is the eighth gate, *Sha'ar ha-Gilgulim*, in which Shmuel Vital collected all the statements concerning the topic of the soul in general and of reincarnation in particular that are found in the *Etz Chaim*.[18] Other, later compilations of Lurianic materials that I will cite in this study include *Olat Tamid*, *Talmud Eser Sefirot*, *Sefer Ta'amei ha-Mitzvot*, and *Sefer Likkutei Torah*.

Shmuel Vital also embarked on his own reformulation of the material found in *Sha'ar ha-Gilgulim*, attempting to express the variegated and complex traditions on the journey of the soul in a more comprehensive and organized way. This reformulation, called *Sefer ha-Gilgulim*, served as a companion text to *Sha'ar ha-Gilgulim*, often paralleling it in content while simultaneously differing from it in some minor respects.[19] These two compilations, along with the voluminous collections of writings organized in *Sefer Etz Chayyim* and the *Shemona She'arim*, serve as the main sources for Luria's oral teachings, and they are the main texts upon which I have based this study.

REVIEW OF SCHOLARSHIP

My study of Lurianic Kabbalah and the findings of this book build upon a significant foundation of research undertaken in the academic field of Jewish mysticism over the past eighty years. What follows is a brief assessment of the most important works of scholarship on Lurianic Kabbalah that provide the academic background and context for this book.

Gershom Scholem was the first modern scholar to present an overview of Lurianic metaphysics, and his summary of the key features of its complex system remains the benchmark of scholarship to this day. However, aside from his influential synopsis of Lurianic Kabbalah in *Major Trends in Jewish Mysticism* and several articles published in the 1940s, Scholem would not publish

---

18 Avivi, *Binyan Ariel*, 30. Avivi notes that two chapters, or *derushim*, in *Sha'ar ha-Gilgulim* are not found in *Sefer Etz Chaim*: *Derush* 11 and 29. See Avivi, ibid., 79. Also see Kallus, "Theurgy," 158–159.

19 On the differences between *Sefer ha-Gilgulim* and *Sha'ar ha-Gilgulim*, see Scholem, "Gilgul," 229: "The two extant recensions of Vital's voluminous notes, *Sefer ha-Gilgulim* and *Sha'ar ha-Gilgulim*, while diverging from one another in certain nuances and formulations, agree on all essential points."

anything of note on this material for the rest of his career.[20] Furthermore, Scholem's treatment of Lurianic Kabbalah remained relegated to the metaphysical and theoretical aspects of Luria's teachings; he never addressed the Lurianic contemplative practices or the interpersonal dynamics between Luria and his students.[21]

A student and contemporary of Scholem, Isaiah Tishby, published *Torat ha-Ra' ve-ha-Qelippah be-Kabbalat ha-Ari* (The Doctrine of Evil and the Shell in Lurianic Kabbalah) in 1942.[22] This slim volume deals with the concept of evil in Lurianic Kabbalah, and along with Scholem's work, it served as the only serious scholarly treatment of Lurianic Kabbalah for the following forty-five years.[23] This neglect of Lurianic Kabbalah in academic discourse has changed in

---

20 Scholem, *MTJM*, 44–286. See Lawrence Fine's discussion of Scholem in *Physician of the Soul*, 7. Menachum Kallus avers that Scholem would return to address and revise some of his positions regarding Luria towards the end of his career. Specifically, he argues that in his encyclopedic entries published in the *Encyclopedia Judaica* [and then collected and published together as the book *Kabbalah* (New York: Plume, 1995)], Scholem refines his view of a strictly theistic understanding of Luria's doctrine of tzimtzum. See Kallus, "Theurgy," 56–63.

21 See, e.g., Fine's statement in *Physician of the Soul*, 8: "Modern authors as well, including Scholem and Tishby ... devoted the vast preponderance of their energies to the study of mythical and theological ideas rather than to the actual rituals and practices of Kabbalah, including the great range of mystical experiences to which kabbalistic sources attest. Nor did they pay much attention either to the social communities in which Kabbalah came to life or the important personalities at the center of those communities." See also Scholem, "Gilgul." In terms of the limitations of Scholem's article, Fine has this to say about the matter: "In a lengthy essay devoted to the evolution and history of the notion of transmigration of souls (*gilgul*) in Jewish mystical tradition, including Lurianic Kabbalah, Scholem does not breath [sic] a word about the practical application of these ideas and beliefs. It is possible to read what Scholem has to say about Luria's conceptions of transmigration without learning anything whatsoever about the central role it played in the religious practices and experiential life of his fellowship" (*Physician of the Soul*, 8).

22 Isaiah Tishby, *Torat ha-Ra' ve-ha-Qelippah be-Kabbalat ha-Ari* [Hebrew] (Jerusalem: Akademon, 1942; rev. ed. Jerusalem: Magnes Press, 1982)

23 On the lack of serious scholarship in the decades following Tishby's work, see Fine, *Physician of the Soul*, 7. On the disproportionate attention paid to Lurianic Kabbalah in the history of modern scholarship compared to other expression of Jewish mysticism, see Yoram Jacobson, "The Aspect of the Feminine in 'Lurianic' Kabbalah," in *Gershom Scholem's "Major Trends in Jewish Mysticism" Fifty Years After: Proceedings of the Sixth International Conference on the History of Jewish Mysticism*, ed. Peter Schafer and Joseph Dan (Tubingen: Mohr, 1993) 239: "In spite of its profound influence on both Jewish thought and history, the Lurianic Kabbalah has not had much success on the stage of modern scholarly research: In comparison with all other fields of Kabbalah ... the negligence of the Lurianic teachings can easily be seen." This quote is also cited by Fine, *Physician of the Soul*, 365n11.

recent years, as more articles have been written that advance our understanding of various aspects of Luria's metaphysical teachings, including several doctoral dissertations and five full-length academic books devoted to the subject.[24]

---

24 The full-length academic books (not including Isaiah Tishby's book cited above in note 22) are those of Avivi, *Binyan Ariel* and idem., *Kabbalat ha-Ari*, 3 vols. (Machon Ben-Zvi: Jerusalem, 2008); Fine, *Physician of the Soul*; Magid, *Metaphysics*; and Devorah Bat-David Gamlieli, *Psychoanalysis and Kabbala: The Masculine and Feminine in Lurianic Kabbala* [Hebrew] (Los Angeles: Cherub, 2006). There are many published traditional or popular books on Lurianic Kabbalah that I am not including in this assessment. Among the many academic articles that explore Lurianic Kabbalah, most only deal with aspects of its metaphysics or cosmology. For exceptions to this general trend, see the references listed on page 36 note 97. For works that treat the specific topic of reincarnation (*gilgul*) in Lurianic Kabbalah see the references listed below, page 25 note 54. On Lurianic Kabbalah in general, the following is a selected list of articles (for a more complete list of references see the bibliography): Rachel Elior, "The Metaphorical Relation Between God and Man, and the Significance of the Visionary Reality in Lurianic Kabbalah" [Hebrew], *Mehqarei Yerushalayim* 10 (1992): 47–57; Lawrence Fine, "The Contemplative Practice of *Yehudim* in Lurianic Kabbalah," *Jewish Spirituality: From Biblical Times through the Middle Ages*, vol. 2, ed. Arthur Green (New York: Crossroad, 1987); Fine, "Maggidic Revelation in the Teachings of Isaac Luria," in *Mystics, Philosophers, and Politicians: Essays in Jewish Intellectual History in Honor of Alexander Altmann*, ed. Jehuda Reinharz and Daniel Swetschinski, with the collaboration of Kalman P. Bland. (Durham: Duke University Press, 1982); Lawrence. Fine, "The Study of Torah as a Theurgic Rite in Lurianic Kabbalah," in *Approaches to Judaism in Medieval Times*, vol. 3, ed. David R. Blumenthal (Atlanta: Atlanta Scholars Press, 1988); Moshe Idel, "'One from a Town, Two From a Clan': The Diffusion of Lurianic Kabbala and Sabbateanism: A Re-Examination." *Jewish History* 7, no. 2 (Fall 1993): 79–104; Yoram Jacobson, "The Feminine Aspect in Lurianic Kabbalah," in Schafer and Dan, *Gershom Scholem's "Major Trends in Jewish Mysticism" Fifty Years After*; Menachem Kallus, "Pneumatic Mystical Possession and the Eschatology of the Soul in Lurianic Kabbalah," in *Spirit Possession in Judaism*, ed. M. Goldish (Detroit: Wayne State University Press, 2003); Yehudah Liebes, "Myth vs. Symbol in the Zohar and in Lurianic Kabbalah," in Fine, *Essential Papers on Kabbalah*; Yehudah Liebes, "Sabbath Meal Songs Established by the Holy Ari" [Hebrew], *Molad* 4 (1972): 540–555; Yehuda Liebes, "'Two Young Roes of a Doe': The Secret Sermon of Isaac Luria Before His Death" [Hebrew], *Mehkarei Yerushalayim* 10 (1992): 113–169; Shaul Magid, "Conjugal Union, Mourning, and Talmud Torah in R. Isaac Luria's *Tikkun Hazot*," *Da'at* 36 (1996): xvii–xlv; Shaul Magid, "From Theosophy to Midrash: Lurianic Exegesis and the Garden of Eden," *Association for Jewish Studies Review* 22 (1997): 37–75; Shaul Magid, "Origin and the Overcoming of the Beginning: *Zimzum* as a Trope of Reading in Post-Lurianic Kabbalah," in *Beginning/Again: Toward a Hermeneutic of Jewish Texts*, ed. Shaul Magid and Aryeh Cohen (New York: Seven Bridges, 2002); Magid, "Lurianic Kabbalah and Its Literary Form": 362–397; Ronit Meroz, "Faithful Transmissions Versus Innovation: Luria and His Disciples," in Schafer and Dan, *Gershom Scholem's "Major Trends in Jewish Mysticism" Fifty Years*; R. Meroz, "Selections from Ephraim Penzieri: Luria's Sermon in Jerusalem and the Kavvanah on Eating Food" [Hebrew], *Mehqarei Yerushalayim* 10 (1992): 211–257; Mordechai Pachter, "Clarifying the Terms *Katnut* and *Gadlut* in the

The doctoral dissertations of note are those of Ronit Meroz and Menachem Kallus.[25] Meroz's study titled "Torat ha-Geulah be-Kabbalat ha-Ari" (The Teachings of Redemption in Lurianic Kabbalah) analyzes the entirety of the Lurianic corpus in order to ascertain the stages of textual development. She discriminates five stages in the development of the Lurianic writings that represent different trends in the evolution of Luria's metaphysical thought. In the course of her study, which is organized around the topic of "redemption" (*geulah*) in the Lurianic texts, she does address to some degree the question of the human soul. However, her examination of this theme is limited to the relational dynamic between Luria and his disciples as it pertained to Luria's wider universal vision for cosmic redemption. That is, she does not address the question of the ontological makeup of the soul itself or its teleological evolution in any detail.[26]

Menachem Kallus's doctoral study titled "The Theurgy of Prayer in Lurianic Kabbalah" attempts to detail a comprehensive theoretical and practical understanding of the Lurianic intentional practices (*kavannot*) associated with the prayer liturgy. Kallus is one of the few scholars to fundamentally challenge Scholem and Tishby's understanding of the basic metaphysical tenets of Lurianic Kabbalah, devoting nearly one hundred pages of his dissertation to

Kabbala of the Ari and a History of Its Understanding in Hasidism" [Hebrew], *Mekharei Yerushalayim* 10 (1992): 171–210; Gershom Scholem, "The Authentic Kabbalistic Writings of Isaac Luria" [Hebrew], *Qiryat Sefer* 19 (1943): 184–199; Gershom Scholem, "The Document on Solidarity of Luria's Disciples" [Hebrew], *Zion* 5 (1940): 133–160; Gershom Scholem, "Physiogonomy of the Face" [Hebrew], in *Sefer Assaf*, ed. Umberto Cassuto (Jerusalem: Mossad ha-Rav Kook, 1952–1953); Elliot Wolfson, "Weeping, Death, and Spiritual Ascent in Sixteenth Century Jewish Mysticism," in *Death, Ecstasy and Other Worldly Journeys*, ed. J. Collins and M. Fishbane (Albany: State University of New York Press, 1995).

25 Ronit Meroz, "Torat ha-Ge'eulah be-Kabbalat ha-Ari" [Hebrew] (PhD. diss., Hebrew University, 1988), and Menachem Kallus, "Theurgy." The only other PhD dissertations on Lurianic Kabbalah I am aware of are Lawrence Fine, "Techniques of Mystical Meditation for Achieving Prophecy and the Holy Spirit" (PhD diss., Brandeis University, 1976) and Don Bresslauer, "Orality and Literacy in Hayyim Vital's Lurianic Kabbalah" (PhD diss., New York University, 1999). There was also a DHL dissertation written on reincarnation in Lurianic Kabbalah. See Raza Leah Hovav-Machboob, "The Ari's Doctrine of Reincarnation" (DHL diss., The Jewish Theological Seminary of America, 1983).

26 See especially her section on the "fourth stage of messianism" (Meroz, "Torat ha-Geulah," 267–328). Meroz articulates a methodology of textual analysis in this dissertation that she would also apply in her later developmental studies of the Zohar. See ibid., 23–38 and her article, "Zoharic Narratives and their Adaptations," *Hispania Judaica Bulletin*, no. 3 (2000): 3–63.

critically deconstruct these two scholars understanding of the basic foundations of Lurianic cosmogony.[27]

Kallus's main criticism pertains to the way Scholem and Tishby understand the internal dynamics of the *tzimtzum* and *shevirah*, and how this "misunderstanding" consequently impacts the way they come to see the process of
tiqun, a big component of which (namely, the *kavannot* of prayer) they never
examined in their writings.[28] However, Kallus directs his main criticism at
Scholem's various formulations of the principle of the *deus absconditus* that he
first articulates in *MTJM*.[29] While Kallus acknowledges that certain aspects of
this approach were revised and refined by Scholem thirty years after the

---

27 On the widespread acceptance of Scholem and Tishby's presentation of Lurianic Kab-
    balah by subsequent scholars in the field, see Joseph Dan, *Kabbalah: A Very Short Intro-
    duction* (New York: Oxford University Press, 2006), 73: "The most important studies
    of Luria's teachings were presented by Gershom Scholem and Isaiah Tishby in 1941,
    and since then, while we have many books and articles dealing with particular problems
    and aspects of Luria's teachings, the main picture they drew is still dominant. Further
    studies may cast some doubts, but as of now presenting their studies is the best that we
    can do." Cf. Kallus, "Theurgy," 29–30, where he says that Scholem and Tishby are "the
    two scholars who have up until the present, continued to shape most of the underlying
    assumptions of researchers into Lurianic Kabbalah"; ibid., 33–34n30: "Scholem's influ-
    ence on the academic presentation of Lurianic Kabbalah, particularly with reference
    to the cosmic origins of evil in his Gnostic-dualist mythological account of Lurianic
    cosmogony is recognizable in the works of nearly every academic writer who offered a
    synopsis of Lurianic Kabbalah." For a list of examples in recent scholarship that demon-
    strate the Scholem-Tishby approach, see ibid., 34n30. Exceptions to this can be found
    in the works of Charles Mopsik [e.g., see his *Les grands textes de la Cabale: les rites qui
    font Dieu* (Lagrasse: Verdier, 1993)], where he criticizes Tishby (and by implication,
    Scholem) for ignoring the teleological dimension to Luria's understanding of free will
    in his presentation of the doctrine of evil, and in Jacobson's article, "The Aspect of
    the Feminine in Lurianic Kabbalah," which levels a more comprehensive criticism of
    Scholem and Tishby's position. My comments on the last two citations are derived from
    Kallus, "Theurgy," 34n30 and 40n79. Other works that challenge certain aspects of the
    Scholem-Tishby approach to Lurianic Kabbalah include Wolfson, "Weeping, Death, and
    Spiritual Ascent in Sixteenth Century Jewish Mysticism" and Liebes, "'Two Young Roes
    of a Doe'": 113–169.

28 *Tzimtzum*, meaning "contraction" or "withdrawal," refers to the process by which the infinite
    source (*ein sof*) withdraws into itself in order to form a vacuum within which creation can
    take place. *Shevirah* refers to the process by which the infinite light (*ohr ein sof*) that fills
    the vacuous space formed by *tzimtzum* shatters the vessels that were created to hold the
    light. *Tiqun* refers to the process through which the cosmic disarray caused by the *shevirah*
    is restored to balance. The metaphysical principles of *tzimtzum*, *shevirah*, and *tiqun* will be
    explained in detail below.

29 See Scholem, *MTJM*, 261 and 271

publication of *MTJM* in his entries to the *Encyclopedia Judaica,* the basic contours of his approach remained the same.[30]

The principle of *deus absconditus* posits that the roots of evil existed within *ein sof* (the infinite mystery) prior to the *tzimtzum* and that the process of *tzimtzum* and the subsequent *shevirah* served to separate out these roots of evil from *ein sof* and to externalize them (this is the "cathartic" expression of the *shevirah* averred by Scholem). This decidedly Gnostic-dualist-theistic model of Lurianic theory sees a strict division between the transcendent realm of *ein sof* and the created realm of the cosmos (which includes the personal God consisting of the *partzufim,* the divine "countenances" that will be explained in more detail below) that takes place within the vacated space of the *tehiru.* Kallus argues that while Tishby does acknowledge that there were other formulations for the reasons for the *shevirah* in Lurianic Kabbalah that would point to a panentheistic understanding rather than a theistic one, he nonetheless implicitly accepts Scholem's theistic approach.[31]

According to Kallus, Scholem and Tishby's preference for a dualistic-theistic approach is the result of a combination of "misinformation" regarding the details of the Lurianic understanding of the "void" (*reshimu*),[32] a lack of attention to certain sections of Vital's writings,[33] a mistaken conflation of the roots of judgment (*din*) with the roots of evil (*qelipah*),[34] and a profound misunderstanding of key Lurianic texts that point to a teleological, rather than a cathartic, interpretation of the *tzimtzum* and *shevirah.*[35]

In lieu of these criticisms, Kallus attempts to demonstrate the fundamentally panentheistic, nondual nature of Lurianic cosmogony (and theodicy) that recognizes the absolutely central role that *ein sof* continues to play in the theurgic processes of *tiqun* following the *tzimtzum* and *shevirah.* In particular, he is interested in how this underlying orientation informs the teleological thrust of the contemplative mechanisms of the *kavannot* of prayer. He does this primarily through rereading the very texts that Scholem uses to prove his theistic-dualistic thesis.[36]

30 See Kallus, "Theurgy," 45 and especially 39–40
31 Ibid., 43
32 Ibid., 37.
33 Ibid., 42–43.
34 Ibid., 77ff.
35 Ibid., 83–111.
36 See especially his comments on 112 concerning Lurianic theodicy: "It is decidedly non-theistic, but is rather, panentheistic and collaborative. It also provides a central role for

Kallus also includes an appendix in his dissertation in which he analyzes what he refers to as "the eschatology of the soul" in Lurianic Kabbalah,[37] which I will discuss in more detail later on in this study. As far as I know, this is the only scholarly treatment of this specific topic. However, Kallus approaches the issue primarily through an analysis of Vital's personal journey of transmigration, and only deals with the complex issues regarding eschatology in a superficial manner. In this appendix Kallus also includes a long footnote that is the first scholarly source that attends to the Lurianic contemplative methods of expediting the process of *gilgul*.[38]

The only full-length scholarly books on Lurianic Kabbalah are those of Yosef Avivi, Devorah Bat-Gamlieli, Lawrence Fine, and Shaul Magid. Yosef Avivi has published two significant works: The first, *Binyan Ariel*, is important for our understanding of the various versions and recensions of Lurianic texts as they evolved over time.[39] An updated and expanded version of *Binyan Ariel* was then published in three volumes under the title *Kabbalat ha-Ari*. In both of these works, Avivi focuses on attempting to discriminate the different strata of the Lurianic texts and reconstruct a timeline of the progression of his thought.[40]

Devorah Bat-David Gamlieli's book *Psychoanalysis and Kabbala: The Masculine and Feminine in Lurianic Kabbala* (Hebrew) is oriented from the academic field of psychology and serves as a model for the possibilities of an interdisciplinary approach to the study of Lurianic Kabbalah. Gamlieli offers a compelling argument for the incorporation of "intuition" into the academic project[41] and within her comprehensive assessment of Lurianic metaphysics through the lens of psychoanalytic theory she includes a psychodynamic interpretation of the development of the "feminine," which serves as an interesting counterpoint to my treatment below of the anatomical development of the feminine *partzuf* of *nuqvah*.[42]

---

human—and Divine—freedom and for creative initiative as the driving force of the process of *Tyqun*." Ibid., 112.

37 This appendix of his dissertation (294–319) serves as the basis of his published article titled "Pneumatic Mystical Possession and the Eschatology of the Soul in Lurianic Kabbalah," in *Spirit Possession in Judaism: Cases and Contexts form the Middle Ages to the Present*, ed. Matt Goldish (Detroit: Wayne State University Press, 2003), 159–185.

38 Kallus, "Theurgy," 296n7.

39 See Avivi, *Binyan Ariel*.

40 See ibid., *Kabbalat ha-Ari*.

41 Gamlieli, *Psychoanalysis and Kabbala*, 25–39.

42 Ibid., 285–318. *Nuqvah* is one of the female "countenances" (*partzufim*) of the cosmic order in Luria's metaphysical system. I will discuss the *partzufim* in more detail below. Also, see my treatment of the anatomical development of *nuqvah* on page 54ff.

In *Physician of the Soul*, Lawrence Fine approaches the study of Lurianic Kabbalah primarily through an interest in the biographical features of Luria's life, his relationship with his fellowship, and through an exploration of the practical, communal, and psychological expressions of his mystical system. He provides us with the most comprehensive biographical outline to date of Luria the person as well as Luria the charismatic saint and master of divinatory arts.[43] Fine's book is the first major study to underscore the importance of the communal, practical, and relational dimensions of Lurianic Kabbalah. It also demonstrates the inseparability of these applied elements of practice with his theoretical system, an orientation that I will continue to develop in the course of this study.

Shaul Magid's book *From Metaphysics to Midrash* examines how the Lurianic project of reinterpreting scripture is inextricably intertwined with the contemporary contexts that informed the cultural reality of sixteenth-century Safed. By treating Lurianic exegetical texts as imaginative "literature," Magid attempts to demonstrate how Luria's mythic reading of the biblical canon deconstructs some of the dualistic assumptions that pervaded earlier forms of Kabbalah. Specifically, he argues that the presence of the Christian and Muslim contexts that shaped the demographic of Safed during Luria's lifetime[44] compelled Luria and his associates to view the world in a different way; a way that thinned some of the exclusivist veils that separated "Jew and non-Jew, man and woman, true religion and false religion, rationalism and mysticism, the human and the divine."[45]

Magid's study opens up new possibilities in our understanding of Lurianic metaphysics and also offers an alternative methodology to approach the textual study of Kabbalah in general. Magid's project is essentially an exploration into

---

43 On Luria's personal history, see Fine, *Physician of the Soul*, chapter 1. In chapter 2, Fine outlines the messianic overtones that saturated the religious communities in Safed in the sixteenth century. In chapters 3 and 5, Fine explores the religious authority attained by Luria in Safed through his charismatic gifts and healing capacities. Fine provides an overview of Lurianic metaphysics in chapter 4; examines the practical applications of *tiqun* through the performance of *mitzvoth* and prayer in chapters 6 and 7; presents the practice of *yiḥudim* in chapter 8; and outlines the messianic relationship between Luria and his disciples through the mechanism of *gilgul* in chapter 9.

44 The Muslim context is the suzerainty of the Islamic Ottoman Empire over Erez Israel beginning in 1516, while the Christian context was established through the settling in Safed of a substantial converso population beginning in the early sixteenth century. On the general contours of this argument, see Magid, *Metaphysics*, 5. Regarding the influence of the conversos on the Jewish community in Safed, see ibid., 37.

45 Magid, *Metaphysics*, 3.

the Lurianic view of "otherness" as expressed in its exegetical texts. He examines this through the philosophical, hermeneutical, and historical perspectives as they interpenetrate Luria's interpretation of scripture. The philosophical perspective examines the tensions of inclusion/exclusion and universalism/particularism; the hermeneutical perspective suggests that Luria's interpretive process is not just an anchoring of his cosmology in canonical material, but rather a means for reconstructing and revaluing scripture itself; and the historical perspective, approached through a "New Historicist" lens, sees Lurianic Kabbalah as a literature that not only interprets but also *constructs* history through its imaginative process of articulating narratives that reflect contemporary issues and dilemmas.[46]

In his study, Magid presents five examples of "otherness," each one taken from one of the five books of Moses. The first chapter, which explores the topic of original sin in the book of Genesis, articulates Luria's conception of the human soul in more detail than other scholarly works to date, with an emphasis on Luria's designation of the highest element of the soul—the *zihara ilah*—and its transmission to Enoch and Elijah, the only two biblical figures who undergo a process of *apotheosis*.[47] Furthermore, in his discussion of original sin, Magid points to the subtle soul dynamics of the mythical figures Cain and Abel who both share a prominent role in Lurianic myth, particularly in his theory of metempsychosis. Both of their souls can be construed to have been conceived as part and parcel of the original sin of Adam, which have implications not only for our understanding of original sin itself, but also for the process of soul construction in Lurianic Kabbalah.[48]

---

46 See ibid., 4 10.

47 The *zihara ilah* is the element of the soul that ascended and did not partake in Adam's sin and thus will not return until the end of days. See *ibid.*, 50. Also see my comments below on page 131 note 94 concerning the use of the term *apotheosis*.

48 See ibid., 55–59. Also see Magid's discussion of the "horizontal" and "vertical" misalignments of Cain and Abel, which has to do with the incongruence between the internal and external aspects of the soul. As Magid points out, this inherent defect cannot be repaired through human action but is consigned to rectification at the "end of days" by divine fiat. See *ibid.*, 60. In chapter two I will argue that the culmination of the process of *tiqun* at the end of days is marked by Luria as the event of resurrection, where the physical body and the supernal element of the soul are unified in a condition of singularity, which includes within its purview both dual and nondual categories of mystical experience, and thus represents a more radical mystical vision than is ordinarily appreciated. This echoes the process of aligning the "internal" and "external" aspects of the soul as pointed out by Magid. See my discussion below on pages 67–68ff and especially note 47.

In chapter two, Magid unpacks Vital's reconstruction of the *erev rav* ("mixed multitude") as a legitimate presence among the Israelites at Sinai, even if their status as both insider/outsider complicates their relationship to both God and Israel.[49] This explains the prominence ascribed by Luria to Moses's mission to gather the *erev rav* and bring them out of Egypt so that they might participate in the revelation at Sinai. The meaning of this impetus by Moses is rooted in the esoteric Lurianic doctrine that sees the *erev rav* as lost parts of Moses's own soul and that must be reintegrated by Moses in order for him to perfect his soul and assume the role of Messiah. Moses's failure to accomplish this task (due to his sin and the sins of the *erev rav* in constructing the Golden Calf) sets the stage for the rehearsing of this drama once again in sixteenth-century Safed, only now the *erev rav* are the conversos and Moses, as Messiah, is Vital (or Luria).

Magid's more nuanced thesis, however, recognizes the subversive paradoxes latent in a kabbalistic reading that uses traditional categories to thin the veils separating self and other in order to reveal that the "other" is nothing but the lost parts of the self that requires inclusion and integration for *tiqun* to take place.[50] The notion that parts of one's soul can inhabit other people (indeed, even a an entire group of people in this case) is a central premise of the Lurianic view of soul dynamics and elements of this will be explored in more detail in chapter one of this study.

In chapter three, Magid explores the Lurianic attitudes towards male-male sex as reflected in Vital's exegetical process, particularly through an analysis of the dynamics of gender transformation that occur in the theater of the *partzufim* as a result of the penetrative act of *mishkav zachar* (male-male sex). Magid argues that Luria's metaphysical explanation of what occurs as a result of male-male penetration implies a tacit recognition of the naturalness of male-male attraction, an attitude that reflects the larger cultural acceptance (and appreciation in some cases) of homoeroticism in the sixteenth-century Ottoman Empire as distinct from the taboo act of male-male intercourse itself. In this exploration, Magid deepens our understanding of Lurianic views on the soul (and *gilgul*) by explicating the dialectics of gender fluidity, transformation, and interpenetration in Lurianic cosmology (and by implication, Magid argues, perhaps in the cultural life of his fellowship as well).[51] Magid's treatment of

---

49 In contradistinction to the Zohar's portrayal of the *erev rav* as pure evil, the midrashic take is more mixed. See Magid, *Metaphysics*, 75–100.

50 See ibid., 75–110.

51 See ibid., 111–142 and especially 136–140.

the Lurianic views on the relationship between gender, sex, identity, and the human soul as it engages the process of *gilgul* will be echoed below in chapter one when I examine the phenomenon of soul dismemberment.

In chapter four, Magid highlights an interesting twist in the Lurianic assessment of Balaam that recognizes that his soul shares the same root as Moses. In contradistinction to the rabbinic and zoharic treatments of Balaam that relegated him to the domain of pure evil, Luria sees Balaam as the split off soulsparks of Moses (originally Abel) that ultimately require reintegration back into the body of Israel in order to attain liberation. This process of reintegration/redemption occurs through the mechanism of *gilgul*, which Magid argues is inextricably linked in Lurianic metaphysics with the process of conversion. Balaam as "other" enters back into Israel (through reincarnating as a Jew) and thus not only redeems his own soul (and that of Moses) but also brings the project of universal *tiqun* closer to fulfillment. Magid exposes the messianic tone of conversion in Luria's metaphysics and its intimate connection with *gilgul*, and thus opens up the door for further research in this direction.

In chapter five, Magid suggests that Luria's understanding of the relationship between the human body and the text of the Torah betrays a line of incarnational thought in Judaism that is similar in certain respects to classical incarnation theology in Christianity. While the seeds of such formulations can be discerned in the deuteronomic code and in intertestamental literature, Kabbalah in general and Luria in particular develop the possibilities of the divinization of the body in more explicit ways. Specifically, Magid examines the usage of the term *tzelem elohim* (divine image) in Lurianic texts and the relationship between one's *tzelem* and the words of the Torah (as the divine incarnate) as internalized into—and perhaps even corporealized as—the physical body through various contemplative rituals (e.g., the recitation of Scripture at spiritually favorable times, for instance on Hoshana Rabbah; the performative rite of Torah study; or the ensubtilization of the body through divine-name meditations).[52] I will echo these themes of incarnation and the divinization of the body in chapter two, which deals with the process of somatic integration and resurrection.

Since the seminal works of Scholem and Tishby there have been many academic articles written on various topics of Lurianic Kabbalah.[53] However, several stand out in terms of our subject of interest; that is, the ontological and

---

52　See ibid., 196–221.
53　See page 16 note 24 for these references.

psychological makeup of the soul and her contemplative journey, specifically as it relates to the *kavvanot* of prayer. Aside from Menachem Kallus's article noted above, there are no specific works of scholarship devoted exclusively to the details of this topic, although there are several that address this issue from the perspective of Luria's architectonic metaphysics in general, and more frequently, through the lens of an inquiry into the phenomenon of *gilgul*, the transmigration of souls.[54]

The first study devoted exclusively to *gilgul* was Scholem's foundational article published as a chapter in his book *On the Mystical Shape of the Godhead*. In this essay, Scholem outlines the history of the concept of *gilgul* over the course of Jewish history and traces the trajectory of its development. He devotes an entire section to the Lurianic period and presents an overview of the Lurianic conception of the soul, its structural architecture, and the complex dynamics of the process of *gilgul*.[55]

Scholem recognizes that the doctrine of "soul sparks" as well as the division of the soul into various parts that features so prominently in Lurianic literature has its roots in thirteenth-century kabbalistic texts.[56] He attempts to trace

---

54 On the history of the transmigration of souls (*gilgul neshamot*) in general and in sixteenth-century Safed in particular, see: Scholem, "Gilgul," 197–250; idem, *Origins of the Kabbalah*, 188–198, 457–460; idem., *MTJS*, 278–284; Elior, "The Doctrine of Transmigration in *Galya Raza*," 243–269; Yehuda Liebes, "*Gilgula*," in "Perakim be-Milon Sefer Ha-Zohar" [Hebrew] (PhD diss., Hebrew University, 1976), 291–327; Werblowsky, *Joseph Karo*, 234–256; Alexander Altmann, "Eternality of Punishment: A Theological Controversy Within the Amsterdam Rabbinate in the Thirties of the Seventeenth Century," in Fine, *Essential Papers on Kabbalah*, 270–287; Hallamish, *An Introduction to the Kabbalah*, 281–309; Giller, *Reading the Zohar*, 37–42; Elyon, *Reincarnation in Jewish Mysticism and Gnosticism*; Arikha, *Reincarnation: Reality that Exceeds All Imagination*; Shekalim, *Torat ha-Nefesh ve-ha-Gilgul b'reshit ha-Kabbala*; Amos, *Be-gilgul Hozer: Gilgul in Kabblah and Other Sources*; Pinson, *Reincarnation and Judaism: The Journey of the Soul*; Mark Verman, "Reincarnation and Theodicy: Traversing Philosophy, Psychology, and Mysticism," in *Be'erot Yitzhak: Studies in Memory of Isadore Twersky*, 399–426; Brian Ogren, *Renaissance and Rebirth: Reincarnation in Early Modern Italian Kabbalah* (Leiden and Boston: Brill, 2009).

55 See Scholem, "Gilgul," 228–241. In the earlier sections of this chapter, Scholem presents important sources that serve as precursors not only to Luria's conception of the soul, but to the different formulations of the makeup of the soul found in earlier kabbalistic texts. Many of these sources-texts (e.g. the Talmudic tradition, found in BT *Haggigah* 13b-14a, of the 974 generations that were foreseen by God before the creation) will serve as metaphysical springboards for more radical understandings of the soul later on in the *Bahir*, the book *Galya Raza*, and in Lurianic Kabbalah.

56 Especially in the Zohar, but in other texts as well. For sources see Scholem, "Gilgul," 305n44. More textual references can also be found in Scholem's article "Towards the

the trajectory and development of these ideas from their earliest instantiations into the more mature, comprehensive and innovative formulations found in the writings of Hayyim Vital. Scholem sees the first developments of the doctrine of the soul sparks arising in response to the question of reincarnation and resurrection. What will happen to all the various bodies that a soul has inhabited over the course of many transmigrations at the time of the resurrection of the dead? The solution is the doctrine of "soul-sparks" that allows the soul to be divided into different parts that inhabit different bodies.[57] Scholem then traces the development of this theme to Luria's innovative propositions regarding the ontological and psychological structure of the soul, the doctrine of soul-sparks, the "lineages" of historically reincarnated characters and in the locus of the soul relative to the body.

However, Scholem focuses his analysis on the "baroque" architectonic structuring of the Lurianic conception of the cosmos as anthropomorphized in Luria's reconfiguration of the earlier traditions on the nature of the human soul. For example, Luria adds two more levels of soul to the three found in the Zohar and organizes them in relation to the five worlds, the five *partzufim*, and more importantly from the perspective of the psychology of the soul, to the cosmic soul of *adam ha-rishon*. The earlier formulations of the doctrine of soul-sparks found in the Zohar and in other thirteenth-century works is consequently refracted through the multidimensional prism of the Lurianic cosmic *anthropos* and hence takes on ever more complexity and nuance than any other earlier system, replete with major and minor soul roots, branches, families, and so forth.[58]

Other topics of note that Scholem discusses include Luria's innovative view that the soul in its various manifestations does not abide in the body, but rather hovers around it as a kind of spiritual aura,[59] and the radical transformation the biblical figure Cain undergoes from his instantiation in the *Tiqunei Zohar* to his prominence as a "great soul" in the Lurianic writings.[60] The significance of the soul categories of Cain (and Abel) in Luria's system pertains most

---

Study of Transmigration in Thirteenth-Century Kabbalah" [Hebrew], *Tarbiz* 16 (1944): 135–150.

57 See Scholem, "Gilgul," 216.

58 See ibid., 228–235.

59 See ibid., 237–238.

60 Scholem was particularly enamored with this dimension of Lurianic thought. See ibid., 236: "This Gnostic element in the reevaluation of Cain's soul, which is now perceived as a "great soul," is one of the most remarkable and one of the strangest parts of Lurianic doctrine, within a system that was strictly Jewish. It is also among the most interesting ideas in Lurianic thought, for which there is no precedent in earlier Kabbalah."

directly to the organization of the various types of souls and the internal laws that govern the way each of these soul-types move through the process of *gilgul*. I will discuss these dynamics in more detail below.

Another important article that deals exclusively with the subject of *gilgul*, although not with Lurianic Kabbalah specifically, is Rachel Elior's study titled "The Doctrine of Transmigration in *Galya Raza*."[61] In her examination of the early sixteenth-century text *Galya Raza*, Elior demonstrates the mythical underpinnings of *gilgul* as a process that is intimately bound up with the doctrine of evil as it is articulated in early kabbalistic texts. Drawing from the highly demarcated dualism between the realms of holiness (*kedusha*) and that of impurity (*qelipah*) found especially in the Zohar, the anonymous author of *Galya Raza* develops a unique metaphysical system that ties together the cosmic drama between good and evil found in the Zohar with the function of the human soul and in particular the need for *gilgul* as part and parcel of the process required for the rectification (and in the case of *Galya Raza*, overtly apocalyptic rectification) of the imbalance initiated in cosmic prehistory.[62]

While this anonymous work does not explore the metaphysical structures of the soul itself, it does provide us with some innovative approaches to the process of *gilgul* that can help us better understand certain aspects of the Lurianic system. In particular, the unique metaphysical system of *Galya Raza* sees holiness and impurity (or good and evil) to be in a necessary symbiosis that is required for the existence of creation. That is to say that existence depends on the attachment of the forces of good to the forces of evil. Most poignantly, the messianic process outlined in *Galya Raza* involves the forces of purity expunging the forces of impurity through a subtle technique of "holy subterfuge" that tricks the *sitra aḥra* (lit. "the other side," a common term denoting the demonic realm) to turn against itself and ultimately self-destruct. The primary means of this subterfuge are the *mitzvot* of the Torah, whose main purpose is to "flatter" the *sitra aḥra* while subversively separating the pure from the impure and good from evil.

---

61 Traditionally, this text is attributed to Rabbi Avraham, a disciple of Luria. However, Elior argues that the text preceded Luria by several decades and could not have been written in the Land of Israel, which necessitates that it was outside of the influence of Lurianic teachings. See Rachel Elior, "The Doctrine of Transmigration," in Fine, *Essential Papers on Kabbalah*, 243.

62 For more on the messianic thrust of *Galya Raza*, see Fine, *Physician of the Soul*, 115 and 117–118.

This radical perspective reached its peak in the author's doctrine of *gilgul*, which is essentially a ruse imposed on the side of *kedusha* ("holiness") by the *sitra aḥra* to maintain its singular power. The forces of purity (the Jews) then manipulate the system of *gilgul* and turn it on its head through the union of great Jews with foreign women and the secret process of transposing holy soul sparks in place of the impure souls of these reincarnated women. This could occur because the doctrine of reincarnation was not known to the *sitra aḥra*. Ironically, even as the *sitra aḥra* imposes *gilgul*, it is simultaneously ignorant of its internal mechanisms of operation.[63]

However, the ultimate purpose of reincarnation for the Jewish people according to this text is for the sake of repentance and purification from the accumulated pollution of the *sitra aḥra*. While this in and of itself is not an innovation of the author of *Galya Raza* (this notion is found in earlier kabbalistic treatises),[64] the author does frame this in a radically meta-historiosophic interpretive model, whereby Israel's subjugation in exile from one seven-thousand-year cycle to another is the necessary arena to which the redemptive process of *gilgul* is inextricably linked. That is to say that the reincarnation of Israel from one meta-cycle of history to another is the very mechanism that God uses to overturn the dominance of the *sitra aḥra* in creation.

In order to demonstrate this point, the author appeals to complex metaphysical interpretations of measurements, particularly the parallels between the earthy measures of a traditional ritual bath known as a *mikvah* (960 *lug*) and the celestial measurements of the divine body (960 limbs of God's body as described in the ancient mystical text *Shiur Komah*).[65] In Rachel Elior's words: "The extent of the process of reincarnation is deduced from the measurements of the ritual bath because metempsychosis is spiritual purification in an earthly ritual bath."[66] The number 960 is also used by the author to predict the end of the messianic process in history (six cycles of 960 years, which comes out to 5760, or 2000 CE).

In light of the relationship emphasized between *gilgul* and the measurements of a *mikvah*, Elior does not mention (in fact, I have not seen any scholars or traditional commentators recognize this) a very interesting and unexplained textual annotation added either by Shmuel Vital (Hayyim Vital's son and editor

---

63 See Elior, "Galya Raza," 243–258.
64 See, e.g., Scholem, "Gilgul," 320.
65 The letters of the Hebrew word *mikvah* (מקוה) are also the same letters as the word *komah* (קומה).
66 Elior, "Galya Raza," 262.

of the *Shemona She'arim*) or by Hayyim Vital himself to the very end of the published editions of *Sha'ar Ha-Gilgulim*. At the conclusion of the text it states: "A *mikvah* for Israel is 40 *se'ah*" (מקוה ישראל מ' סאה) with no further explanation or explication. Although there is no explicit mention of the relationship between *gilgul* and *mikvah* in Lurianic literature, perhaps Shmuel Vital was familiar with the tradition in *Galya Raza* that correlates the two and was pointing to it with a cryptic textual allusion.

This begs the question to what degree the broader metaphysical orientation of *Galya Raza* informs the Lurianic formulations and perspective on *gilgul*. As we will see in more detail in chapter two of this book, the mystical function of the *gilgul* process was ultimately rooted in a radical messianic vision of the equalization of all hierarchy in existence, resulting in an epistemologically intuited unification of all reality.[67] Thus, the association between *gilgul*, *mikvah* and the messianic age may have followed a trajectory of development that continued into the redaction of the Lurianic texts penned by Vital.

Another innovation by the author of *Galya Raza* is his markedly different view of the reason for the number of times a soul reincarnates. The traditional view found in earlier texts (and, as we will see later on in this book, this is also the view of Luria) as to the number of possible reincarnations for a particular soul is either three or a thousand; typically it is three, but can go up to a thousand if the person is very wicked and requires more refinement through the process of transmigration.[68] However, the author of *Galya Raza* inverts this: The wicked only reincarnate three times but those who are less sinful can reincarnate up to a thousand times to aid them in their process of purification and enable them to enter the Garden of Eden.[69] As Elior points out, *Galya Raza* also emphasizes the possibilities of reincarnating into animals (even vermin and crawling things) to a more extreme degree than what is found in earlier texts.[70] To be sure, all this points to the fact that *Galya Raza* is an important influence in the development of the concept of *gilgul* in sixteenth-century Kabbalah and

---

67 The correlation between the ritual act of immersing in the *mikvah* and its epistemological function has already been pointed out by Maimonides, who refers to the waters of the *mikvah* as the "waters of knowledge." See Maimonides, *Mishnah Torah, Hilchot Mikva'ot* 11:12. On the phenomenological implications of Maimonides's statement, see my article "Not-Knowing and True Knowledge—The Essence of Purim," *Spectrum: A Journal of Renewal Spirituality* 2, no. 1 (Winter–Spring 2006); especially 37.

68 See Scholem, "Gilgul," 321.

69 See Elior, "Galya Raza," 268n73.

70 See ibid., 259.

further investigation into the extent of this influence remains a desideratum in the academic study of Jewish mysticism.

The most comprehensive scholarly treatments of the construction and nature of the soul in Lurianic Kabbalah is found in the chapter titled "Metempsychosis, Mystical Fellowship, and Messianic Redemption" in Lawrence Fine's book *Physician of the Soul: Healer of the Cosmos*; in sections of Shaul Magid's book *From Metaphysics to Midrash*; and in Menachem Kallus's published article titled "Pneumatic Mystical Possession and the Eschatology of the Soul in Lurianic Kabbalah."[71]

Like Scholem, Fine examines the topic of the soul mainly in the context of his study of *gilgul*, and more specifically through the lens of his agenda to demonstrate the personal and practical relevance of Luria's teachings for Luria himself and for his fellowship.[72] Fine argues that the metaphysical dynamics of *gilgul* were deeply relevant to Luria precisely because of who he imagined himself to be relative to these cosmic processes, and perhaps even more poignantly, relative to his students. For example, Fine uses the testimonies of Hayyim Vital and Solomon Shlomiel of Dresnitz about a pilgrimage undertaken by Luria to the presumed site of the *idra rabbah* to demonstrate that Luria believed that he was the reincarnation of Rabbi Shimon bar Yochai and that his students were the reincarnation of bar Yochai's students. Fine writes:

---

71 See Kallus, "Pneumatic Mystical Possession." A corollary to Kallus's published article is found in Appendix II of his doctoral dissertation, titled "Pneumatic Mystical Soul-Impregnation and the Eschatology of the Soul in Lurianic Kabbalah" (Kallus, "Theurgy," 294–354). My analysis will draw from both of these versions, although they are similar in content.

72 This methodological perspective permeates Fine's entire book. See especially his comments on the "embodied" study of Lurianic Kabbalah—*Physician of the* Soul, 9–15, and the following statement: "Lurianic Kabbalah was no mere theoretical system or set of intellectual or theological abstractions dressed up in mythic guise. Rather, the central argument of this study is that Lurianic Kabbalah was first and foremost a lived and living phenomenon, the actual social world of a discrete, historically observable community" (10); "The complex relationships among the members of this community, and the way in which they viewed those relationships, do not form a minor subtext of this study, but one of its main subjects" (12). Specifically, with regard to the topic of *gilgul*, Fine writes: "While Luria's teaching on this subject include a great deal of theoretical discussion, as already noted, his primary motivation was neither speculative nor abstract, but personal and practical" (306). For more on the tradition of idealizing Luria, primary through the hagiographical text *Shivḥei Ha-Ari*, see Eitan Fishbane, "Perceptions of Greatness: Constructions of the Holy Man in *Shivḥei ha-Ari*," *Kabbalah: Journal for the Study of Jewish Mystical Texts* (2012): 195–221.

Luria's elaborate teachings bearing upon the subject of gilgul ... are thus far more than a set of theoretical doctrines. They had to do with his most intimate and personal concerns, especially during the latter months of his life, when his interest in the soul-ancestries of his students assumed increasing significance to him. Luria's quest for tiqqun in its many forms— personal, communal, cosmic, and historical—was inexorably tied to his beliefs concerning his own soul-ancestry and those of his disciples."[73]

Since Luria saw himself as the earthly embodiment of the cosmic generative force and a reincarnation of both Moses and Shimon bar Yochai, his messianic role in bringing the final *tiqun* to completion included both a cosmic and communal dimension; in fact, the two things are inseparable insofar as Luria and his fellowship were the earthly expressions of these very supernal dynamics.

In the course of explicating the messianic thrust of Luria's self-perception and its practical implications for him and his fellowship, Fine presents an outline of the five categories of soul,[74] the doctrine of the soul-garments,[75] the five forms of *zivvugim*, or *hieros gamos*, that form the soul-garments by way of "wasted" seminal emissions,[76] as well as the central importance of determining one's soul-history of transmigrations for the fulfillment of the task of *tiqun*.[77]

Of particular relevance to our study are the Lurianic teachings on the soul garments (*levushim*), which are highly developed and are inextricably intertwined with his entire metaphysical system. Fine demonstrates that the soul-garments are constructed out of the "wasted" seminal emissions of various righteous figures over the course of history. This tradition originates from Luria's interpretation of the rabbinic statement that when the biblical patriarch Joseph resisted the seductions of the wife of Potiphar, his semen dripped through his fingernails.[78]

For Luria, this narrative points to a parallel cosmic process, whereby ten drops of semen flowed from the supernal Joseph (i.e. the *sefirah* of *yesod*) but were not received properly in the cosmic womb of *nuqvah*. As a result, these "wasted" drops of semen descended into the *qelipot* where they transformed

---

73 Fine, *Physician of the Soul*, 303–304.
74 Ibid., 306–307.
75 Ibid., 309, 324, and especially 326–330.
76 Ibid., 310–314; on the third *zivvug*, see 312.
77 Ibid., 270.
78 BT Sotah, 36b inter alia; for more sources, see Fine, *Physician of the Soul*, 437n18.

into garments whose function was to protect the souls stuck there.[79] Just as Joseph emitted semen as an esoteric rite to form the necessary souls-garments for his generation, so must each central righteous figure do so for his respective time and place. Fine argues that Luria saw himself as the Joseph, or *yesod*, of his generation and was thus responsible for the secret esoteric function of producing the proper soul-garments for his generation, and especially for the students in his fellowship.[80]

The soul garments themselves are constructed from the substance of "wasted" seminal fluids, which, in turn, result from five sacred cosmic unions (*zivvugim*), each one of which produce garments for a particular group of souls trapped in the *qelipot*. The third type of *zivvug*, or union, described by Fine, that between Jacob and Leah, is responsible for the formation of the soul-garments of Luria's students (these garments are actually the result of the two *zivvugim* of this pair, the first that takes place immediately after midnight and produces ten drops of semen and the second *zivvug* that takes place before dawn that produces another two drops). This means that Luria himself is the *yesod* in this *zivvug* from which these twelve drops emitted.[81]

However, it is the determining of one's personal soul history of transmigration that is of central importance to the task of *tiqun*. This is a key point Fine emphasizes:

> The primary importance of all this from the Lurianic point of view has to do with its existential significance for Luria's own contemporaries, and most particularly for Luria's own personal soul-history and those of his disciples. For the souls of righteous individuals correspond in precise ways to the various dimensions of divinity of which the cosmos is composed ... that is to say, the different gradations and configurations of the divine find earthly expression in the lives of earthly individuals in every generation, linking them to the past in a complex chain of transmigration. Mythic history and personal history combine in such a way as to shape both the identities of individuals and the collective identities of certain groups of people.[82]

---

79 Ibid., 308–309.
80 Ibid., 309, 324, and especially his discussion of the sermon "Two Young Roes of a Doe," 326–330.
81 Ibid., 310–314; on the third *zivvug*, see 312.
82 Ibid., 307–308.

Another reason for the importance of recognizing one's soul-ancestry has to do with Luria's doctrine of the "soul-roots." This teaching posits that each soul is an intrinsic part of a larger constellation of souls that share a common root in Adam's original soul. These soul-roots and soul-families have a special attraction and affinity for each other and even have a kind of responsibility for each other: "The knowledge of one's soul-ancestry—knowledge that Isaac Luria was able to give to his disciples—was thus of absolutely crucial importance to them."[83] This familial relationship of souls to each other also serves as the functional basis for the Lurianic practice of *yiḥudim* (meaning "unifications"), which sought to establish contemplative communion with the soul of a righteous member of one's own soul-ancestry through performing specialized meditations at his gravesite.[84]

In his examination of Luria's techniques of "diagnostics," Fine also briefly discusses the relationship between the twenty-two letters of the Hebrew alphabet and the three primary levels of soul: *nefesh*, *ruaḥ*, and *neshama*. He recognizes that the letters manifest differently (mostly in size) depending on the level of soul that they are expressing. In this discussion, Fine makes a casual statement that attempts to articulate the ontological makeup of the soul, although he does not discuss it in any detail and offers no textual support for it. He writes:

> These three dimensions of the soul clothe one another, as it were, with the body's skin constituting the outer covering of all. The skin is tantamount to the husk or shell of materiality, the qelippah, which surrounds all the lights of holiness in the world. The lights, or letters of the various parts of the soul, on the other hand, are manifestations of divinity itself, in as much as the constituent elements of the soul are identical with God.[85]

Fine also briefly mentions the *tzelem*, or subtle body, that mediates between the body and the *nefesh* level of soul,[86] but omits any detailed discussion of the ontological makeup of the soul, nor does he address the interplay of the various soul-parts (one's own soul-parts as well as the inclusion of others) in the processes of *gilgul* and *ihbur*. For example, the phenomenon of soul-splitting

---

83 Ibid., 270.
84 Ibid.
85 Ibid., 155. For more on the concept of the *tzelem*, see Scholem's chapter titled, "Tselem: The Concept of the Astral Body" in his *On the Mystical Shape of the Godhead*, 251–273 and the discussion by Shaul Magid in chapter 5 of his *Metaphysics*.
86 Fine, *Physician of the Soul*, 95–96.

or dismemberment, whereby different parts of the same soul can inhabit several bodies simultaneously in a single incarnation, or whereby a single body constitutes the soul parts of several different souls, is not even mentioned by Fine.[87] He also does not address the centrality of the convert (*ger*) in the phenomenological mechanics of *gilgul*,[88] the mystical function of resurrection in the *gilgul* process, and the explication of the contemplative practices specifically associated with the integration of soul-parts.[89]

In his book on Lurianic exegesis, Shaul Magid develops our understanding of Lurianic views of the soul in provocative ways. While the Lurianic doctrine of the soul is not the central topic of his study, he explicates certain aspects of Luria's views of the soul that had not been previously explored. In particular, he demonstrates how Luria utilizes the concept of soul-construction and *gilgul* as a mechanism of subverting classical rabbinic attitudes towards the "other." I have already discussed Magid's thesis in detail above and there is no need to rehearse it again here.[90]

In his article on spirit possession, Kallus examines the topic of the soul in Lurianic Kabbalah primarily through the mechanism of soul impregnation, or *ibbur*, and how these processes expressed themselves in the pneumatic experiences of Hayyim Vital.[91] To this end, Kallus outlines the different levels of relationship that exist between souls that share a common soul-root. The first level that he discusses is that of the righteous one (*tzaddik*) who impregnates

---

87 Scholem mentions these various phenomena in his article on *gilgul*, but does not explicate them in detail. See Scholem, "Gilgul," 216 and also see Kallus, "Theurgy," 296n7, where he does discuss these matters in some detail.

88 Fine does not discuss the place of the convert (*ger*) in Lurianic Kabbalah at all, except superficially in a footnote. See *Physician of the Soul*, 441n92. Fine also briefly mentions *gerim* in the context of discussing Moses's responsibility to redeem the "mixed multitude" (*erev rav*), which Fine says "refers to the souls of Egyptians who sought to convert (*gerim*)." Ibid., 323.

89 Fine briefly mentions these practices, as does Scholem, but offers no explanation of the practices themselves. See Fine, *Physician of the Soul*, 306–307. Kallus is the first to discuss these practices in more detail (see Kallus, "Theurgy," 296n7, and see my discussion below).

90 The most salient points that pertain to our subject of interest is his analysis of Lurianic texts that deal with the soul constructions of Adam, Cain, and Abel; his analysis of conversion (*gerut*) as a messianic trope and his discussion of "incarnation" as text/body in Lurianic praxis. See my discussion above on page 21ff.

91 Kallus notes the distinction between *gilgul* and *ibbur* in Lurianic literature: while *gilgul* refers to the incarnation of a soul in a body at the time of birth, *ibbur* points to the sharing of a body by different souls that share the same soul root, or origin, in soul of Adam. See M. Kallus, "Pneumatic Mystical Possession," 160.

(*ibbur*) himself into the soul of a sinner who shares the same soul root in order to inspire him with thoughts of repentance. In this type of *ibbur*, the *tzaddik* is not required to remain bound to the sinner's soul if he continues to sin since he is not under any personal obligation to help the sinner.

A second, higher form of relationship is when a *tzaddik* impregnates himself in another soul in order to complete the rectification of a sin that he committed in a past incarnation. In such an *ibbur*, the *tzaddik* enters another soul in order to test himself by encountering a similar situation of sin that he failed in a prior lifetime. If he succeeds then both the *tzaddik* and the impregnated soul receive the merit of the successful encounter; if he fails, however, the living soul still receives the edenic merit of the *tzaddik*'s prior lives.

A third level of impregnation is when a person performs a righteous deed that is similar to the meritorious act of a dead *tzaddik* in his soul-family. When this occurs, the living soul can attract an *ibbur* from that very great *tzaddik* that originally performed such a deed and accumulate the merits of that great *tzaddik*. Kallus also mentions that the impregnations can compound one upon the other until the person can attain his "ultimate root," and in some cases, even go beyond the ultimate root of one's personal soul. These compounded impregnations can even occur simultaneously such that a single person can be impregnated by up to three souls at a given time.[92]

Kallus then outlines the different levels of soul and how they relate to the practice of *yiḥudim*,[93] and the composite picture of Hayyim Vital's soul and the actual and potential impregnations that he experienced or believed himself to possess based on the teachings imparted to him by his teacher. The particular soul-lineage of Vital is self-reflectively discussed a great deal in his *Sefer Ḥezyonot* and in *Sha'ar ha-Gilgulim*, the two primary texts upon which Kallus bases his study. The portrait of Vital's soul and its pneumatic vicissitudes leads Kallus to conclude that the following elements were required to succeed in Luria's complex system of impregnation mysticism: 1) Knowing one's "tree of impregnations," generally by means of revelation, 2) Attaining a clear picture of how the system of soul evolution works, 3) Practicing cosmic *yiḥudim* in addition to personal *yiḥudim*, 4) Possessing a self-image that enables absolute self-confidence, and 5) Wholehearted devotion in practicing Lurianic pneumatic techniques.[94]

---

92 See ibid., 161–162.
93 Ibid., 162–163.
94 Ibid., 163 and 168.

Kallus also discusses some of the possible techniques that were taught by Luria to ascertain one's past lives,[95] and presents unresolved questions related to the subject of the evolution of the soul in Lurianic Kabbalah that require further study. Some of these undecided issues are: whether or not Lurianic Kabbalah displays a "nominalist" or "realist" perspective; whether or not all the rectified souls "telescope" back into the united soul of *adam ha-rishon* at the completion of the process of *tiqun*; whether the final *tiqun* extends to the world of *asiyah* (the domain of the *qelipot*) or does the world of *asiyah* return to its ontic station before the fall (that is, to *tiferet* of *yetzirah*); whether the transformation enabled by *tiqun* effects the current state of the world to come and how this interpenetrates with the state of resurrection (indeed some Lurianic texts conflate the two); and the meaning of the mention of the *qelipah* in the "seed" of *adam qadmon*.[96]

To conclude this section, I will recap some of the key takeaways. Despite the formidable advances in scholarship since Scholem's first foray into Lurianic metaphysics nearly seventy-five years ago, there are still remarkably few studies dedicated to the practical, contemplative and communal dimensions of its mystical system.[97] Furthermore, there is to date no comprehensive treatment of the doctrine of the soul or of *gilgul* in Lurianic literature, despite the centrality of these topics to the entirely of his metaphysical and practical systems.[98] Luria's understanding of the soul is grounded in a radical view of the inherent multiplicity of individual identity, and the mechanism of *gilgul* is thus designed in

---

95 These practices are deduced from various later texts, since there is nothing explicit in this regard in Lurianic literature. Some of these practices include the adjuration of angels with oaths, dream yoga, and psychological methods. Kallus admits that these are all speculative (see ibid., 168–169).

96 A reference to *Likkutei Torah* 43b. See ibid., 170–173.

97 Most of the studies that deal with Lurianic Kabbalah are still focused on various aspects of his metaphysical system. The exceptions include Magid, "Conjugal Union, Mourning, and Talmud Torah in R. Isaac Luria's Tikkun Hazot": xvii-xlv; Fine, "'The Contemplative Practice of Yehudim in Lurianic Kabbalah" and throughout Fine, *Physician of the Soul*; Moshe Idel, *Messianic Mystics* (New Haven: Yale University Press, 1998), especially appendix 2; and Kallus's unpublished doctoral dissertation, "Theurgy." Shaul Magid's recent study of scriptural interpretation in Lurianic literature also addresses the communal dimensions of Luria's fellowship in various ways, most notably in its assessment of the larger historical and sociological context of the converso community in Safed in the sixteenth century. See *Metaphysics*, 75–110. Also see Reuven Kimmelman's study of the prayer *L'cha Dodi*, which discusses certain dimensions of the Lurianic *kavvanot* of prayer: *Lekha Dodi ve-Kabbalat Shabbat: Their Mystical Meaning* [Hebrew] (Jerusalem: Magnus, 2003).

98 The centrality of the doctrine of *gilgul neshamot* to Luria's entire metaphysical system is acknowledged by Shaul Magid (See, e.g., Magid, *Metaphysics*, 55 and 159) and Fine, *Physician of the Soul*, 8.

accordance with this composite structure of the human being. The theoretical, psychological and practical implications of this complex anthropological view has yet to be explored by scholars.

It is also striking that scholars have not recognized that the redemptive project of *gilgul* is not only central to Luria's drama of *tiqun*, but that its ultimate success is dependent on the role of the soul of the convert in the process.[99] The contemplative mechanisms through which the Lurianic practitioner intentionally splits off parts of his soul in order to hasten the final completion of the transmigratory journey have also been overlooked by scholars in the field, as have the metaphysical implications of the doctrine of resurrection of the dead.

This last lacuna in the academic study of Lurianic Kabbalah will be the primary focus of this study. The contemplative practices developed by Luria to intentionally fragment the soul and expedite the process of rebirth provide us with an opportunity to understand more thoroughly the central dialectical tension that underlies all of Lurianic metaphysics and practice. This tension between the manifold on the one hand and the unity on the other—between dualism and nondualism—is the same tension that expresses itself in Luria's multidimensional understanding of the human soul. That the human being must undergo a process of excessive disunity in order to more readily realize its unitive nature points to this extreme tendency of Lurianic practice. As we will see, it is this re-membering in death of the dis-membered body in life, that represents the radical paradoxicality of the Lurianic mystical vision.

This radical eradication of the boundaries that separate life and death, body and soul, human and cosmic, in Lurianic practice has never been appreciated by scholars, despite its importance for fully appreciating the monistic implications of Lurianic metaphysics and practice. By exposing this esoteric dimension to the Lurianic teachings, this book can perhaps help us understand more fully certain key questions in the academic study of Mysticism in general and of Lurianic Kabbalah in particular.

OVERVIEW OF LURIANIC METAPHYSICS

Before we unpack the mystical practices designed to expedite the journey of rebirth, we must first properly understand their broader metaphysical context.

---

99 The one exception is Shaul Magid, who recognizes the act of conversion as a central trope in Lurianic mysticism and one that is necessary for *tiqun* to be completed. See his *Metaphysics*, 75–110.

In this section, I will provide an overview of the main features of Lurianic cosmology, a summary of his unique doctrine of *gilgul,* and a review of his understanding of the different categories of soul and how each one fits into his teachings on reincarnation.

According to Luria, three main events in cosmic prehistory account for the current state of the universe and the human's role within it. He calls these events *tzimtzum* (contraction or withdrawal), *shevirat ha-kelim* (breaking of the vessels), and *tiqun* (restoration). *Tzimtzum* is the process by which *ein sof* (the infinite mystery/source; lit. "no end") manifests a vacuous, "empty" space within which the finite universe is formed. This resolves an inherent paradox of creation: How can there be space for a finite, physical universe, if infinity spans all of reality? The doctrine of *tzimtzum* explains how *ein sof* withdraws itself back into itself, vacating a tiny point within its own vastness that is devoid of the quality of infinity. The light of *ein sof* then reenters this vacuum and the *sefirot* (s. *sefirah,* divine potencies), which exist only in potential in the infinite vastness, manifest and self-organize into a form known as *adam qadmon* ("primordial human"). This "human" form is the first shape reality assumes in the vacuous space after the *tzimtzum.*[100]

As the process of creation unfolds and the infinite light emanates through the interface of *adam qadmon,* special cosmic "vessels" of dense light manifest to hold the purer light of the *sefirot* which now begin to separate into distinct entities.[101] While some of these vessels do their job properly by containing the light, others shatter under the impact, and the shards of the vessels, as well as some of the light that is attached to them, fall into the depths of the vacuous space, called the *tehiru.*[102] This event is known in Lurianic terminology as *shevirat ha-kelim* (the breaking of the vessels).

---

100 When the divine ray of light (*kav ha-middah*) emanates into the *tehiru,* or the vacuous space, in the form of *adam qadmon,* it first manifests in a series of concentric circles, only afterwards forming itself into the shape of a "line," or a human body. This is the Lurianic theory of *iggul v'yosher,* described by Vital in *EH,* gate 1, chs. 1–5 (Jerusalem, 1975), 21–29. On the history of *tzimtzum* in Kabbalah in general, see Moshe Idel, "On the Concept of Zimzum in Kabbalah and Its Research," *Jerusalem Studies in Jewish Thought* 10 (1992): 59–112; Magid, "Origin and Overcoming of the Beginning."

101 Only the light that shines through the "eyes" of *adam qadmon* atomize to the degree that special vessels are required to contain them. See *EH,* gate 8, ch. 6. This process is also described in Scholem, *MTJM,* 265; Fine, *Physician of the Soul,* 133–134; Fine, "Yichudim,"67 and Kallus, "Theurgy," 203n3.

102 The vessels that were designed to hold the three upper *sefirot* that shone through the "eyes" of *adam qadmon,* namely, *keter, ḥokhmah* and *binah,* did not shatter. Only those that were intended to hold the six lower *sefirot,* namely, *ḥesed* through *yesod,* broke under the impact.

The shards from the shattered vessels that descend into the *tehiru* (void) produce the *qelipot* (husks) that are the source of evil in the Lurianic system, as well as the physical world itself. The pure, divine light that remains attached to these material shards in turn became "trapped" in the gross, material world, forever yearning to be redeemed from its state of "exile" in order to be reunited with its source in the upper worlds. The process by which the divine light is extricated from the *qelipot*, and the universe restored to its original harmonious state, is known as *tiqun* (restoration).

This process of *tiqun* constitutes the central framework of the Lurianic contemplative system. It includes specialized *kavvanot* (mystical intentions) that are designed to theurgically realign the cosmic imbalances caused by the breaking of the vessels. The bulk of the *kavvanot* that are attributed to Luria constellate around the daily prayer liturgy and are to be performed while reciting these prayers or while performing the daily regimen of obligatory commandments. There are also other categories of *kavvanot* that are even more specialized: for example, the practice of *yiḥudim* (unifications) involves entering into a meditative state that is conducive to communicating with the souls of dead *tzaddikim* (righteous beings).

Another facet of *tiqun* relates to the restoration of the human souls that descend into the *qelipot* (lit. husks) as a result of the breaking of the vessels and of the sin of *adam ha-rishon* (the first human). This aspect of *tiqun* is intimately tied up with the evolutionary process of *gilgul* and will be discussed in more detail below.

Immediately following the breaking of the vessels, a divine damage control mechanism automatically activates in order to fix the fallen state of the universe. This mechanism reorganizes the sefirotic light that emanates through *adam qadmon* into a series of *partzufim* (supernal constellations). The word *partzufim* means "faces," but as S. Magid points out, they are better understood as the "interfaces" where the infinite meets the finite.[103]

Malkhut, the last *sefirah*, cracked but did not shatter like the others. Furthermore, most of the light that had already emanated into these shattered vessels returned above to its divine source, while only some of this light descended below and attached itself to the scattered shards. See Scholem, *MTJM*, 266 and 412n63; Fine, "Yichudim," 67. For a more detailed discussion of the precise dynamics of the *shevirah*, including the Lurianic (de)construction of the divine names associated with this process, see Kallus, "Theurgy," 203n3.

103   See Magid, *From Metaphysics to Midrash*, 24. For a rich retracing of the Lurianic principle of the *partzufim* back to key sections of the Zohar, see Melila Hellner-Eshed, *Seekers of the Face: Secrets of the Idra Rabba (the Great Assembly) of the Zohar* (Stanford: Stanford University Press, 2021) [original Hebrew version published in 2017 by Yidiot Achronot Press].

These *partzufim*, which are divine organizing principles, restructure the universe to correct the damage caused by the breaking of the vessels. In this process, the *sefirot* are reconstituted into five *partzufim*: *keter* (the first *sefirah*) becomes *arikh anpin* (long-faced), *hokhmah* (the second *sefirah*) becomes *abba* (father), *binah* (the third *sefirah*) becomes *imma* (mother), the six *sefirot* from *hesed* through *yesod* became *zeir anpin* (short-faced), and *malkhut* (the tenth and last *sefirah*) becomes *nuqvah* (female), also called by the name *rahel* (or Rachel)."[104]

The *partzufim* are the primary players in the Lurianic cosmic drama. They are the dynamic principles that constitute the supernal realms and serve as the relational organisms that are impacted by the theurgic activities of the human contemplative. Since each of these five divine personalities are constituted by particular configurations of the ten *sefirot*, then more precise references can be made to the interior regions of any one of the *partzufim*. This allows Vital to discuss *yesod* (the ninth *sefirah*) of *zeir*, or *binah* (the second *sefirah*) of *imma*, for example. The intricacy of this system is further compounded by the fact that each of the *partzufim* are also found in each of the four primary worlds, to be discussed in the next section. This architectonic design makes for an intricate network of living loci within the celestial realms that are accessed and manipulated by the theurgist in the performance of the various Lurianic *kavvanot*.[105]

The erotic relationships between the *partzufim* represent the central metaphysical and theurgic elements of the Lurianic tradition. At first *abba* and *imma*, as well as *zeir* and *nuqvah*, are united in perpetual union. Through the *zivvug* (mating) of these two mystical couples, the divine light that emanates through *adam qadmon* is able to channel and organize itself in a way that restores order and harmony to the chaos caused by the breaking of the vessels.

However, while this reconfiguration of the celestial spheres improves the situation, it does not fully redeem all the sparks of light that remain trapped in the *qelipot*. The task of providing the finishing touches to the restorative process is left to *adam ha-rishon* (the first human) whose soul contains within it all the worlds and whose body is in essence a microcosm of *adam qadmon*. His essential task, as a completely spiritual being, is to complete the process of

---

104 On the formation of the *partzufim*, see *EH*, gate 11, ch. 7. On the place of the *partzufim* in Lurianic myth, see Scholem, *MTJM*, 269–273; Fine, *Physician of the Soul*, 138–141; Fine, "Yichudim," 68–70. There are really twelve or thirteen *partzufim* in total, but only these five serve as the primary players in this drama. See Magid, *Metaphysics*, 24–29.

105 Ibid., 24–29; Kallus, "Theurgy," 130–131.

tiqun through performing certain contemplative exercises, designed to elevate the last of the trapped sparks. As we will see in the next section, ultimately this project fails and the task of completing the rectification of the universe falls upon the shoulders of the human Lurianic practitioner.

Luria's teachings on the *partzufim* are extremely complex, and they also make up the bulk of the traditions we have in his name, especially those recorded by Hayyim Vital. However, for the sake of brevity and for the purposes of this book, I have outlined the basic dynamics of the *partzufim* that are necessary to understand his theory of reincarnation and the contemplative practices explicated by Vital. More details of these dynamics will be discussed in the following sections of this study.

Another important Lurianic metaphysical category is that of the five worlds, or cosmic dimensions, that are constituted and organized by the ten *sefirot* and the *partzufim*. They are called, from below to above: *asiyah* (making), *yetzirah* (formation), *beriyah* (creation), *atzilut* (emanation), and *adam qadmon* (primordial human). On the human plane, these five worlds correspond with the five levels of soul: *nefesh* (person), *ruaḥ* (spirit), *neshama* (soul), *ḥayah* (life-force), and *yeḥidah* (singularity). After the breaking of the vessels, the lowest world, *asiyah*, which had until then been a completely spiritual world, descends and becomes mixed up with the *qelipot* and the forces of impurity. This "fall" of *asiyah*, which is also the counterpart of the *sefirah* of *malkhut*, leads to the formation of the material world.[106]

When the process of *tiqun* begins and *malkhut* is reconfigured into the *partzuf* of *raḥel*, and *raḥel*, in turn, is united with the upper worlds through her union with *zeir anpin*, the world of *asiyah* is once again elevated to its former spiritual status. Adam's task at this point is to perform certain contemplative exercises in order to redeem the last remnants of divine sparks that are trapped in the realm of the *qelipot*. Adam, whose body is a microcosm of *adam qadmon* and whose soul contains within it all the worlds, is the only being capable of performing such a feat. Standing at the very nexus of the spiritual world of *asiyah* and the nether realms of impurity, yet containing within himself all the worlds, Adam is the ideal figure to redeem the trapped light from the *qelipot* and integrate it back into the upper worlds.

---

106   On the doctrine of the worlds, see *EH*, gate 47, chs. 1–6. Also see Magid, *Metaphysics*, 29–30; Fine, "Yichudim," 69 and Scholem, *MTJM*, 275–276 and 279–280. For more on the development of the four worlds doctrine, see Gershom Scholem, "*Hitpatchut Torat Ha-Olamot Bi-Kabbalat Ha-Rishonim*," in *Tarbiz* 2 (1931): 415–442 and *Tarbiz* 3 (1932): 33–66.

However, due to Adam's sin, this final *tiqun* does not take place. Instead of redeeming the final sparks of light from their entrapment, Adam attaches himself to the realm of impurity, and all the worlds, which had almost been elevated to their proper place, once again are left in disarray. Adam himself, along with the world of *asiyah* to which he is associated, fall below into the realm of the *qelipot*. Good and evil are again thoroughly mixed together as Adam, along with the whole world of *asiyah*, become materialized.[107] The fall of Adam also forces *nuqvah*, or *raḥel*, to be separated from her union with *zeir anpin*.

This broken state of affairs is then left to the terrestrial human to rectify. The Lurianic practitioner is now the theurgist *par excellence*, inheriting a litany of meditations that constitute the hidden mechanisms to re-unify *nuqvah* with her mate *zeir*, thereby bringing the cosmos back into alignment.[108]

The *zivvug*, or mating, of *raḥel* and *zeir anpin*, which is described in overtly sexual language in the Lurianic literature, consists of an exchange of erotic "fluids." *Raḥel* initiates the mating process by causes her "waters" to ascend to *zeir* in order to arouse him to allow his own "waters" to flow back down to her. Unification then occurs when both the female waters ascend and the male waters descend in an uninterrupted and unceasing flow. As a result of Adam's sin, the female waters that ascend from *raḥel* in order to arouse *zeir anpin* to mate with her are stopped up and the male waters that descend to nourish *raḥel* cease to flow.

Therefore, one aspect of the process of *tiqun*, or rectification, calls for the theurgist to facilitate the ascension of *nuqvah*'s female waters back up towards *zeir* in order to stimulate his male waters and thus initiate the intimate union of these two dissociated parts of the cosmic body. As we will see later on in this book, the contemplative plunging of the practitioner's soul into the ethereal realm of *nuqvah* (and at times into the depths of the *qelipot* themselves) is the primary method of arousing *nuqvah* female waters; indeed, this is only possible because the human soul is the embodiment of the female waters themselves.[109]

One major consequence of Adam's sin, and one that serves as the foundation for Luria's understanding of reincarnation, is the descent of all human souls into the realm of the *qelipot*. Adam, as the microcosm of the entire

---

107 Since *asiyah* is also the parallel term for the *sefirah* of *malkhut* and the *partzuf* of *raḥel*, these two mystical entities also descended along with Adam. Therefore, this fall is also expressed in Lurianic literature as the "exile" of *malkhut*, or *shekhinah*, or as the separation of *zeir anpin* and *nuqvah*. See Scholem, *MTJM*, 275–276.

108 See Fine, *Physician of the Soul*, 141–144.

109 On the male and female waters, see *EH*, gate 39, chs. 1–15; Fine, "Yichudim," 69 and see my discussion below on page 78ff.

emanated universe, also contains within his own soul all the souls of humanity.[110] Thus, when Adam falls into the nether realms, all human souls likewise become imprisoned in this web of corporeality. In the Lurianic system, *tiqun* therefore demands two distinct actions from the individual: 1) to elevate the divine sparks of light trapped in the *qelipot*, and 2) to redeem the pure souls that remain imprisoned in these impure realms.[111]

Luria describes the fulfillment of this sacred mission in extraordinary detail. The individual's task is essentially a contemplative one. Every mundane act—especially the performance of the commandments and the recital of the liturgical prayers—must be accompanied by an appropriate intention designed to realign and reunite the upper worlds. As mentioned above, the primary focus of such meditations is the reunification of the *partzufim* of *zeir* and *nuqvah*. Lawrence Fine describes this process:

> Every action done in the world below—the material world—accompanied by concentration on the dynamics being initiated through such action, causes the "female waters" within *Nukva de-Zeir* to become aroused and ascend with the 288 sparks that were believed to be attached to the broken vessels. The "female waters" act as spiritual "chemicals" which bring about—even if only temporarily—*zivvug* or harmony between male and female within the Godhead.[112]

These mystical intentions, or *kavvanot*, are highly complex, comprising endless combinations of divine names transposed and permuted one upon the other with mind-boggling sophistication. These specialized practices are both for the performance of specific commandments as well as for nearly every word of the liturgical prayer. There are also more advanced *kavvanot* called *yiḥudim* that may be performed by highly trained adepts under specific conditions.[113] As we said above, the point of all these exercises is to restore the universe to its pristine state of wholeness by reintegrating the fallen sparks of light back into their source in the upper worlds.

---

110 Scholem points out that this notion is based on a mystical interpretation of an *aggadah* on Adam found in *Midrash Tanchuma, Ki Tisa*, §12 and *Exodus Rabbah*, §40. See Scholem, *MTJM*, 278 and 414n105.

111 Fine, *Physician of the Soul*, 144 and "Yichudim," 69–70.

112 Fine, "Yichudim," 70. On the 288 sparks of light see ShHK, RaPaCH Nitzotzim, 101–109; Scholem, *MTJM*, 268n73.

113 See Vital's *Sha'ar ha-Yiḥudim* for a description of these practices.

Aside from raising up the sparks trapped in the *qelipot*, the individual is also charged with redeeming his or her own soul from its entrapment in the material realms. The mission of every individual soul is to return to the cosmic Adam, the root of all souls and the place where all souls are united in oneness. According to Luria, this can only happen by performing all 613 commandments.[114] This position is based on an ancient tradition correlating the commandments with the 613 different parts of the body; specifically, the 248 positive commandments with the limbs and the 365 negative commandments with the sinews.[115] According to Luria, the soul is also divided into 613 parts, each one in turn corresponding to one of the 613 commandments. These different parts of soul are "activated" or reach their fullest manifestation, when the particular commandment that parallels it is fulfilled. Only souls that have restored all their 613 "soul sparks" through the performance of the commandments are able to extricate themselves from the *qelipot* and reintegrate into the cosmic Adam. All those who, for whatever reason, are unable to perform all the commandments in their lifetime must, after death, reincarnate into another body. Indeed, until they accomplish their mission, their soul will continue to return in an endless cycle of transmigration until all 613 commandments have been fulfilled.

There are different opinions among the kabbalists as to how many times a person may transmigrate. The most common position, based on older texts, is that a person can reincarnate a maximum of three times. However, Luria modified this position to apply only to completely wicked people; as long as the individual performed one good act during their lifetime they can reincarnate again. However, even according to Luria there was a limit: no soul, even the most righteous, can transmigrate more than one thousand times.[116]

Another aspect to Luria's doctrine of metempsychosis concerns the acquisition of the different levels of soul. The notion that the soul is made up of different parts was inherited from earlier kabbalistic texts; the Zohar, for example, had already described three levels of the soul: *nefesh, ruaḥ, and neshama*.[117] In Luria's

---

114 *ShG*, ch. 4, 11 (Jerusalem: Vitebsky, 1986), 20, 39. All page references to *ShG* refer to the Ashlag edition.

115 On the association of the commandments with the bones and sinews of human anatomy, see Scholem, "Gilgul," 231 and Daniel C. Matt, "The Mystic and the Mitzwot," in Green, *Jewish Spirituality*.

116 See *ShG*, ch. 4, 21–22 and Scholem, "Gilgul," 211–212. On the need to perform all 613 commandments in order to complete the cycle of *gilgulim*, see *ShG*, chs. 4, 11, 20, and 39; Scholem, *MTJM*, 282; Scholem, "Gilgul," 232–237.

117 See Isaiah Tishby, *Wisdom of the Zohar*, trans. David Goldstein, vol. 2 (Oxford: Oxford University Press, 1989), 677–748.

system, two additional layers were added on to these three; namely, *ḥaya* and *yeḥidah*.[118] These soul levels, in turn, both parallel, and are comprised of, the five worlds as well as the *partzufim*. For example, the lowest level of soul, called *nefesh*, parallels both the world of *asiyah* and the *partzuf* of *raḥel*. However, within the *nefesh* is also contained all five worlds as well as all five *partzufim* in all their stages of development. Furthermore, each of the worlds also contains within it all the levels of soul. Within each of the levels of soul are also contained the other levels of soul as well as the *sefirot*. These endless layers of associations are unique to Luria and characterize what Scholem has called his "baroque" style.[119]

When a person is first born they automatically receive a *nefesh*, the lowest level of soul. If, through fulfilling the Torah, they purify their *nefesh* sufficiently from the dross of the *qelipot*, they may then acquire the next highest level of soul. The parts of soul that are not integrated into the individual during their lifetime must return in future lifetimes in order to continue its process of purification. Even though according to Luria the soul consists of five parts, only the three lower levels of *nefesh*, *ruaḥ*, and *neshama* need completion and integration in order for an individual to be freed from the cycle of reincarnation.[120] When all three levels of soul are united within the individual, he is freed from the cycle of reincarnation, and he returns above to his place in the unified cosmic soul.

Vital describes in extraordinary detail how and under what circumstances these different soul parts transmigrate. Firstly, only a "new" soul—that is, a soul that is in its first incarnation—has the potential to acquire all three levels of soul in a single lifetime.[121] At birth they receive a *nefesh*; at the age of thirteen, if they have proven worthy through their good deeds, they receive a *ruaḥ*; and if, by the age of twenty, they have still remained pure, then they also acquire a *neshama*.[122] However, if during this person's first lifetime they do not merit to receive higher levels of soul, those soul parts must return in future incarnations until they have become completely realized.[123] Vital describes this process:

118 *ShG*, ch. 1, 9.
119 See Scholem, *MTJM*, 271. Also see *ShG*, ch. 1, 12.
120 See ibid., ch. 2, 12–16.
121 There are two types of "new" souls in the Lurianic system, both of which have the potential to free themselves in one lifetime from the need to transmigrate, although the methods are different for each of these respective soul types. I shall discuss these differences below.
122 The attainment of the different parts of soul at these respective ages only applies to one category of "new soul," as I shall explain below.
123 *ShG*, ch. 2, 13. The notion that the higher levels of soul descend at the age of thirteen and twenty, respectively, is based on a passage from the *Zohar* (II: 94b).

Indeed, if he did not restore his *nefesh* completely the first time [i.e. during his first lifetime], and he expired from the world, then his *nefesh* must return in a *gilgul* numerous times until it completely purifies itself. At that point, even though [the *nefesh*] is completed its *ruah* does not enter it, since the *nefesh* can only be restored by means of *gilgul*, except under extreme effort, as will be explained later, God willing. Therefore, he must [first] expire from the world, [so] the *nefesh* [can] return in a *gilgul*, and then it [i.e. the *nefesh*] merits [to receive] its *ruah*. And if he restores also his *ruah*, then he must expire from the world and reincarnate again, so that his *neshama* can enter him, in the same way the *ruah* entered him before. But if he does not restore his *ruah*, then the *nefesh* together with the *ruah* must reincarnate numerous times until the *ruah* is restored. Then the man dies, and the *nefesh*, *ruah* and *neshama* reincarnate together until all three are restored. Then he does not need to reincarnate any more, since once the *neshama* is restored he is considered a "completed man" as is known.[124]

In this passage, Vital outlines a major difference between "new" and "old" souls. While "new" souls have the potential to integrate all three parts of their souls in one lifetime, and thus be spared from the burden of reincarnation, "old" souls—any soul that has not freed itself during its first incarnation—are destined for a longer more complicated process.[125] "Old" souls cannot draw down

---

124 *ShG*, ch. 2, 13. All translations in this book are mine:

ואמנם אם לא תקן את הנפש לגמרי בפעם א' ונפטר מן העולם אז צריך שתחזור הנפש ההיא בגלגול עד
כמה פעמים עד שתזדכך כל צרכה לגמרי ואז אע"פ שנשלמה אין הרוח שלה נכנס בה כיון שלא נתקן
הנפש אלא ע"י גלגול אם לא בדוחק גדול כמו שיתבאר לקמן בע"ה ולכן צריך שיפטר מן העולם ותחזור
הנפש להתגלגל ואז תזכה אל הרוח שלה ואם יתקן גם הרוח אז צריך שיפטר מן העולם ואח"כ יתגלגל
ותבא בו גם הנשמה ע"ד הנזכר בענין הרוח ואם לא תקן הרוח צריך שיתגלגלו כמה פעמים הנפש עם
הרוח עד שיתוקן הרוח ואז ימות האדם ויחזור ויתגלגל הנפש והרוח וגם הנשמה עד שיתוקנו שלשתם
ואז איל לו צורך עוד להתגלגל כלל כי בהיות גם הנשמה נתקנת הרי הוא אדם שלם כנודע.

Elsewhere Vital presents a different, conflicting, version of how this process occurs. There he writes that after the individual dies his *nefesh* remains above in the upper worlds while his *ruah* descends into his body, "garbing" itself in the *nefesh* of a convert, or *ger*. This happens because the *nefesh*, which has been completely purified, cannot serve as the dwelling place of a *ruah* that is still impure. However, once he completely restores his *ruah*, his true *nefesh* then descends to replace the *nefesh* of the *ger* as the "chariot" of his higher levels of soul. See *ShG*, ch. 1, 12 and see my discussion of this topic and references on page 34 note 88 and page 87 note 95.

125 *ShG*, ch. 7, 28. The division between "new" and "old" souls is a little bit more complicated in *ShG* than I have presented it here. For a more detailed exposition on their differences, see *ShG*, chs. 6–7, 25–32, and ch. 12, 42–43.

higher levels of soul while they are yet alive; rather, once they have completely purified one level of soul (and this itself may require numerous lifetimes), they must then die before they can acquire the next.

So, if someone works on purifying his *nefesh* for a number of lifetimes, and then finally succeeds, he must then wait until the body that he inhabits during that lifetime expires. Then, in his next incarnation he receives a *ruah*, and once he perfects that, he must again wait to die before he receives a *neshama* in the following transmigration. Only once the *neshama* is rectified is the individual considered to be "completed" and is henceforth freed from the cycle of rebirth.[126]

However, there are certain measures that specific people can take in order to shorten the duration of this often long and painful process. In the passage cited above, Vital refers to these measures when he writes that "the *nefesh* can only be restored by means of *gilgul*, except under extreme effort, as will be explained later, God willing." The "extreme effort" he refers to is the performance of specialized meditations that, if done under the proper conditions, enables certain souls to draw down higher levels of soul during their own lifetime, thus sparing them future incarnations. These meditations will be explored in detail in chapters one and two.

As mentioned above, according to Lurianic myth the original fall of Adam had dire consequences for both the celestial and terrestrial worlds. His sin not only caused the descent of the entire spiritual world of *asiyah* into the realm of impurity, but it also caused many of the souls contained within his own to fall and become trapped in the *qelipot*. These souls manifested in the material world as individual human beings whose sole/soul mission is to both extricate the divine sparks of light from the *qelipot* as well as redeem their own souls from this realm of impurity.

126　The question of what happens to a person once their *nefesh* is completed and they are stuck waiting around to die before they are able to acquire a *ruah* or *neshama* is addressed by Vital in a number of interesting ways. One solution he offers is that of the "secret of impregnation," or *sod ha-ibbur*. According to this doctrine, once a person has perfected his *nefesh*, the *ruah* of righteous people, or *tzaddikim*, who have already freed themselves from the cycle of reincarnation and who now dwell above in the upper worlds, can descend and dwell upon the *nefesh* of this individual. The same is true of a person who has perfected his *nefesh* and *ruah* and is now waiting to die in order to receive his *neshama*. Depending on the merits of the individual, even great souls from Jewish history, including the forefathers themselves, can inhabit one's body in order to help them perform various good deeds. Although, as Vital points out, the motives of these great souls are not always altruistic: they too receive merit above in paradise for the commandments performed through their agency, and they often descend for their own benefit. See *ShG*, ch. 2, 14–15.

Luria describes Adam's fall into the material realm as the "diminishment" of his stature. His cosmic limbs "shrunk," so to speak, as his garments of light (אור) were transformed into garments of skin (עור).[127] Some of Adam's cosmic limbs fell off of him altogether, descending deep into the nether worlds. As Adam's cosmic dimensions diminished in order to accommodate their new abode in the material world, all the souls that were contained within his own soul responded in one of three ways. The souls that emanated from the highest sources in the cosmic world abandoned Adam altogether and returned to the upper worlds. Some souls, however, remained with Adam after his fall and helped him restore his own soul substance, albeit in a more material context. Most souls, however, fell, along with some of Adam's own "limbs," into the depths of the qelipot.[128]

The first category of souls—those that returned to the upper worlds after Adam's sin—are called by Luria "completely new souls."[129] When a soul of this type descends into the material world and is born into a human body it can very easily free itself in its first lifetime from the need for future incarnations. Only a soul from this category automatically receives a ruah at the age of thirteen and a neshama at the age of twenty, provided that they have remained free from sin.[130]

The second category of souls—those that remained with Adam after his sin and helped reconstitute his soul substance—are called by Luria "new souls" (as opposed to "completely new souls"). Adam later transferred these souls to his sons Cain and Abel. Vital describes this transference of soul substance to Cain and Abel as a direct "inheritance" from their father, one that took place during Adam's own life, and thus does not fall under the category of gilgul at all. The human souls that have their roots in the souls of Cain and Abel are considered to be "great souls" since they had the strength to remain with Adam after his sin and resisted falling into the qelipot.[131]

---

127 Ibid., ch. 7, 28; Scholem, "Gilgul," 229–230.

128 ShG, ch. 7,28; also see Scholem, "Gilgul," 232. Vital offers a somewhat different division of the categories of soul in ShG, ch. 12, 42–43 and in ibid., ch. 39, 164. See this last reference for the inclusion of the souls of gerim, or converts, as a separate category in its own right. On the souls of gerim, see page 86ff and especially note 95. For prior scholarly attempts to outline the various categories of soul according to Luria, see Fine, Physician of the Soul, 306–307.

129 ShG, ch. 7, 28: The phrase here is נשמות חדשים לגמרי. I cannot explain the obvious grammatical error in this phrase except to assume it was an editorial oversight by Hayyim or Shmuel Vital.

130 Vital interprets the passage from the Zohar II: 94b outlining the different ages that one receives the different levels of soul as referring only to this type of soul. ShG, ch. 7, 28.

131 Ibid., ch. 7, 28–32. Scholem points out that the gilgulim of the souls that have their roots in the souls of Cain and Abel hold a major place in Luria's mythological system. Many of the great souls of Luria's generation, including Luria himself, are described as coming from this

When a soul of this type inhabits a physical body, it too has the potential, like a "completely new soul," to acquire all the necessary soul parts in a single lifetime. The difference is that a plain "new soul" must work exceedingly hard in order to make this happen, unlike the first type of soul, for whom this task comes quite easily. Furthermore, the only way for this second type of soul to actually accomplish this feat is by performing specialized meditations on the verse from Isaiah 26:9, "My *nefesh* desires You at night," as the individual goes to sleep at night. These *kavvanot*, which I shall discuss more fully in the next parts of this book, have the effect of bypassing the rules of the game, so to speak, in that they enable the individual to draw down the next highest level of soul without having to first die and reincarnate in another body.[132]

The third category of souls—those that descended into the *qelipot* after Adam's sin—are considered to be descendants of the soul of Seth, Adam's third child. These souls have no way of drawing down the higher soul levels in a single lifetime and therefore must undergo a minimum of three incarnations before they even have the possibility of becoming free.[133] The *kavvanot* that are designed to shorten the duration of the transmigration process do not work for souls of this type.[134] Therefore, before we outline the details of these meditations it is important to understand that these practices only work for souls of the second type; namely, those souls that have their roots in the souls of Cain and Abel.

Despite articulating the most detailed and consequential metaphysical and contemplative system in all of Jewish history, Lurianic Kabbalah remains largely unexplored territory by scholars of Jewish mysticism.[135] Nearly all of the academic contributions to our understanding of Lurianic Kabbalah to date builds upon the assumptions put forth in the foundational studies of Gershom Scholem and Isaiah Tishby conducted in the 1940s. With only a few exceptions,

---

soul category. See Scholem, "Gilgul," 235–236 and 309n95. In another place, Vital writes that most souls in the world today are from this category. See *ShG*, ch. 6, 26.

132 Ibid., ch. 7, 29.

133 The first lifetime is spent restoring the *nefesh*, the second the *ruah*, and the third the *neshama*. Therefore, a soul of this type requires at least three lifetimes to complete its mission. Ibid., ch. 7, 30.

134 *ShG*, ch. 7, 28–29.

135 See, e.g., Lawrence Fine's statement: "The cosmological myth Isaac Luria taught is without doubt the most elaborate such story in all of Jewish tradition" (*Physician of the Soul*, 124). Also see Elliot Wolfson's comment positioning Lurianic Kabbalah as "unquestionably the most complex body of Jewish mystical literature" (published on the back cover of Magid, *Metaphysics*).

the basic orientation of these scholars to Lurianic Kabbalah as an expression of mystical dualism has remained unquestioned and unchallenged.

This study will call into question some of these assumptions by exposing a more radical mystical process at the heart of Lurianic teaching. Not only does Luria celebrate the reconstitution of the anatomical structure (in resurrection) through the transgression of physiological limitation (in intentional death), but in the process the cosmos is also neutralized of all comparative status. That is, the deconstruction of the human soul is in a dialectically reciprocal relationship with the reconstruction of the cosmos: as the self is deconstructed (through the *kavvanot* to expedite rebirth), the cosmos is reconstructed (through the anatomical development and sexual union of the male and female aspects of the Godhead), and as the self is reconstructed (through resurrection of the dead), the cosmos is deconstructed (of hierarchical rank).

This radical expression of mystical paradox is a far cry from the sterile architectonic (as Scholem put it, "baroque"[136]) and normatively constructed dualistic character of Lurianic Kabbalah portrayed in the limited works of scholarship devoted to its explication. Indeed, Luria's mystical vision represents a remarkably nuanced and precise metaphysical perspective that is refracted throughout the voluminous treatises of Vital and embodied in the extensive network of contemplative practices that make up the primary modes of practice in this tradition. It is my wish that this book help illuminate for the seasoned scholar—as well as for the contemporary student of mysticism—these core mystical dynamics at the heart of Lurianic Kabbalah.

---

136 See Scholem, *MTJM*, 271.

CHAPTER 1

Sleep and Rebirth

> Life does not proceed by the association and addition of elements, but by
> dissociation and division.
>
> —Henry Bergson

In the remaining sections of this book I will examine the meditative techniques
taught by Luria to help the mystic achieve in a single lifetime what would ordinarily require many. In chapter one, I will examine those *kavvanot* that pertain to
the recitation of the bedtime *shema*, and are to be performed when going to sleep
at night. The next set of *kavvanot*, explored in chapter two, are to be performed
during the *nefilat apayim* prayer in the morning service immediately following
the *amidah*. As far as I know, these are the only descriptions in all of Jewish literature that advocate the intentional splitting of one's soul.[1] As such, a detailed
exploration of these practices is crucial to more fully appreciate the implications
of the Lurianic doctrines concerning the pentapartite soul and the dynamics of
its dismemberment in the process of reincarnation.

Through the translation and analysis of these Lurianic sleep-time meditations, I will also demonstrate how the internal dynamics of these *kavvanot* are
patterned on the metaphysical template of cosmogenesis as articulated in Lurianic mythology. Just as cosmic human, in the form of *adam ha-rishon*, undergoes a primordial process of sleep and dismemberment, so too the soul of the
Lurianic practitioner is nocturnally severed as a transitional stage towards the
optimal and ultimate development of the individual consciousness. By mimicking the anatomical fragmentation of the divine body (i.e. the severance of the
partzufim), the human adept ironically serves to embody the divine more fully,

---

1   Scholem briefly mentions these practices (see Scholem, *MTJM*, 271) although he does
    not discuss them in any detail. Menachem Kallus devotes only a footnote in his doctoral
    book to the subject of these exercises and admits that "these fascinating practices deserve
    separate analysis" (Kallus, "Theurgy," 296n7). Also see Kallus, "Pneumatic Mystical Posses-
    sion," 175n7. I am not aware of any other references to these practices in any published work
    to date.

ultimately leading to the reintegration of the fragmented soul into the unitive cosmic womb and the re-somatization of the individual body at the time of resurrection.

THE ANATOMY OF SLEEP

The sleep time practices designed by Luria to free the soul from the need for future incarnations are inextricably linked to both the supernal dynamics of his cosmic drama as well as with the larger context of the Lurianic *kavvanot* of prayer that provide the script for these contemplative performances.[2] For Luria, the act of sleep is seen to be the human parallel of the *tardemah* (primordial process of slumber) that overtakes *zeir* in his elaborate myth of cosmogenesis. In this metaphysical narrative, the two lower *partzufim* of *zeir* and *nuqvah* reach developmental maturation through the infusion of *mohin* (*consciousness*) from the more sublime *partzufim* of *abba* and *imma*.[3]

---

2 The mystical function of sleep in Lurianic Kabbalah develops themes already established in earlier kabbalistic texts, particularly in the Zohar. The Zohar's treatment of the subject is in turn based on earlier formulations in rabbinic literature, particularly on the Talmudic correlation of sleep with death. See, e.g., *BT Berachot* 57b, where it states that "sleep is one sixtieth of death." On the concept of sleep in aggadic literature see Woolf Hirsch, *Rabbinic Psychology*, vol. 2 [Hebrew] (London: E. Goldston, 1947), 199–203 (cited in Tishby, *Mishnat HaZohar* [Jerusalem: Mosad Bialek, 1971] 125). However, the Zohar develops the relationship between sleep and death in much more explicit and provocative ways than we find in rabbinic literature. There are several sub-themes underscored by the Zohar in terms of this mystical correlation. The first is the principle that during sleep the animating life force almost completely leaves the physical body, rendering it ontologically similar to death. See, e.g., Zohar II: 215b and I: 83a. The second sub-theme regards the associative nexus of *shekhinah*, *sitra ahra* (the "other side," i.e., the realm of evil), nighttime, and death. See Zohar II: 215b and I: 35b, where the *shekhinah* is called the "tree of death" when separated from *tiferet* and the other *sefirot*. Other associated themes include the relationship between the *shekhinah* and the term "night" and with nighttime in general (See, e.g., Zohar II: 38b), and on the correlated dominance of the *sitra ahra* during the night, and on its association with the term "death" (see Zohar III: 119a). On the specific dynamics of the soul's ascent to the upper realms during sleep, see the passage in Zohar II: 142a. Other kabbalistic texts from the same period as the Zohar also make this correlation. See, e.g., *Sefer Shoshan Sodot, Sod Keriyat Shema she-al ha-Mita*, 42, and Recanati's *Peirush al ha-Torah, Bereishit*. For an example of a kabbalistic text authored during the period between the Zohar and Luria that develops these themes, see Meir ibn Gabbai, *Tola'at Ya'akov, Sod Tefillat Aravit*, 12. For another example of the synthesis of these themes, see the Zohar's articulation of sleep as an act subject to the realms of *shekhinah*, death, and the *sitra ahra* (Zohar I: 206a–206b).

3 On the transference of *mohin* into *zeir* and the development of his (and *nuqvah's*) anatomical stature, see *EH, Heychal Zeir Anpin, Shaar Ha-mohin*, chs. 1ff; *ShK, Rosh*

There are two different accounts in Vital's writings describing this process. The first posits that the *mohin* that descend into *zeir* in order to form his consciousness (that is, his upper three *sefirot*) are exclusively derived from the *netzah, hod,* and *yesod* of *imma*. In other passages, however, his language implies that the *mohin* that animate *zeir* and affect his development stem from both *imma* and *abba*.

Vital addresses this apparent contradiction by explaining that there is a difference between the ontological status of *abba* and *imma* and that of *zeir* and *nuqvah*. Since *zeir* and *nuqvah*'s union is temporally conditioned, when they are not actively engaged in *hieros gamos*, their ontology remains distinct. However, *abba* and *imma* are established in a condition of continuous or permanent union (*zivvug temidi*), which precludes any possibility for ontological rupture between the two. Therefore, Vital admits that whenever he states that the *mohin* descend from *imma* into *zeir* (clothed in her *netzah, hod,* and *yesod*), he is implicitly including *abba* in that process, since he is perpetually embedded inside *imma*.[4]

However, while *zeir anpin* attains full maturation by means of the *mohin* he receives directly from *imma* (and by association, *abba*), *nuqvah*'s development is arrested since she is still a mere "point" embedded in *zeir*'s backside, specifically in his posterior ribs. As such, the *mohin* that she receives at this point is restricted to those that filter through the back of his body.[5]

Ha-Shanah, chs. 1–9; ShK, *Inyan Derushei ha-Laylah*, ch. 6; PEH, *Sha'ar Keriyat Shema she'al ha-Mitta*, ch. 3.

4 See, for example, ShK, *Inyan Derushei ha-Laylah*, ch. 6, 358:

נודע שיש חילוק בין או"א לברא וברתא כי ברא וברתא הם חלוקים זה מזה ...

אבל או"א כחדא שריין וחשובים כא'. ואבא תדיר אתגניז גו אימא. ונמצא שאעפ"י

שתמצא תמיד כתוב בדברינו שהמוחין דז"א נעשו מין נה"י דאימא ודאי שג"כ הם מכח אבא.

(Know that there is a difference between *imma* and *abba* and the son and daughter [i.e. *zeir* and *nuqvah*], since the son and daughter are separate from each other. But *imma* and *abba* abide as one and are considered one. And *abba* is always hidden within *imma*. And it is found that even though you will always find it written in our words that the consciousness [*mohin*] of *zeir anpin* is made from the *netzah, hod* and *yesod* of *imma*, they are certainly also from the power of *abba*.)

5 See ShK, *Inyan Derushei ha-Laylah*, ch. 2, 341. Elsewhere, Vital states that before the *nesirah* (the anatomical "sawing," or dismemberment, of *zeir* and *nuqvah* that I will discuss in more detail below), *nuqvah* is positioned as a "small point" inside *zeir*'s *yesod*, in the aspect of face-to-face union. See ShK, *Inyan Rosh ha-Shanah*, ch. 1, 216 and ShK, *Inyan Derushei ha-Laylah*, ch. 6, 361, where Vital accounts for the two positions of *nuqvah*: "And you need to know that this "point" is able to stand face-to-face with *zeir anpin* at all times." The reason for this is presented by Vital in ShK, *Inyan Tefillin*, ch. 5, where he explains that when *nuqvah* is in the condition of a "small point" she embodies the aspect of *keter* and thus is capable of face-to-face union with *zeir*.

The complex process of *zeir* and *nuqvah*'s anatomical development is outlined in greater detail in several places in Lurianic literature, and not surprisingly the most comprehensive treatment of this topic can be found in texts that deal primarily with the mystical meaning of sleep.[6] One such passage is in his introduction to the *kavvanot* for the blessing *hamapil*, recited during the bedtime *shema*, where Vital rehearses the central Lurianic drama of the creation of Adam and Eve (*ḥavah*) and the cosmological correspondences in the anatomical formations of *zeir* and *nuqvah*. In this version of the narrative, when *zeir* was first created on the sixth day of creation he consisted of only the lower six *sefirot* and lacked the upper three of *ḥokhmah*, *binah* and *da'at*. To remedy this deficiency, *imma* projected her lower *sefirot* of *netzaḥ*, *hod*, and *yesod* into *zeir*

ודע כי הנקודה הי' הנזכרת היא בחינת הכתר שברחל והיא שרשית ועיקרית בה. והט"ס האחרות הם התחתונות שמן החכמה שבה ולמטה. ואלו הם הבאים לה בסוד תוספת כמבואר אצלנו ... ואז אותה נקודת הכתר דרחל להיותה שרש רחל ועצמותה לכן בעלותה באצילות יושבת עם ז"א פב"פ.

(And know that this point of the ten [*sefirot*] that was mentioned is in the aspect of *keter* that is in *raḥel*, and it is fundamental and essential to her. And the other nine *sefirot* are the lower ones from *ḥokhmah* and below. And these are those that come to her in the secret of "addition" as it is explained by us ... and then that point, the *keter* of *raḥel*, since she is the root and essence of *raḥel*, therefore when she ascends to *atzilut* she sits with *zeir anpin* face-to-face.)

In terms of the maturational process itself, the specific *moḥin* that descend in order to develop the *partzuf* of *zeir* are garbed in the *netzaḥ*, *hod*, and *yesod* of *imma* (or *binah*) when she is in the aspect of *tevunah*. They enter into *zeir* and provide him with the nourishment necessary for his development, at the culmination of which he is referred to by the name "Adam." Since *nuqvah* is situated at the back torso of *zeir* (according to one version) through a small opening at the back of his chest, these *moḥin* are then transmitted to *nuqvah*, providing her with some degree of nourishment but not enough to complete her developmental process. See *ShK, Inyan Derushei ha-Laylah*, ch. 2, 240–341:

בתחילה בהיותה דבוקה באחוריו קודם הנסירה היה חלק אור המוחין שבתוך ז"א הראוי להגדיל הנוקבה נכנס תחילה תוך ז"א ואח"כ יוצא האור מתוכו דרך נקב אחורי החזה לחוץ ובונה הכלים של הנוקבא והיתה היא צריכה לקבל ולינק ממנו ולכן לא יכלה להגדיל לגמרי.

(At the beginning when she is attached to his backside before the sawing [*nesirah*], the part of the light of consciousness that is within *zeir anpin* and that is fitting to develop the female [*nuqvah*] enters first into *zeir anpin* and afterwards the light goes out from him through the way of the hole at the back of the chest to the outside and builds the female's vessels. And she was required to receive and suckle from him and therefore she was not able to fully develop.)

6   See *ShK, Inyan Derushei ha-Laylah*, ch. 6 and the companion version in *PEH, Sha'ar Keriyat Shema she'al ha-Mitta*, ch. 3. Also see *EH*, gate 29, *Sha'ar ha-Nesirah*, chs. 1–9; *ShK, Rosh HaShanah*, ch. 1 and especially ch. 3; *ShK, Inyan Tefillin*, ch. 5; *ShK, Inyan Sukkot*, ch. 3; *ShK, Inyan Derushei ha-Laylah*, ch. 4–6.

and from these three *sefirot* (also categorized as *zeir*'s *moḥin*) *zeir*'s upper three *sefirot* were formed.[7]

At the same time that *imma*'s *sefirot* emanate down into *zeir*, the original three *sefirot* that serve as *zeir*'s upper triad (*ḥesed*, *gevurah*, and *tiferet*), ascend into *zeir*'s cephalic region to form the three cranial cavities which are then infused with the three *moḥin* that descend from *imma*. The *moḥin* received from *imma* then interpenetrate with the *ḥesed*, *gevurah*, and *tiferet* that form the cranial cavities of *zeir* and from them a new triad are constructed. This new triad then descends to form the standard *ḥesed*, *gevurah*, and *tiferet* of *zeir*.[8]

Once these three newly refurbished *sefirot*, and in particular, *tiferet*, descend from *zeir*'s cranium in order to establish his torso, a small hole is bored into the posterior side of his chest within which the "head" of *nuqvah* is formed. At this stage, *nuqvah* only consists of one-tenth of the *sefirah* of *malkhut*, and thus she is referred to as a "small point." From this "small point," *nuqvah*'s stature develops in the following manner: first, her *keter* is formed from *zeir*'s *tiferet*. Then the nine *sefirot* from *ḥokhmah* through *malkhut* are formed from the backside of *zeir*'s *netzaḥ*, *hod*, and *yesod*.

Vital explains that this is why *nuqvah* is symbolically referred to by the letter *dalet* ('ד), since she is formed from only these four *sefirot* (*tiferet*, *netzaḥ*, *hod*, and *yesod*) of *zeir* and she is also dependent on *zeir* for sustenance (the word דלת alludes to the word דלה, which means "poor"). As we will see below, Once the *nesirah* is successfully carried out and *nuqvah* accomplishes the repositioning of her embrace with *zeir* in face-to-face anatomical alignment, only then she is referred to with the letter *hey* (ה), which represents a state of "wealth," referring to the completed form of her stature.[9]

Vital notes that the process outlined above is undertaken only while *nuqvah* is relating to *zeir* from the position of back-to-back, which is a position of subservience and subordination towards *zeir*. While in this position, she receives sustenance from *zeir* in the form of "illumination" that emanates from his eyes as he gazes into her through the hole in the back of his chest.[10]

---

7 See *ShK, Inyan Derushei ha-Laylah*, ch. 6.

8 Ibid.

9 Ibid., 359.

10 Ibid: והוא פותח עיניו להשגיח ולהביט בה אבל אינו מביט אלא במקום החזה שבו ומשם נוקב אור עיניו ויוצא לאחור ומאיר בה. (And he opens his eyes to watch and gaze upon her, but he only gazes in the location of his chest, and from there the light of his eyes pierces through and exits out the back and illuminates into her).

Commensurate with *zeir*'s gazing at *nuqvah* is *arikh anpin*'s illuminating gaze at and into *zeir*, which inspires a chain reaction of "gazing" that culminates in the construction of *nuqvah*'s body.[11]

As mentioned above, this process takes place on the sixth day of creation, which corresponds with Friday afternoon before the onset of the Sabbath (and it is also the first day of Rosh HaShanah, which becomes relevant in our discussion below). It should be noted that when *nuqvah* is first constructed (in the manner outlined above, from the four *sefirot* of *zeir*), she is positioned back-to-back from *zeir*'s posterior chest and caudally toward his feet.

Originally, this divine union was designed to progress into a face-to-face *zivvug*, so that male-female equalization would assert itself in the place of female subjugation to *zeir*. With the onset of gender equity, the cosmic totality would have then attained a condition of permanent balance. The reversal of the coital position was meant to be performed on Sabbath eve, but was subsequently sabotaged by the serpent's seduction of Eve. According to Luria, Eve was sexually penetrated by the serpent and inseminated with its venom (*zohama*) before the pre-Sabbath coitus with Adam could take place. This resulted in the birth of Cain and Abel, whose souls are mixtures of both Adam's and the serpent's seed and thus contain both "good" and "evil."[12]

As a result of the lust generated by the serpent's sexual activity with Eve, she and Adam had premature intercourse before the onset of the Sabbath which then disrupted the natural flow of the creative process. This disruption necessitated that their union be relegated to the status of back-to-back union rather than the more optimal condition of face-to-face union that was required for the harmonization of all the worlds.

Henceforth, a more elaborate mechanism was required to bring the female to an equal status with the male and thereby achieve face-to-face union. On the cosmic plane, this more elaborate mechanism involves the structural development of *nuqvah* over the course of the ten days of repentance (the ten days between the holidays of Rosh HaShanah and Yom Kippur) and the painstaking and piecemeal anatomical severance of her body from that of *zeir* (i.e. the

---

11 See *Yafeh Sha'ah*, 359, who interprets this act of gazing as referring to the transfer of *gevurot* from *zeir* to *nuqvah* in order to help build her structure. For an example of Vital's usage of the term "body" (גופא) to refer to *nuqvah*'s structure, see ShK, *Inyan Derushei ha-Laylah*, ch. 6, 360.

12 For a synopsis of this narrative, see ShK, *Inyan Rosh HaShanah*, ch. 1, 211 and the parallel version in PEH, *Rosh HaShanah*, ch. 4. Also see Magid's discussion of this myth in his study of the Lurianic formulation of original sin—*Metaphysics*, ch. 1

"sawing," or *nesirah*). With the successful completion of this process a proper face-to-face *zivvug* with *zeir* is able to ensue.[13] To be sure, this intricate drama contains an implicit overture towards the necessity of gender equality in the calibrations of cosmic harmonization.[14]

As discussed above, the anatomical dismemberment of *nuqvah* from *zeir* is made possible through the slumber (*tardemah*) of *zeir*. According to Luria, when *zeir* falls asleep all that remains is a mere remnant of sentience (*kista d'ḥiyuta*). This condition is actually a regression of *zeir*'s consciousness to an earlier stage of development prior to the descent of *moḥin* from *imma*, in which *zeir* only consists of the six lower *sefirot*. In this state, he is essentially a body without a soul, since the *moḥin* that he receives from above constitute the actual substance of his soul, and it is this *moḥin* that ascends while he sleeps.[15] Furthermore, the gazing of *arikh anpin* into *zeir* ceases during sleep (in fact it is the withdrawal of this gazing that is the *cause* of sleep) and consequently *zeir* loses his capacity to gaze into *nuqvah* through the portal in the back of his chest.

In this state of *zeir*'s insentience, *nuqvah* is also deprived of the nourishment that she received through *zeir*'s backside and consequently her stature is also diminished, regressing back to its original condition of a mere "point." In this state, she is able to be severed from his body. Once detached, *nuqvah* is brought to the rostral end of *zeir*'s cranium, and facing his face she receives the cosmic gaze directly from *arikh anpin* (and in some versions, she receives the *moḥin* from *imma*).[16] This infusion completes the structural development of *nuqvah*, and her stature now matches that of *zeir*. Facing each other in

---

13 See *ShK, Inyan Rosh HaShanah*, chs. 1–4 and especially ch. 3. Also see the version presented in *ShK, Inyan Sukkot*, ch. 3 which goes into more detail regarding the dynamics between the *ḥasadim* and *gevurot* as expressed exegetically through the verse "His left arm is under my head and his right arm embraces me" (Sg. 2:6).

14 On the fluidity of gender and identity in Lurianic Kabbalah in general, see Charles Mopsik, *Sex of the Soul: The Vicissitudes of Sexual Difference in Kabbalah* (Los Angeles: Cherub Press, 2005) and Magid, *Metaphysics*, ch. 3. For a psychoanalytic interpretation of the development of *nuqvah* and the *nesirah*, see Gamlieli, *Psychoanalysis and Kabbalah*, 285–317.

15 See page 53 note 4.

16 See *ShK, Inyan Derushei ha-Laylah*, ch. 6, and especially the commentary *Yafeh Sha'ah* there, 360, who points out that this is the only passage in all of Lurianic literature where Vital suggests that *nukvah*'s development occurs through the direct infusion from *arikh anpin* rather than from *imma* (and indirectly, from *abba*).

anatomical alignment and proportional symmetry, the pair can now fully engage in face-to-face union:

> Just as *zeir anpin* returned to his original status so too *nuqvah* after she developed into a complete *partzuf* [in the aspect of] back-to-back [union] as we have mentioned, she returned to her original status to be in the secret of a small point through [*zeir's*] falling into a deep sleep as we mentioned. Therefore, now she is called a צלע ("side" or "rib") and not a *partzuf*. And this is what is referred to in the verse: "And he took one of his ribs [and fashioned eve out of it]." And after she was diminished, the emanator sawed her from his backside and elevated her above, opposite *zeir anpin's* face. Then *arikh anpin* shined light into her and her rectification was completed and she grew and was built into a complete structure like her husband was at the beginning. And now they both became really equal; each to the other, Adam and Eve. And then *binah* returned to garb her *netzaḥ, hod,* and *yesod* in *zeir anpin's* head to make for him consciousness (*moḥin*) as we have said. And then the two of them were face-to-face.[17]

It should be noted with regard to the theurgic elements of *nuqvah's* structural development, that her full anatomical structure is established by the Lurianic *mekhaven* during the first section of the *amidah* prayer in the morning service, during the *avot* blessings. It is only at the end of the *amidah*, with the implementation of the *kavvanot* for the *sim shalom* blessing, that the face-to-face *zivvug* is accomplished.[18]

---

17 *ShK, Inyan Derushei ha-Laylah*, ch. 6:

> ונמצא כי כמו שז"א חזר למדתו הראשונה כן נוקבא אחר אשר הגדילה אחור באחור פרצוף שלם כנזכר חזרה
> למדתה הראשונה להיותה בסוד נקודה קטנה ע"י הפלת התרדמה כנזכר ולכן עתה נקראת צלע ולא פרצוף. חש"ה
> ויקח אחת מצלעותיו ואחר שנתמעטה נסרה המאציל מאחוריו והעלה אותה למעלה כנגר הפנים דז"א
> ואז האיר בה ה א"א והשלים תקונה והגדילה ובנאה בנין שלם כמו שהיה בעלה בתחילה ונמצאו עתה שניהם
> שוין ממש זה כזה אדם וחוה. ואח"כ חזרה הבינה להלביש נה"י שלה בריש דז"א לעשות לו מוחין כנ"ל
> ונמצא כי אז היו שניהם פב"פ.

On the two different types of face-to-face unions, see *ShK, Inyan Derushei ha-Laylah*, ch. 6, 360.

18 See *ShK, Inyan Kavvanat ha-Amidah*, chs. 1 and 6 (especially toward the end); *ShK, Inyan Rosh HaShanah*, ch. 6. Also, for the critical role of the blowing of the *shofar* in the cosmic mechanism of the *nesirah*, particularly in the "waking up" of *zeir* from his slumber, see *ShK, Inyan Rosh HaShanah*, ch. 7 and *PEH, Derush ha-Shofar*, chs. 1–3.

SLEEP AND DISMEMBERMENT

As explained in the previous section, for *nuqvah* to fully develop into a *partzuf* in her own right, she must first attain anatomical independence from *zeir*. This is achieved through a cosmic surgical procedure called *nesirah* (sawing) that dismembers *zeir*, anatomically separating *nuqvah* from him and establishing her as an independent cosmic entity.[19] As mentioned above, in order for this procedure to take place, *zeir* must first be "anesthetized"; that is, he must be rendered insentient in order for the *nesirah* to properly take place and in order to allow the appropriate *mohin* to flow into her directly from *imma* and *abba* without first traversing through him.

In this process, *zeir* falls unconscious and the *mohin* that were transmitted to him from above alight from him and enter directly into *nuqvah* who is attached to *zeir*'s backside. This is how Luria understands the "slumber" that overtakes Adam that is reflected in Genesis 2:21: "And YHVH *Elohim* caused a deep sleep (*tardemah*) to fall upon Adam." Before *zeir* falls asleep, the *mohin* that *nuqvah* received came through a small opening at the back of *zeir*'s chest; however, once he falls asleep his *mohin* departs his body and is free to enter into *nuqvah* directly without first filtering through him at all.

This direct transference of *mohin* occurs by first entering into the *partzuf* of *leah*, which is the aspect of *nuqvah* that is anatomically aligned with the top part of *zeir* (along his backside), from his chest and above. Then the *mohin* descend into *rahel*, who is positioned below *leah* in anatomical alignment with *zeir*'s lower sections. This firsthand infusion of *mohin* allows these two *partzufim* of *leah* and *rahel* to develop such that they integrate into one unified *partzuf* whose measure equals that of *zeir*. With the achievement of male-female anatomical alignment, the stage is then set for the *nesirah* to take place, which establishes the mutual independence necessary for face-to-face *zivvug* to take place.[20]

Elsewhere, Vital explains the primordial roots of this process. The slumber and ascent of *zeir*'s soul stimulates the union of *imma* and *abba* and as a

---

19 Concerning this, see the exegetical comment by Vital in *ShK, Inyan Derushei ha-Laylah*, ch. 4, 341: "And this is what the verse says, "And he took one of his ribs" (Gen. 2:21): the meaning is: "He sawed him."" For sources on the *nesirah*, see the previous note. For Lurianic sources that address different elements of this myth, see *EH*, gate 29, *Sha'ar ha-Nesirah*, chs. 1–9; *ShK, Rosh HaShanah*, ch. 1 and especially ch. 3; *ShK, Inyan Tefillin*, ch. 5; *ShK, Inyan Sukkot*, ch. 3; *ShK, Inyan Derushei ha-Laylah*, ch. 6

20 See ibid., ch. 4.

result of their intercourse, *mohin* descend into *nuqvah* in order to develop her structural stature.[21] In this same passage, Vital formulates the *nesirah* as a process whose main objective is to separate the forces of "judgment" (*dinim*) from the backside of *zeir* and merge them into the backside of *nuqvah*, leaving *zeir* in a condition of pure *hesed* ("love") and *nuqvah* possessing only *gevurot* (literally "strengths," equivalent to "judgments" or *dinim*). Then through back-to-back union, the unification is achieved, and *nuqvah* 's "judgments" are "sweetened" by *zeir's* "love."[22]

Thus, we see that this intricate process of divine slumber begins when the *mohin* first enter into the *partzuf* of *leah*, which is the aspect of *nuqvah* anatomically aligned with the top part of *zeir* (along his back), from his chest and above. Then the *mohin* descend into *rahel*, who is positioned below *leah* in anatomical alignment with *zeir's* lower sections. This firsthand infusion of *mohin* allows these two *partzufim* of *leah* and *rahel* to develop such that they integrate into one unified *partzuf* whose measure equals that of *zeir*.

A remarkable event then occurs as result of *zeir anpin's* act of sleep: the twofold rupture of the divine body. The first aspect of this involves the severance of *zeir's* "soul" from his body while he is asleep in the condition of *tardemah*. Vital writes:

> Concerning the matter of the deep sleep of *zeir anpin*, for behold "A deep sleep fell upon him and he slept" (Gen. 2:21), and then his *mohin* departed from him, and it is known that his *mohin* are in the aspect of his soul and his spirit; that is, his soul ascends above to *abba* and *imma*.[23]

---

21 *ShK, Inyan Rosh Hashanah*, ch. 1, 216.

22 In this scenario, the act of *nesirah* occurs through the agency of pure *hesed* as embodied in *imma*. This is anchored by Vital in the verse from Lev. 20:17: "And if a man takes his sister it is a *hesed* ." This verse is interpreted as follows: When a man (*zeir*) takes (i.e. saws off) his sister (*nuqvah*), it is through the act of *hesed* (that is, through *imma*, this is accomplished). See *ShK, Inyan Rosh Hashanah*, ch. 1, 216.

23 *ShK, Inyan Derushei ha-Laylah*, ch. 4, 348:

בענין הדורמיטא והתתרדמה של ז"א כי הנה נפלה עליו תרדמה וישן ואז המוחין שלו מסתלקין ממנו ונודע שהמוחין שלו הם בחינת נשמתו ורוחניותו ועולה נשמתו למעלה עד או"א.

Elsewhere, Vital specifies that when *zeir's* "soul" ascends during the *dormita*, all that is left inside *zeir* is a mere remnant of sentience that maintains the animation of *zeir's* "body." See *ShK, Inyan Rosh HaShanah*, ch. 1. There, Vital also equates the *mohin* with the soul explicitly: "For at the time of the slumber of *zeir anpin*, his soul, which is his *mohin*, ascends." See *ShK, Inyan Rosh Hashanah*, ch. 3, 226 and compare with the nearly identical statement in *PEH, Sha'ar Rosh HaShanah*, ch. 3.

This dislocation of *zeir*'s soul from his body serves as the general template for the ascent of the human soul during sleep that we will encounter in more detail later on in this study. To be sure, the Lurianic adept is explicitly encouraged to view himself as mimicking this process of somnolence and severance that permits *zeir*'s soul to ascend to more recondite spheres in the cosmic hierarchy:

> And behold concerning the issue of the intention of sleep, the matter is that the person must intend that also during the time of sleeping he is serving his Creator, in the secret of "In all your ways, know Him" (Prov. 3:6). And that is, that the person should intend that he himself is the aspect of the male *zeir anpin*, that the emanator cast upon him a slumber and he slept.[24]

A striking parallel to this Lurianic principle that calls upon the worshipper to see himself as *zeir* can be found in the Hindu lineage of Advaita Vendata, where the texts claim that in deep sleep the practitioner unites with God. In the words of Swami Nikhilinanda: "we learn that in dreamless sleep the *jiva* becomes united with *Isvara*."[25] If we compare the Vedantic *jiva* and the Lurianic *mekhaven* ("worshipper"), and *zeir* with *Isvara*, we see that just as the human soul unites with *zeir* (albeit through the agency of *nuqvah*) in the Lurianic *kavvanot* of sleep, so does the contemplative Advaitin merge with *Isvara*.

24　*ShK, Inyan Derushei ha-Laylah*, ch. 4:

> והנה ענין כונת השינה ענינה הוא שצריך האדם לכוין כי גם בעת השינה עובד את בוראו בסוד בכל דרכיך
> דעהו. והוא שיכוין האדם שהוא עצמו הוא בחינת ז"א דכורא אשר הפיל עליו המאציל תרדמה וישן.

Cf. Vital's articulation of the ascension of the soul to *imma* in *ShK, Inyan Rosh HaShanah*, ch. 1, 215:

> ואז ז"א לבדו בבחינת נשמתו המסתלקת ממנו בעת התרדמה והשינה עולה למעלה בסוד מ"ן אל אימא עילאה
> כדרך האדם המפקיד נשמתו ביד המלכות לצורך מ"ן שבה

(And then *zeir anpin* alone, in the aspect of his soul that departs from him at the time of the deep sleep (*tardemah*), ascends above in the secret of female waters to upper *imma* in the manner of the person who deposits his soul in the hand of *malkhut* for the needs of the female waters that are within her.)

Also Cf. the rather explicit expression of this correspondence in *PEH*, ch. 11, 337: "And as we have explained, when the soul ascends at night at the time of sleep so it is also the secret of the slumber (*dormita*) of *zeir anpin*." On the direct homology of *zeir* with both *adam ha-rishon* and the human Lurianic practitioner, see Kallus, "Theurgy," 143n27.

25　See Swami Nikhilinanda, *Vedantasara or the Essence of Vedanta of Sadananda Yogindra* (Calcutta: Advaita Ashrama, 1968), 35.

If *zeir*'s deep sleep serves as the template for the human being's deep sleep (or if *zeir* and the human are homologous, as they ultimately are in Lurianic practice), we find a similar association in Advaita Vedanta. After presenting primary texts that illustrate these points, the Advaitia Vedanta scholar Arvind Sharma writes: "The striking result that is achieved by adopting these approaches is the equation of *prajna* or the self in dreamless sleep on the micro scale with Isvara or God on the macro scale."[26] This statement echoes some of the formulations in Lurianic texts in which the practitioner is encouraged to be like *zeir* in performing the appropriate sleep-time practices.[27]

There are other interesting correlations between Lurianic teachings on sleep and the nondual tradition of Advaita Vedanta, which reflect some of the epistemological considerations that we have explored above. First, the broader metaphysical questions of dualism and nondualism are of central concern as much for the Advaitin as they are for Luria.[28]

Secondly, Advaita Vedanta also maintains a sophisticated doctrine describing the stages of consciousness that are traversed during the various phases of sleep, and also correlates these processes with dimensions of self-identity and with the journey of reincarnation.[29] Third, in Advaita

---

26 Arvind Sharma, *Sleep as a State of Consciousness in Advaita Vedanta* (Albany: SUNY Press, 2004), 91.

27 See, for example the following passage from *ShK, Inyan Derushei ha-Laylah*, ch. 4:

And behold concerning the issue of the intention of sleep, the matter is that the person must intend that also during the time of sleeping he is serving his Creator, in the secret of "In all your ways, know Him" (Prov. 3:6). And that is, that the person should intend that he himself is the aspect of the male *zeir anpin*, that the Emanator cast upon him a slumber and he slept.

See the original Hebrew and my discussion above, page 61 note 24.

28 See my discussion of these parallels below on page 147. Also see especially the classic philosophical reconstruction of these metaphysical questions in Elliot Deutch, *Advaita Vedanta: A Philosophical Reconstruction* (Honolulu: University of Hawaii Press, 1980).

29 On the relationship between states of consciousness and sleep in Advaita Vedanta, see Sharma, *Sleep as a State of Consciousness in Advaita Vedanta*, vii: "One of the well-known doctrines associated with Advaita Vedanta is that of *avasthātraya*, or of the three states of consciousness: waking (*jāgrat*), dreaming (*svapna*), and deep sleep (*susupti*). Out of these three states of daily experience, Advaita Vedanta often draws on that of deep sleep to validate an argument, point a moral, or even adorn a tale." There are several obvious correlations between the Advaitin understanding of deep sleep and that of Luria. In classic Advaitin philosophy, while the mind ceases to function in deep sleep, the persistence of identity remains due to the presence of the "witnessing consciousness" (See ibid., 59). For an interesting study of the question of identity in Advaita Vedanta specifically, see Arvind Sharma, "Dreamless Sleep and Some Related Philosophical Issues, *Philosophy East and West* 51, no. 2 (April 2001): 210–231.

Vedanta texts, deep sleep is commonly referenced as a mechanism to impart mystical teachings about the nature of reality.[30] Fourth, Advaita Vedanta recognizes only a subtle distinction between the cessation that occurs at death and the suspension of mind that occurs during sleep, echoing the rabbinic tradition that sleep is one-sixtieth of death and the subsequent Lurianic practices that build upon this principle.[31]

SLEEP AND DREAMS

Vital not only outlines the precise anatomical mechanics of *zeir*'s slumber in terms of the ascent of his *mohin*, but he also unpacks the implications of the *kista de-ḥiyuta*, the "remnants of consciousness" that remain behind during his ascent. In this account, *zeir*'s lower six *sefirot* remain behind, garbed in the surrounding light of *imma*'s lower three *sefirot* that are lodged inside the throat of *zeir*. This configuration of sentience is the source for the inner vision that becomes available during sleep and that produces dreams. See, for example, the following passage:

> When the three "greater" *mohin* of the divine names spread through the body of *zeir anpin*, by necessity they pass through his throat, where they are garbed within the "smaller" *mohin* of *elohim* [i.e. of *imma*] and are covered over when they are within them. And when *zeir anpin* sleeps in the secret of the *tardemah* as mentioned, dreams come to him from the "greater" divine names that remain within the "smaller." Because they [i.e. his greater consciousness] did not completely ascend, and from what remains of them, the dream is drawn to *zeir anpin*, who sees and envisions as if he were awake.[32]

---

30 See the sources cited in the previous note.
31 Many Advaitin teachers go much further than this in their equation of the state of deep sleep with that of both death and the ultimate state of liberation from *avidya*, the "ignorance" that is the condition that leads to rebirth. See the citations in Sharma, *Sleep as a State of Consciousness in Advaita Vedanta*, 68–69.
32 See ShP, *Vayeshev*, "ויוסף הורד מצרימה":

בהתפשט ג' המוחין דגדלות דהוי"ת תוך גופא דז"א, עוברים בהכרח דרך הגרון, ושם מתלבשים תוך
המוחין דקטנות דאלהים, ומתכסים בהיותם שם בתוכם. וכשישן ז"א בסוד התרדמה כנזכר, אז בא
אליו החלום, מן בחי' הוי"ת דגדלות, שנשארו תוך הקטנות, כי לא נסתלקו לגמרי, וממה שנשאר
מהם, שם נמשך מהם החלום לז"א, שרואה ומביט כאלו הוא בהקיץ.

In this passage, Vital positions dreaming as emanating from the expanded consciousness that is latent within the contracted consciousness that is located in the throat. This is articulated more clearly in the following passage:

> Sleep and slumber, which are the absence of perception, are drawn from "small consciousness" (*moḥin de-katnut*). And dreaming, which has a degree of perception but is covered and hidden, comes from "big consciousness" (*moḥin de-gadlut*) that remains in them, garbed within the "small consciousness" that is in the throat.[33]

In Lurianic Kabbalah, the dreaming consciousness is thus understood to be anatomically centered in the throat, a correspondence that is also found in both the Hindu tantric tradition of Kashmiri Shaivism and also in the Tibetan Buddhist tantric teachings of the Bon School.[34] For example, in the spiritual autobiography of Shaivite teacher Swami Muktananda, the throat center is a central locus of inner experience in sleep. He writes:

> When you go to sleep to remove your fatigue, at night or during the day, it is in the throat center that your fatigue is dispelled. Only there do you fall asleep. ... This proves that sleep is a treasure, which lives in the throat center and which I call Shveteshwari, the white goddess.[35]

Elsewhere, Swami Muktananda elaborates more on the function of the white goddess Shveteshwari: "The subtle body, which is shaped like a thumb and which I have hitherto spoken of as Shveteshwari, is the means by which the individual soul experienced the dream state."[36] Since Shveteshwari lives in the throat center, here we see that in Muktananda's lineage of Hindu tantra, the dream-center is also located in the throat.

---

33 Ibid. Also Cf. with ShP, Bo, "בא אל פרעה."
34 For an example of the Shaivite correspondence where the throat center is associated with sleep, see Swami Muktananda, *Play of Consciousness* (South Fallsburg: SYDA Foundation, 1978), 7–8. In Tibetan Buddhism, the throat is correlated with dreaming specifically. See, e.g., Tenzin Wangyal Rinpoche, *The Tibetan Yogas of Dream and Sleep* (Ithaca: Snow Lion, 1998) 117. Also see Andrew Holecek, *Dream Yoga* (Boulder: Sounds True, 2016), 65. See my discussion below on the Buddhist correspondences.
35 Muktananda, *Play of Consciousness*, 8.
36 Ibid., 116.

This correspondence is also evident in the Vajrayana teachings of Tibetan Buddhism, where an entire system of yogic practice is performed during sleeping and dreaming. For example, according to Tenzin Wangyal Rinpoche, the main meditation practice utilized to induce lucid dreaming begins with the instruction to visualize "a red, luminous *A* in your throat chakra."[37] According the aforementioned scholar, the throat center is also the seat of dreams, as he writes: "The teaching says that focusing on this chakra produces gentle dreams."[38] This practice is explained in more detail by Andrew Holecek:

> When you lie down to go to sleep, bring your mind to your throat, which is where your consciousness gathers when you dream. Visualize a red pearl or red AH there. ... In this visualization, you are pulling consciousness (the drops) from waking consciousness to dreaming consciousness.[39]

In this passage, Holecek clarifies some of the metaphysical elements of the practice. When the practitioner performs the appropriate visualization of the Tibetan syllable *AH* in the throat center, "drops" of consciousness (called *bindus*) are concentrated there.[40] In particular, these "drops" are understood to fall from the head center down to the throat, where they gather and concentrate to enable dreaming.[41] Thus, this contemplative maneuver focuses the mind in the throat—an anatomical location associated with the experience of lucid dreaming.

Vital describes a similar process in his explication of the cosmic dynamics of sleep and dreaming. The consciousness (*moḥin*) first descends from the

---

37 Rinpoche, *The Tibetan Yogas of Dream and Sleep*, 116. Cf. with his description of the practice on page 94, where focusing on the throat chakra is positioned as the first step for entering into the sleep and dream state.

38 Ibid., 85. Note the following passage from the same page, which describes this practice in more detail:

> Visualize a beautiful red lotus with four petals in the throat chakra. The throat chakra is at the base of the throat, closer to where the neck meets the shoulders than to the head. In the center of the four petals, facing forward, is an upright, luminous Tibetan A, clear and translucent, like crystal made of pure light. Just as a crystal laid on red cloth reflects the color and appears red, so does the A pick up the red of the petals and appear red. On each of the four petals is a syllable: RA to the front, LA to your left, SHA to the back, and SA to the right. As sleep comes, maintain a light, relaxed focus on the A. This part of the practice is meant to bring the mind and prana into the central channel. The quality is peaceful, and as we merge with the deep red A we find peace within ourselves. The teaching says that focusing on this chakra produces gentle dreams.

39 Holecek, *Dream Yoga*, 65.

40 Ibid., 61.

41 Ibid., 66.

head center (from the *sefirot* of *ḥokhmah, binah,* and *da'at*) down into the throat, where the dynamic between the expanded consciousness (*moḥin de-gadlut*) and contracted consciousness (*moḥin de-katnut*) interact to produce dreams.[42] Interestingly, this dynamic of contraction and expansion that is clearly correlated with the throat center in Lurianic Kabbalah is similarly understood in Tibetan Buddhism. For example, in his presentation of the first sequence of dream yoga practices, Tenzin Wangyal Rinpoche writes: "The chakra used is the throat chakra, which is energetically connected to potentiality and expansion and contraction."[43]

In the above analysis, I have noted some striking parallels between Tibetan Buddhism, Hindu Tantra, and Lurianic Kabbalah in terms of the relationship between sleeping, dreaming, and the throat center of consciousness. Since historical lines of influence between these traditions and Lurianic Kabbalah are unlikely, these similarities may point to common mystical insights that arose across cultures and wisdom streams. While this suggestion is rife with epistemological problems,[44] it nonetheless beckons us to consider the possibility that certain dimensions of human experience share a common core across traditions and cultures.[45]

---

42 See *ShP, Vayeshev,* "ויוסף הורד מצרימה" and my translation of this passage above.

43 Rinpoche, *The Tibetan Yogas of Dream and Sleep,* 117. For another interesting parallel see *ShP, Yechezkel, Siman* 21, where Vital states: "All pride is in the throat." Compare this with the statement by Tenzin Wangyal Rinpoche that "Pride is associated with the chakra in the throat." See ibid., 39.

44 On the epistemological limitations of language in the study of comparative mysticism, see Steven T. Katz, "Language, Epistemology, Mysticism," in *Mysticism and Philosophical Analysis,* ed. Steven Katz (New York: Oxford University Press, 1978), 22–74.

45 While some scholars maintain the position that there is an essential core to all mystical experience, others contend that all experience is determined by one's particular cultural, linguistic, religious, and environmental context. The essentialist (or perennialist) position was first articulated by William James in his lecture on mysticism published in *Varieties of Mystical Experience* (New York: Penguin, 1982), 206–233, and has been followed up and developed further by figures such as Wayne Proudfoot, Aldus Huxley, and Huston Smith. The contextualist position was first professed by Katz in his "Language, Epistemology, Mysticism," and in a second article titled "The Conservative Character of Mystical Experience," in Steven Katz, *Mysticism and Religious Traditions* (New York: Oxford University Press, 1983), 3–60. Katz's approach has also been developed by other scholars such as Robert Gimello; see his "Mysticism in Its Contexts," in ibid. On the contours of this debate in general and for more recent contributions to this question, see the collection of essays published in *On the Problem of Pure Consciousness: Mysticism and Philosophy,* ed. Robert Forman (New York: Oxford University Press, 1997) and especially the critique of Katz's argument presented there in Donald Rothberg's "Contemporary Epistemology and the Study of Mysticism," 163–210.

SOUL RUPTURE AND COSMIC UNION

Thus far we have clarified the first dimension of *zeir*'s process of slumber, which is the severance of *zeir*'s "soul" from his body while he is asleep in the condition of *tardemah*. The second aspect of cosmic dismemberment induced by *zeir*'s sleep involves the anatomical dislocation of *nuqvah* from *zeir*'s body. As we saw above, this process, termed *nesirah* in Lurianic parlance, serves to complete the structural development of *nuqvah*'s body by establishing her anatomical autonomy and resourcing her sustenance directly from *imma*.[46]

The parallels between the slumber of *zeir* and the human practitioner are further established during the performance of certain *kavvanot*, whereby the ascent of the soul during sleep is utilized as an occasion for the intentional dismemberment of the soul. In this process, the metaphysical premise that the soul is divided into multiple parts allows for the different soul-parts to be contemplatively dislocated from each other during sleep for the evolutionary/messianic goal of integrating all souls back into the universal soul of *adam ha-rishon*. In other words, just as *nuqvah* is anatomically severed from *zeir* in order to prepare her for a more optimal (and equitable) union, so too the human soul is dismembered during sleep in order to achieve a more complete condition of maturity, expressed in the release from the bonds of rebirth.

According to Lurianic teachings, prior to the destruction of the second temple in Jerusalem in 70ce, the formal liturgical prayers were sufficient to raise up both the internal and external dimensions of the worlds, which respectively correspond to the soul and the physical body.[47] However, following the destruction of the temple only the inner dimensions, which are synonymous with the soul, could be elevated through the performance of the *kavannot*.[48] That is, only the soul of the worlds, but not its vessels, or external casings, are restored to its primordial condition through human effort (through the ascent of the human soul in sleep or in the raising up of the sparks through

---

46 In some versions, the function of the *nesirah* is to resource *nuqvah*'s nourishment directly from *arikh anpin*, not *imma*. See *ShK, Inyan Derushei ha-Laylah*, section *Kavvanot* for Bedtime *Shema*, and page 57 note 16, above.

47 See, e.g., the statement in *EH, Heichal Nuqvah de-Zeir anpin*, gate 40, *Sha'ar ha-Hashmal*, ch. 1: "The souls are called inner and the vessels which are the body are called outer." The constructs of "inner" (*penimiyut*) and "outer" (*chitzoniyut*) layers of the soul also reflect the larger metaphysical design that has the same categories describing the cosmic realms. For more on this topic, see *EH, Sha'ar Penimiyut v'Chitzoniyut* and Pachter, "Clarifying the Terms *Katnut* and *Gadlut* in the Kabbala of the Ari and a History of Its Understanding in Hasidism": 171–210.

48 See, e.g., *ShK, Inyan Rosh HaShanah*, ch. 2, 220.

contemplative practice). Therefore, through the dismemberment of the soul in the *gilgul* process, this inner dimension of the worlds is restored to a perfected state through the proper ascent of the multiple soul-parts to its locus of origination in the cosmic realms.

However, this process of dismemberment only marks the penultimate fulfillment of the journey of *tiqun*, since while it restores the internal essence (*penimiyut*) of creation to its primordial roots, it does not rectify its external expressions (*ḥitzoniyut*). In order to properly cap the theatrical project of creation, the external manifestation of the world, represented by the physical world and the human body, must also be completely divinized (and the divine, materialized). As we will see in more detail in chapter two, the apotheosis of the physical body through the mystical process of resurrection (*teḥiyat ha-metim*) represents the terminal transformative event that integrates body and soul as the microcosmic expression of total cosmic fulfillment.[49]

To understand how the mystic intentionally dismembers his soul as the first stage of this ultimate process of *tiqun*, we need to appreciate the broader theurgic system of the Lurianic *kavvanot* of prayer, whose primary function is to re-establish the cosmic order that fell into disarray following the primordial rupture of the vessels. The *kavvanot* accomplish this by executing hyper-focused

---

49 On the divinization of the physical body, see Luria's exposition on the transformation of the physical bodies of the ten martyrs in *ShMRshB*, 166–168, and see my discussion of this theme throughout chapter two of this book. At play is an interesting inversion of the theme of "descent for the sake of ascent" (*yeridah k'tzorekh aliyah*), a central trope in Lurianic metaphysics and theurgy in general. Here, we see a movement of "ascent for the sake of descent." I.e. the adept's soul (like *zeir* in the primordial creative process) ascends in order to be refreshed and renewed only that it might descend again, now mystically restored and in a higher spiritual condition than it was prior to its original ascent. See, e.g., the statement in *ShK, Derushei ha-Laylah*, ch. 2: "And we find that by means of the slumber (*dormita*) he attains a higher level." Based on this metaphysical template established by the *tardemah* of *zeir*, we can also speculate as to why according to Luria women do not reincarnate. On this Lurianic principle, see *ShG*, chs. 9, 20 and *SeG*, ch. 13. Since the process of reincarnation is intimately linked to the mystical dynamics of sleep, only the soul of the male (qua *zeir*) would technically ascend above during sleep, since it is only the male that is *zeir anpin* incarnate. Thus, there is no need for women (qua *nuqvah*) to reincarnate since they do not need to sleep in the mystical sense. However, this suggestion must be explored further, especially in light of the fact that under certain circumstances women may enter into the body of someone who is already alive (See, e.g., *SeG*, ch. 13) and that there is also evidence that there are distinct masculine and feminine souls. For a more elaborate discussion on the nature of a feminine soul incarnated in a masculine body, see *ShP, Parshat Vayera* and the discussion in Kallus, "Theurgy," 299n20. Also see the important study regarding this question in Mopsik, *Sex of the Soul*.

contemplative exercises to stimulate the sexual activity of the *partzufim*. Through the mutual exchange of erotic fluids, the agitated disruption in the cosmic nervous system is regulated, and creation above and below is saturated with blessings.[50] This cosmic inter-coursing of sexual fluids and aroused genitalia are reflected in the human consciousness in the form of Hebrew letters; specifically, the letters that coalesce to articulate the various divine names.[51] Cathecting one's contemplative intention, or *kavvanah*, onto these divine names, and then manipulating the letters and names in precise ways, impacts which sexual position will be engaged by the divine paramours.[52]

There are three categories of *zivvug* that are affected by the contemplative's *kavvanot*, and each category has two components. The first category pertains to which cosmic couple will be stimulated to coition: *abba* and *imma* or *zeir* and *nuqvah*.[53] The second category relates to the sexual position: back-to-back or face-to-face.[54] The third category addresses the type of copulation: "Priming

---

50 The sexual functioning of the *partzufim* is implicit throughout Lurianic Kabbalah and can be found on nearly every page of Vital's writings. On the centrality of *eros* and desire in Lurianic Kabbalah, see Magid, *Metaphysics*, 31. On the centrality of sexual union in Kabbalah in general, see Moshe Idel, *Eros and Kabbalah* (New Haven: Yale University Press, 2005) and Mopsik, *Sex of the Soul*. For a possible textual influence on Lurianic conceptions of sexual activity, see the erotically charged passage in R. Moses Cordovero's *Teffilah le-Moshe*, vol. 1 (n.p.: Premyshlan, 1892), 213a-b.

51 Indeed, even the letters are sexually active. See, e.g., the vaginal penetration of *nuqvah* by Imma's fingers, embodied as the letters מנצפ"ך. See *ShK, Inyan Derushei ha-Laylah*, ch. 3, 345 and my discussion below on page 81ff.

52 For an overview of the main formulations of the divine names and how they correspond to the *partzufim* and the various other cosmic forms see Kallus, "Theurgy," 134–140 and Magid, *Metaphysics*, 31–33.

53 There are also sub-categories for each of these unions. For example, in the *zivvug* of *zeir* and *nuqvah*, it could be either Jacob or Israel copulating with either Rachel or Leah. The same applies to *imma* and *abba*, each of which also manifest as different forms at different times (e.g., as *yisrael saba* and *tevunah*). For more on the different forms of each of the *partzufim*, see Magid, *Metaphysics*, 24–29; Kallus, "Theurgy," 130–131 and the notes there; Fine, *Physician of the Soul*, 138–141. Which specific forms of a given *partzuf* are sexually engaged at a given time depends on many factors including the time of day or night, the day of the week, the coordinates on the annual cycle of the season and/or holy days, etc. However, the primary framework that governs the patterns of inter-divine sex is the daily prayer cycle. At each of the formal prayer services, as well as at other contemplatively strategic times (e.g. going to sleep or *tiqun hatzot*), the various combinations of *zivvugim* are stimulated in different ways. These complex and interpenetrating dynamics make up the bulk of the theoretical material that frames the practices of the *kavvanot* of prayer.

54 On the differences between the back-to-back and face-to-face unions and each of their respective relationships to the *kavvanot* of prayer, see Kallus, "Theurgy," 144–156.

penetration," which readies the womb of either *imma* or *nuqvah* for impregnation, or "conception penetration," which initiates the fertility process.[55]

The daily prayer cycle governs these patterns of inter-divine penetrative sex. At each of the formal prayer services as well as at other contemplatively strategic times various unions (*zivvugim*) are contemplatively stimulated by the Lurianic kabbalist. The meditations that we are concerned with, those designed to free the soul from the cycle of rebirth, are executed during the larger series of *kavannot* associated with the bedtime *shema* and are to be performed upon going to sleep at night. The corresponding *zivvug* that is enacted through the performance of the *kavvanot* for the bedtime *shema* has two functions. The first is to benefit the ascending souls themselves, that they be restored and refreshed.[56] The second is to support the cosmic coupling of *zeir* and *nuqvah* that is to take place after midnight. The latter union falls under the category of "priming penetration," discussed above, which prepares *nuqvah* or *imma*'s reproductive organs for the more primary *zivvug* that takes place at midnight and in the morning prayer service.[57]

The primary *zivvug* of *imma* and *abba* takes place during the recitation of the *shema* during the morning service, followed by *zeir* and *nuqvah* (in the aspect of Jacob and Rachel) during the *sim shalom* prayer at the end of the morning *amidah*. Since the sexual functioning of *zeir* and *nuqvah* is dependent on the influx of orgasmic fluids from above, the general pattern of the *zivvugim* requires that first *imma* and *abba* merge in sexual union followed soon after by that of *zeir* and *nuqvah*.[58]

---

55 These are terms that I have devised to refer to the two types of sexual intercourse found in the Lurianic literature. Vital refers to them as "the first intercourse" (*bi'ah rishonah*) and "the second intercourse" (*bi'ah sheniyah*). This notion is based on the passage in BT Yevamot 34b and on several sections of the Zohar (see, e.g., Zohar II: 99b–100b) that suggest that the first intercourse prepares the female as a vessel for future impregnations. For more on the differences between "first" and "second" penetrations, see my discussions throughout chapter two of this book, and Kallus, "Theurgy," 248–249.

56 See *ShK, Inayn Derushei ha-Laylah*, ch. 3; *PEH, Shaar Rosh HaShanah*, ch. 3.

57 Vital explains that the reason why *imma* also requires "priming" with a "first intercourse" has to do with the *moḥin* that she transmits to *zeir* (encased in her *netzaḥ, hod,* and *yesod*). In the course of the transmission, the spirit that she was inseminated with in her first intercourse with *abba* (called the *avira dakhyah*) is lost and must be replenished with further "first intercourses." See *ShK, Inyan Derushei ha-Laylah*, ch. 8.

58 See *ShK, Inyan Derushei ha-Laylah*, ch. 8. See as well, e.g., *PEH, Sha'ar Rosh HaShanah*, ch. 3. These "orgasmic fluids" are my poetic translation of the Lurianic term *itrin* lit. "crowns," that flow from the sexual union of *imma* and *abba* and descend in order to arouse the union of *zeir* and *nuqvah*.

These introductory remarks have outlined the metaphysical background and theurgical context for the performance of the specialized *kavvanot* designed to free the practitioner's soul from future incarnations. These *kavvanot*, embedded within the meditations of the bedtime *shema*, express the logical and practical implications of Luria's metaphysical view that posits:

1) A divine slumber (*zeir's tardemah*) resulting in
2) The dismemberment of *zeir's* body/soul (the dismemberment/*nesirah* of *nuqvah* from his body and the concurrent ascent/dislocation of his soul/*moḥin* and its transference to *nuqvah*) and
3) The somatic integration of the dislocated parts in the face-to-face union of *zeir* and *nuqvah*, resulting in the unification of these two divine bodies.

Furthermore, as these metaphysical principles telescope through the assumption that *zeir* is the ontological prototype for the human practitioner and that the *mekhaven* (the "worshipper") is explicitly exhorted to intend that "he is *zeir anpin*" when he goes to sleep, it thus makes sense that the Lurianic adept would also go through a parallel process of sleep, body/soul dismemberment, and somatic integration. The contemplative mechanics of these first two processes will be examined in the next sections. The third step of somatic integration is realized in the resurrection of the physical body, and will be explored in chapter two of this book.

KAVVANOT FOR BEDTIME SHEMA

As explained above, when a "new soul," or a soul that descends from the souls of Cain and Abel, is born into a physical body and the individual succeeds in purifying his *nefesh*, he is then poised to receive his *ruaḥ* from the upper spheres. Generally speaking, even a soul of this caliber must wait until its next lifetime before it can acquire its higher soul parts. However, as Vital explains, there are ways this person can accomplish in one lifetime what would ordinarily take many:

> With extreme effort, it is possible for a "new soul" [i.e. those that descend from the souls of Cain and Abel] to attain in a small degree the three souls—*nefesh*, *ruaḥ* and *neshama*—together, at one time and in one body, so that he does not require many *gilgulim*, and that he complete the

restoration of those three [soul parts] in one single *gilgul*. At the beginning, when the *nefesh* first reincarnates alone, if it is completely restored but the *ruaḥ* cannot yet descend as we have explained ... there is one *tiqun* [that may be performed] ... and that is, when the person goes to sleep at night and "deposits" his *nefesh* into God's hands, as is known, it is possible that his *nefesh* remain above, cleaving to the "upper well" in the secret of the female waters ... and when he awakens from sleep in the morning, then his *ruaḥ* alone enters him, and this is as if he actually reincarnated another time in another body. Then he continues to restore [the *ruaḥ*] until it is completely restored, at which point the *nefesh* can return to the body as it was before, since both [the *nefesh* and *ruaḥ*] are now restored. Then the *ruaḥ* garbs itself in the *nefesh*, and the *nefesh* becomes a chariot [for the *ruaḥ*]. Afterwards, if the *ruaḥ* is completely purified, it is possible that both the *nefesh* and *ruaḥ* go out at night at sleep time, in the secret of a "deposit" as was mentioned. They remain there above, and then in the morning when he wakes from sleep his *neshama* enters him and he restores it. After he has completed its restoration, the restored *nefesh* and *ruaḥ* return and enter [him], and the three unite together in his body, each one being a chariot for the other, as is known. Then he will not need any more *gilgulim*.[59]

In this passage, Vital outlines how this process works. When a "new soul" that has restored his *nefesh* wishes to acquire his *ruaḥ* without reincarnating, he can "deposit" his *nefesh* in the "upper well in the secret of the female waters" when he goes to sleep at night. His *nefesh* then remains above in this celestial realm while his *ruaḥ* descends into his body. In the morning, he wakes up to find a new *ruaḥ* and a new mission; his task now becomes to purify and restore his

---

59 *ShG*, ch. 3:

בדוחק גדול אפשר שיזכה החדשה קצת להשיג שלשתם ביחד נר"ן בפעם אחד בגוף אחד ולא יצטרך לגלגולים רבים
וישלים תקון שלשתם בגלגול אחד לבדו. והענין הוא כי הנה כי כאשר נתגלגל הנפש לבדה בתחילה אם נתקנה בתכלית
התכוך לגמרי והנה אז אין הרוח יכול לבא עמה כנ"ל לפי שהיא שלימה והוא חסר התקון אמנם יש לו תקנה אחת
כיון שנתקן הנפש לגמרי כנ"ל והוא כאשר אדם ישן בלילה ואז מפקיד נפשו בידו יתברך כנודע אפשר שתשאר
נפשו למעלה דבוקה בבאר העליון בסוד מיין נוקבים כמבואר אצלינו בשער התפילה בשכיבת הלילה וע"ש וכאשר
יעור משנתו בבקר יכנס בו הרוח לבדו והרי זה כאלו נתגלגל ממש פעם אחרת בגוף אחר והולך ונתקן עד שיושלם
לגמרי ואז יכולה הנפש לחזור בגוף כבראשונה כיון ששניהם נתקנים ויתלבש הרוח בנפש ותהיה הנפש מרכבה
אליו. ואח"כ אם יזדכך הרוח לגמרי אפשר כי גם יצאו הנפש והרוח בלילה בעת השינה בסוד פקדון כנזכר וישארו
שם למעלה ואז בבקר בהקיצו משנתו תכנס בו הנשמה ותתקן בו. ואחרי שנשלם תקונה יחזרו לבא הנפש והרוח
המתוקנים ויתחברו שלשתם יחד בגוף הזה
ויעשה זה מרכבה לזה כנודע ולא יצטרך עוד לגלגולים אחרים.

Cf. the description in *ShG*, ch. 7 and *ShK*, *Inyan Derushei ha-Laylah*, ch. 10.

ruaḥ. When he completes this task, his *nefesh,* which until now had remained above, returns to his body and serves as a dwelling place for his newly restored *ruaḥ.* If the person is worthy, this same process can then repeat itself in order to acquire his *neshama.*

To be sure, this passage raises a number of questions that must be answered before we can begin to understand how this process works. Firstly, what does it mean to "deposit one's *nefesh* in the upper well"? What are the upper well and the female waters in this context? Finally, how exactly does one go about doing this? The answers to these questions are bound up in the intricate Lurianic myths that explain the relationship between sleep, soul, and the upper worlds. Therefore, before we can understand the mechanism of this *kavvanah* we must first turn our attention to these matters; specifically, to the manner in which the soul ascends to the upper worlds as the body sleeps.

Vital addresses this ascent of the soul in several different places.[60] In one section in *Sha'ar ha-Kavvanot* that deals with the meditations performed during the recitation of the bedtime *shema,* Vital explains at length how one ensures that his soul ascend to the proper place in the upper worlds as he goes to sleep at night. By meditating on the verse "Into Your hand I deposit my spirit, You have redeemed me, Lord God of Truth" (Psalms 31:6) in a specific way, certain sefirotic dynamics are catalyzed that condition the *sefirah* of *malkhut,* or the *partzuf* of *nuqvah,* to receive the individual's soul as he sleeps at night. Vital writes:[61]

> Let us explain well the verse "Into Your hand I deposit my spirit, You have redeemed me, Lord God of truth" (Ps. 31:6). You should meditate upon what I have showed you many times; namely, the two "hands" of the upper mother (i.e. *binah*), each one of which contains five fingers. They have been made a vessel for *malkhut,* in order that the matter of the female waters manifest for her within them. This is the secret of the five double letters of מנצפ״ך.[62] They flow to her from the divine name בוכ״ו which is

---

60 ShK, *Inyan Derushei ha-Laylah,* ch. 10; PEH, *Sha'ar Keriyat Shema she-al ha-Mitah,* chs. 7 and 12; *Olat Tamid,* 118; *Sha'ar M"N M"D, Derush* 4; ShK, *Inyan Tefilat ha-Shachar,* 115b; *Sefer Likutim, Tehilim,* 34; EH, part 1, *Sha'ar ha-Melachim,* ch. 6.

61 For an alternate version of the following *kavvanah* in which the soul is deposited in the *yesod* of Leah, rather than Rachel, see my discussion below on page 76ff.

62 I.e. each one of these letters represents one of the five fingers on the hands of *binah.* That each of these letters has both a middle and final form alludes to her two hands. Later on, Vital notes that *binah's* left hand is also reflected in the second "hand" alluded to in the verse "In Your hand I deposit my spirit." The first "hand" is the first word, בידך, "In Your hand." The second "hand"—ידך—is formed by the last letters of the first three words in this verse,

derived from the name which אהיה is within *binah*,[63] and whose *gematria* (numerical equivalence) is 34, the same as the word יד"ך ("Your hand," from the verse above). So, when you say the word בידך ("In Your Hand"), you should meditate on the name בוכ"ו, which has the same *gematria* as יד. By means of this name, *nuqvah* becomes a "well" (באר) and a vessel for the female waters, as alluded to by the acronym formed from the first letter of each word in the verse "In Your hand I deposit my spirit" (בידך אפקיד רוחי). You should meditate on elevating your soul towards there in the secret of the female waters, in order that afterwards *malkhut* receive male waters from her husband, and become filled from them. Then she will be called "well," as is known.[64]

בידך אפקיד רוחי. *ShK, Inyan Derushei ha-Laylah*, ch. 10, 371. On the metaphysical background for this process, see *EH*, gate 6:39, ch. 1, 132 in the Warsaw edition.

63 Each letter in the name בוכ"ו is one letter removed from its parallel letter in the name אהיה, the name traditionally associated with the *sefirah* of *binah* in Lurianic texts. Thus, it is "derived" from that name. This is a common technique utilized by Luria to reveal secret relationships between various words and divine names. For a more detailed explication of the numerical and linguistic equivalents of the name בוכ"ו and, in particular, on its role in the development of *nuqvah*'s anatomical structure, see *ShK, Kavvanat ha-Amidah*, ch. 5, 225. In this passage, we also have an interesting correlation established by Vital between this developmental process and resurrection of the body, which I think alludes to a more radical nondual perspective echoed in other Lurianic texts. See my discussion below, page 142 note 114.

64 *ShK, Inyan Derushei ha-Laylah*, ch. 10, 371:

נבאר פסוק בידך אפקיד רוחי כו' באר היטב מכמה כוונות והוא כי צריך שתכוין אל מה שהודעתיך
פעמים רבות ענין השני ידים דאימא עלאה אשר יש בהם חמשה אצבעות בכל יד והם נעשו כלי אל
המלכו' להיות לה בתוכם ענין המ"ן ואלו ה"ס ה' אותיות כפולו' דמנצפ"ך ואלו נמשכים לה משם
בוכ"ו הנמשך מן שם אהיה שבבינה שעולה בגי' ל"ד כמנין יד"ך כמבואר באורך בברכת אתה גבור
וע"ש ותכוין מלת בידך אל שם בוכ"ו הנז' העולה גי' ידך והנה ע"י השם הזה נעשית הנוקבא באר
וכלי דמ"ן הנרמז בר"ת בידך אפקיד רוחי ותכוין להעלות שם נשמתך בסוד מ"ן כדי שתקבל אחר כך
המלכות מבעלה מ"ד ותתמלא מהם ואז תהיה נקרא באר כנודע.

For a slightly different version of this meditation see *PEH, Sha'ar Keriyat Shema She'al ha-Mittah*, ch. 11, 334–339. This *kavvanah*, which appears in several places in Lurianic texts, is based on the following passage from *Zohar III: 119a*:

א"ר אלעזר כתיב בידך אפקיד רוחי פדיתה אותי יי אל אמת האי קרא אית ליה לאסתכלא ביה חמיתון מאן
דאפקיד בידא דמלכא מידי. אלא ודאי זכאה הוא בר נש דאזיל באורחוי דמלכא קדישא ולא חטי קמיה. תא חזי
כיון דעאל ליליא אילנא דמותא שליט בעלמא ואילנא דחיי אסתלק לעילא לעילא. וכיון דאילנא דמותא שליט
בעלמא בלחודוי כל בני עלמא טעמין טעמא דמותא. מ"ט בגין דההוא אילנא גרים וכד בר נש בעי לאקדמא
ולמפקד בידיה נפשיה בפקדונא בפקדונא דבר נש דיהיב פקדונא לאחרא דאף על גב דאיהו אתחיב לגביה יתיר
מההוא פקדונא לאו כדאי לאתאחדא ביה האי ובפקדונא אתמסר לגביה. ואי יסרב ביה ודאי נבדוק אבתריה
דלאו מזרעא קדישא הוא ולאו מבני מהימנותא. כך ההוא אילנא בני נשא אקדימו ויהבין ליה פקדונא דנפשייהו
וכל נשמתין דבני עלמא נטיל. וכלהו טעמין טעמא דמותא בגין דהאי אילנא דמותא הוא ובגין דכל אינון נפשתא

The goal of this meditation is to prepare *nuqvah* or *malkhut* to receive the soul of the one who is going to sleep at night. First the adept must focus his attention on the divine name בוכו as he utters the word בידך. By concentrating on this divine name, which has the same *gematria* as the word ידך and is derived from the name אהיה, the adept stimulates the energies in the *sefirah* of *binah*—particularly her two "hands" composed of the two forms of the five double letters מנצפ"ך—to come together to form a receptacle, or a "well," in the womb of *malkhut* below.[65]

אע"ג דכלהו אתחייבו לגביה ולאו כדאי הוא לאתבא פקדונא לגביה דבר נש אלא כיון דכלהו אתמסרי ליה
בפקדונא אתיב כל פקדונין למאריהון.

(Rabbi Elazar said: It is written, "Into Your hand I deposit my spirit, redeem me YHVH the God of Truth" (Psalms 31). There is something to see in this verse. Do you recognize who deposits something in the hand of the king? Certainly, the person who walks in the way of the holy king and who does not sin before him is innocent. Come and see: At the time that night comes, the tree of death rules in the world, and the tree of life ascends far above. Since the tree of death alone rules in the world, all the children of the world taste the taste of death. What is the reason? Because that same tree [i.e. the tree of death] causes [it]. And the person needs to first deposit his soul into his hand [i.e. in the upper realms] as a deposit, in [the manner of] a deposit that one person gives to another. Even though he is more indebted to him because of the deposit, it is not sufficient to detain him, since the deposit is transferred to him. And if he refuses him, he will definitely check him that he is not from the holy seed, and not of the sons of faith. So too with that tree. People first give to it their souls as a deposit, and all the souls of the people of the world are taken. And they all taste the taste of death, since that tree is the tree of death. And since all those souls, even though they are all indebted to it, and it's not fitting to return the deposit to the person [himself], but rather since all of them are given to it as a deposit, therefore all the deposits are returned to their owners.)

In this passage, the Zohar also employs the verse from Ps. 31:6 to unpack the themes of sleep, death, and the depositing of the soul. However, Luria appropriates this zoharic passage for his own metaphysical and redemptive ends by situating its phenomenological mechanisms within his elaborate metempsychotic system, a dimension of meaning that is completely lacking in the Zohar.

65 On the formation of the womb of *malkhut* into a vessel see *EH, Heychal Mayin Nukvin*, gate 39, ch. 1. There Vital indicates that the contours of the womb are the female waters themselves, which receive the spirit through insemination by the male. For more on the soul's attachment to the "well," see *ShK, Nefilat Apayim*, ch. 5. The attribution of the term "well" to *malkhut* is found throughout Lurianic texts, and has its roots in the Zohar (see, e.g., *Zohar* I: 151b–152a). In his treatise *Olat Tamid*, Vital presents a different picture of the establishment of the vessel as distinct from the female waters. He clarifies that there are two aspects that constitute the vessel in *malkhut* that holds the female waters. The first relates to the more recondite process of the insertion of the three names of 72 (*yhvh* filled with the letter *yud*) from the *yesod* of *abba* into the *yesod* of *imma* in the first act of insemination. Since the numerical value of these three names is 216, Vital refers to this process as the "secret of 216." He suggests that the three forms of the name of 52 that are consequently transmitted

However, the above procedure was not the only way to perform this practice. In a personal account, Vital testifies that one night Luria "saw through his wisdom" (i.e. through pneumatic vision) that it was necessary for Vital to deposit his *ruaḥ* in the *yesod* of *leah* instead of *raḥel*, and therefore a different manner of executing the above *kavvanah* was required. However, Vital does not provide us with any more details as to what conditions necessitated this shift of focus.[66] This alternate version of the practice involves the concentration on the "prior" letters of the divine name אהיה in addition to the "subsequent" letters that appear in the standard version:

> And this is the matter of this *kavvanah*: Behold we explained earlier that with the word בידך)"in your hand"([we count] the first mention of [the word] ידך ("in your hand"). And with the last letters of [the phrase] בידך אפקיד רוחי ("in your hand I place my spirit") we have the second time [the word] בידך)"in your hand") [appears]. Behold they are [the] two hands. And you must intend that the first "hand" is the name אהיה since *leah* is the upper world that is called אהיה. And intend that the prior letters for the name אהיה are אדט"ד, and the subsequent letters are בוכ"ו, which is the numerical value of ידך. And behold אדט"ד and בוכ"ו have the numerical value of 52, for they are the aspect of the name of 52 of the female waters, which is in the *yesod* of *leah*. And afterwards intend on the first letters from [the phrase] בידך אפקיד רוחי (i.e. באר) which is the aspect of the name of 52 as we mentioned, which is אדט"ד and בוכ"ו, and the name אהיה filled with [the letter] ה', which adds up to 151. And behold 52 and 151 equals [the value of] באר in isopsephy. And this is the secret of the upper well of *leah*.[67]

---

from the *yesod* of *zeir* into the *yesod* of *nuqvah* and that serve as a vehicle to carry the female waters up to *binah*, derive ontologically from these more primordial three names of 72 that are transferred from *abba* to *imma* at the commencement of their first *zivvug*. See *Olat Tamid*, 116–119. On the five double-letters of מנצפ"ך see page 73 note 62.

66 See *ShK, Inyan Derushei ha-Laylah*, ch. 10, 371–372.

67 Ibid.:

וזה ענין כונה זו הנה נת"ל שבתחבת בידך נזכר פעם אחת ידך. ובס"ת בידך אפקיד רוחי פעם שנית ידך, הרי
הם ב' ידות. וצריך לכוין כי יד הא' הוא שם אחיה לפי שלאה הוא עלמא עלאה הנקרא אהיה. ותכוין כי אותיות
הקודמות לשם אהיה הוא אדט"ד ואותיות שלאחריו הם בוכ"ו כמנין ידך. והנה אדט"ד ובוכ"ו גימטריא ב"ן
שהם בחינת שם ב"ן של מ"ן שביסוד של לאה. ואח"כ תכוין בר"ת בידך אפקיד רוחי באר והיא בחינת שם
ב"ן הנזכר שהוא אדט"ד ובוכ"ו ושם אהיה במלוי ההין העולה קנ"א. והנה ב"ן וקנ"א גימטריא בא"ר ה. ח"ס
הבאר העליון דלאה.

On the same night that Luria imparted this practice to Vital, Luria also instructed him to perform a specialized *kavannah* upon his recitation of the bedtime *shema*. This practice entailed focusing on the two appearances of the word *shem* (שם) and the two appearances of the word *ayd* (עד) in the *shema* prayer. The first instance of the word *shem* is in the first two letters of the word *shema* (שמע); the second instance is the coupling of the first letter, *shin* (from שמע), with the last letter, *mem* (from the last word אלהיכם).[68] The first occurrence of the word *ayd* (עד), is the combination of the *ayin* from the last letter of the word *shema* (שמע) with the *dalet* from the last letter of the word *eḥad* (אחד); the second occasion is from the last two letters from the phrase *barukh shem kevod malkhuto le-olam va'ed* (ברוך שם כבוד מלכותו לעולם ועד).[69]

This is significant for our study because the very next word in this section of *ShK* begins the explanation for the *kavvanah* cited above from *ShG*, ch. 3, pertaining to the methods for achieving liberation from rebirth. In the passage from *ShK*, the *kavvanah* is much more elaborate than what is found in *ShG*, and the requirement that the adept deposit his soul specifically in the *yesod* of *raḥel* is absent. In fact, the text stipulates that the gilgul-liberation practice requires that the adept deposit his soul in the *yesod* of *leah*, not *raḥel*. This is indicated by Vital's explication of the term *be'er* (באר), where he states that "the word *be'er* alludes to what we have explained, that the *nefesh* ascends to the upper well and remains there."[70]

Furthermore, the following passage follows Vital's explicit discrimination between the upper well as referring to *leah* and the lower well signifying *raḥel*:

> And this is the secret of the upper well that is *leah*; and we have already explained that the lower well of *raḥel* is the merging of *yhvh* and *elohim*, *yhvh* and *adonay*. And behold they are two wells."[71]

The fact that Vital records this *gilgul*-liberation *kavvanah* immediately following a specialized practice transmitted to him by Luria that involved the depositing of

---

68   The last word, אלהיכם, is from the end of the third paragraph of the traditional *shema* liturgy.

69   After recording this transmission from his teacher, Vital confesses that Luria taught him an "awesome" *kavvanah* related to this but that he forgot it. See *ShK, Inyan Derushei ha-Laylah*, ch. 10, 372: "And behold concerning this teaching he [i.e. Luria] explained to me a great and awesome *kavvanah* and I forgot it." והנה בענין הדרוש הזה ביאר לי כוונה גדולה ועצומה ושכחתיה.

70   *ShK, Inyan Derushei ha-Laylah*, ch. 10: מלת באר לרמוז אל מה שביארנו שעולה הנפש אל הבאר העליון ונשארה שם.

71   Ibid: ר התחתון דרחל היא חיבור הויה ואלהים הויה ואדני והרי הם "ס הבאר העליון דלאה וכבר ביארנו כי הבא"ח שתי בארות.

his soul in the *yesod* of *leah* further clarifies that the *kavvanah* of *gilgul*-liberation examined above requires the deposit of the soul into the *yesod* of *leah* rather than into the *yesod* of *raḥel*.

This is also the formulation of the primary version of the *gilgul*-liberation *kavvanah* found in *ShG*, ch. 3, where Vital specifies that the soul is deposited in the "upper well." Since the standard version of the *kavvanah* בידך אפקיד רוחי that is performed on a nightly basis requires the deposit of the soul into *raḥel* for the duration of the night, and the *gilgul*-liberation practice requires the deposit of the completed soul-part into *leah*, thus we can deduce that the alternate version of the בידך אפקיד רוחי *kavvanah*—that deposits the soul in *leah*—is called for in such a case.

Based on this passage, we can also speculate that Luria told Vital to perform the alternate version of the nightly *gilgul*-expedition practice of "into your hand I deposit my spirit" because in Luria's estimation Vital had completed his *nefesh* and was now ready to draw down his *ruaḥ*.

THE FEMALE WATERS

The ascent of the soul during sleep thus serves two primary functions: the first is to stimulate the *zivvug* of *zeir* and *nuqvah* by functioning as female waters in enacting "priming penetration," and the second is to refresh and revive the "old" souls (that is, souls that are already incarnate in physical bodies) by "depositing" themselves inside the *yesod* of *nuqvah* at night.[72] If performed properly, the soul of the meditator will then ascend into this "well" and, as the embodiment of the female waters, play a vital role in the reunion of *nuqvah* and *zeir anpin*.[73]

---

72 See *ShK, Derushei ha-Laylah*, ch. 3, 345–346.

73 In the *kavvanot* for *nefilat apayim*, Vital describes an alternative mechanism that creates a "well" as a vessel within *nuqvah* designed to receive the practitioner's soul. The intention there is to give oneself over to "death," which is associated both with the realm of the *qelipot* as well as with *malkhut*. There are three levels of contemplative death outlined by Vital: the first, which is accomplished through the rehearsal of the *kavvanot* for *nefilat apayim*, is the basic expression of giving oneself over to death, which creates a "well" as a vessel for the female waters in *malkhut*. The second is giving oneself over to death as an act of sanctifying God's name. This can be accomplished either on the inner level through the meditative performance of *keriyat shema* (see *ShK, Inyan Kavvanat Keriyat Shema*, ch. 6, 153ff) and its attendant *kavvanot* or through the literal death of the body as an act of *kiddush hashem* as occurred, e.g., with the ten martyrs. The third is the extreme act of sacrificing one's actual physical life while in anatomical contact with the Torah. This was attained by Rabbi Akiva, when he was literally wrapped in the Torah scroll and burned alive by the Romans. (On the death of R. Akiva, see *PT Berakhot* 9:14b and *BT Brachot* 61b.) Each one of these categories

As we explained above, according to Luria the reunion of these two separated lovers is the ultimate goal of all human action and contemplation. In this particular case, the souls of the righteous help realize this union by ascending into the prepared vessel—the "well"—while their bodies sleep below. These souls themselves constitute the female waters that then ascend and arouse *zeir* to satiate *nuqvah* with his male fluids.[74]

Elsewhere Vital explains the relationship between righteous human souls and female waters more fully. According to Luria, before the second temple in Jerusalem was destroyed, *zeir* and *nuqvah* were still unified in perpetual union. At that time *zeir*, through the agency of *yesod*, "fertilized" *nuqvah* with his seed, filling and fulfilling her with nourishment from all the upper worlds. From this seed sprouted the righteous human souls, who then descended into the physical world and inhabited human bodies. However, after the destruction of the temple, *zeir* and *nuqvah* were torn from each other. The fertile seed that flowed to *nuqvah* from *zeir* ceased, putting to a halt both her own nourishment from *zeir* as well as the development of new souls from this union.[75] From that point onward, the "seed" that constitutes *nuqvah*'s main nourishment would derive from those righteous souls that once grew in her fertile soil:

---

of contemplative death in turn correlates with specific combinations of divine names and fulfills particular functions in the project of cosmic maintenance. The first level serves to implement the supernal union of *malkhut* and *tiferet* in the aspect of the "lower kiss"; the second level catalyzes the union of *hokhmah* and *binah* in the aspect of the "upper kiss." In contradistinction to the prior two practices which effect only temporary states of union through upper and lower "kissing," the third level of contemplative death establishes a permanent condition of cosmic union. See *ShK, Inyan Nefilat Apayim*, ch. 5: "It does not become a permanent chariot for this unless he gives himself over to death on the Torah, on the commandments, and for the sanctification of God in action, as R. Akiva did." The thematic constellation of death, sleep, and sex will be addressed in depth in chapter two.

74　There are many places in Lurianic literature that identify human souls with the female waters. See, e.g. *ShMRsh*, 167: "The aspect of female waters are the essence of the terrestrial human souls themselves, and understand this well and remember it, for it is a great principle, in order that you know what female waters are." בחינת מים נוקבין הם מציאות הנשמות של א"ב התחתונים עצמם והבן זה הטב וזכרהו כי הוא כלל גדול כדי שתדע מהו מים נוקבין. For other examples of this equivalency, see, *ETI*, gate 39, ch. 1, 2; *ShK, Inyan Nefilat Apayim*, ch. 5; *ShY*, 4a. On the centrality of the female waters in the theurgic processes of Luria in general see page 75 note 65 and Kallus, "Theurgy," 247. On the mythical and psychological background of the female waters in earlier kabbalistic and rabbinic literature, see Yehudah Liebes, "Ha-Mashiach shel ha-Zohar," in *Harayon ha-Mishichi be-Yisrael* (Jerusalem: The Israel Academy for Sciences and the Humanities, 1982), 179n314.

75　This is the reason why, according to Luria, after the destruction of the temple no new souls from the world of *atzilut* are able to descend into the physical world. *ShG*, ch. 6, 26.

> After the destruction of the temple, *zeir anpin* was separated from *nuqvah*, and the upper gardener, who is *yesod*, no longer seeded his garden. However, his garden was seeded by her own means; namely, from the after-growth that had already gone out and sprouted from her. From them [i.e. the after-growth] she returned and sprouted. Now these after-growths are the souls of the righteous, whom the upper gardener seeded in the upper garden before the destruction and whom sprouted in her. When they expire from this world, they return and ascend to her in the secret of the female waters ... and from them she returns and sprouts.[76]

The souls of the righteous that had grown in *nuqvah*'s garden while she was still being fertilized by *zeir* now return to her garden after they expire from this world. These souls now constitute the female waters that ascend to arouse *zeir* to once again—if even momentarily—unite with his lover below. If successful, the arousal stimulated by *nuqvah*'s waters will cause *zeir* to respond in kind with a downpouring of his own male waters, an act that should harmonize and realign the heavenly and earthly spheres.

To be sure, the souls of the righteous not only return to *nuqvah* as female waters when they die, but also when they go to sleep.[77] By concentrating on the hidden dynamics initiated by reciting the verse "Into Your hands I deposit my spirit," the righteous man prepares *nuqvah*'s "well" to receive his soul when he goes to sleep at night. If performed properly, his soul then ascends into the upper well in the secret of the female waters, thus helping to provide the necessary stimulus to arouse *zeir* to unite with *nuqvah* and consequently

---

76 *ShG*, ch. 18, 51:

אחר החרבן נתפרדו ז"א מנוקבא והגנן העליון שהוא יסוד איננו זורע גנתו. אמנם גנתו מזרעת מאיליה מן הספיחים שיצאו וצמחו בה מתחלה ומהם חזרת וצומחת. והנה חספיחים הם נשמות הצדיקים אשר טרם החרבן זרעם הגנן בגנה העליונה וצמחו בה. וכאשר חחרת ונפטרים מן העה"ז חחרים לעלות שם בה בסוד מ"ן או ביסוד שהוא הגנן העליון בסוד מ"ד ומהם חחרת וצומחת.

77 The intimate relationship between sleep and death has roots in earlier rabbinic tradition, where we find the statement that sleep is one-sixtieth of death (*BT Berakhot* 57b). Also see the comment by Ibn Ezra on Psalms 13:4 where the phrase "sleep of death" is used. This correlation is expanded in the Zohar (see, e.g., *Zohar* I: 206b–207a; *Zohar* III: 119a; *Zohar* I: 83a; *Zohar* II: 142a) and developed by Luria into a central trope of his applied system. See page 73 note 60 for more references. Entering into the sleep state is—in terms of its contemplative function—the same as death for Luria. Note, e.g., the repeated use of the term "really" or "actually" (*mamash*) in the following statement (*ShK, Nefilat Apayim*, ch. 2, 304): "And so too really (*mamash*) in this way is it really (*mamash*) in the matter of the person's sleep at night that it is also too in the secret of death." Also see Kallus, "Theurgy," 261.

provide nourishment to the lower worlds. This exercise also renews the spirit by returning it—if only for the night—to its cosmic source above. Then, in the morning the same soul that ascended the night before now returns to the body.

Thus far we have unpacked the ontological makeup of the female waters and their correlation with the souls of the righteous. However, Vital outlines two additional elements at play in the ascent of the female waters that are important for this exploration. The first relates to the "vessel" of *nuqvah*'s womb that is constructed by the five double letters of מנצפ"ך, and the second pertains to the spirit that the male leaves inside the female after coitus. With respect to the first element, Vital explains:

> The vessel of the woman's womb that receives the drop [of semen] from the male. ... This vessel itself is constituted by the upper hands of *binah*, which are her *ḥasadim* and *gevurot*. ... This is the secret of the letters מנצפ"ך which are doubled and they descend below to *nuqvah* and make her vessel.[78]

Elsewhere Vital explicates this in more detail, outlining the anatomical genesis of the letters מנצפ"ך and their transformation into the vessel of *nuqvah*. According to this version, the vessel is none other than the *yesod* of *nuqvah*, also referred to with the terms "womb" (בית רחם) and "hand" (יד) which represent the loci to which the souls ascend when going to sleep at night. As we saw above, it is called "hand" because this "womb" is constituted by five *gevurot*, which are represented by the five letters מנצפ"ך as well as by the five letters of the divine name אלהים. These five letters, in turn, derive from five anatomical "roots": the nose, mouth, arms, hands, and fingers.

While all five of the *gevurot* are included in each one of these five anatomical locations, only one of these *gevurot* is dominant in any particular location. Furthermore, it is only the singular dominant *gevurah* that is recognizable in the anatomical form; the other four are implicit and encompassed within it. However, at the most distal end of these five anatomical landmarks are the digits (i.e. the fingers), which are unique in that they are the only ones of the five loci in which all five of the *gevurot* are explicitly recognizable and revealed in

---

78 See *EH*, part 2, *Sha'ar M"N M"D 39*, ch. 1, 132:

כלי של בית הרחם של האשה כדי לקבל טפת הזכר בתוכה ... וכלי זה נעשה ע"י ידים עליונים דבינה שהם
ח"ג שלה ... ח"ס ה' אותיות מנצפ"ך שהם כפולות והם יורדים עד שם למטה בנוקבא ונעשית כלי

the anatomical form. That is, each individual finger embodies one of the five gevurot.[79]

This brings us to a remarkable event: the vaginal penetration of *nuqvah* by *imma*'s fingers in order to prime her reproductive organs for conception. This is outlined by Vital in the following passage:

> And behold in earlier times they would remove the virgins [i.e. the hymen] with a finger and would break it with the hand. And the reason was in order that the first intercourse not be a waste. And they would fix the vessel within her with a finger in order that she conceive also from the first intercourse. And this matter of breaking [the hymen] occurred above in the supernal *nuqvah* of *zeir anpin*, because the celestial hand of *imma* descended into her *yesod* and broke it [i.e. her hymen] with her finger and fixed it and made it into a vessel. And the aspect of *imma*'s five fingers remained there always for the needs of the vessel of *nuqvah* of *zeir anpin*.[80]

The source for this sexual act is a passage in the Talmud that explains that although Tamar was a virgin when Judah had intercourse with her, she was still able to conceive since she had ruptured her hymen with her finger prior to their coitus.[81]

The *zivvug* that is stimulated at night by performing the bedtime *shema* does not produce new souls like the *zivvug* that is stimulated during the day in the morning prayers. Rather, the vessel of the *yesod* of both *imma* and *nuqvah* are being prepared so that the morning *zivvug* has the potential to properly produce new souls. Therefore, it is in the aspect of the "first intercourse" or "priming penetration," while the "second intercourse" or "copulation penetration" occurs in the morning.[82]

---

79 See *PEH, Shaar Rosh HaShanah*, ch. 3 and *ShK, Inyan Derushei ha-Laylah*, ch. 3.
80 *ShK, Inyan Derushei ha-Laylah*, ch. 3, 345:

> והנה בזמן הראשונים היו מוציאים הבתולים באצבע והיו ממעכין ביד. והטעם היה כדי שגם הביאה ראשונה לא
> תהיה לבתלה וחיו מתקנין הכלי שבה באצבע כדי שתתעבר גם מביאה ראשונה. וענין מיעוך זה היה למעלה בנוקבה
> העליונה דז"א כי היד העליונה דאימא ירדה ביסוד שלה ומעכה אותו באצבע ותקנה אותו ועשאתו כלי. ונשאר שם
> בחי' ה' אצבעות אימא עלאה תמיד לצורך הכלי דנוקבא דז"א ...

Also Cf. *PEH, Sha'ar Rosh HaShanah*, ch. 3; *ShK, Inyan Keriyat Shema*, ch. 6; *PEH, Keriyat Shema*, ch. 9.
81 See *BT Yevamot* 34a. Also see *Ohr ha-Chayyim*, Gen. 49:3.
82 See page 70 note 55.

Practically speaking, *imma*'s womb is primed through the recitation of the first line of the bedtime *shema*. *Nuqvah*'s vessel is prepared, in turn, through the recitation of the second line, "Blessed is the name of the glory of His kingship forever" (ברוך שם כבוד מלכותו לעולם ועד). However, while the nighttime *shema* does not have the power to produce new souls, it does have the capacity to renew and refresh old souls; that is, souls that are already incarnated. The practitioner takes advantage of this property during sleep, when the souls ascend to this "womb" in order to be mystically renewed.[83]

The second element that fuels the ascent of the female waters pertains to the spirit that the male leaves inside the female after coitus. This is the "name of 52" (i.e. the tetragrammaton filled in with the letter *hey* and that has the numerical value of 52)[84] and is identified with the spirit inserted into *nuqvah* by *zeir* at the time of their first coitus. This divine name then serves as the vehicle that transports the female waters to her husband for subsequent unions.[85]

Elsewhere Vital suggests that the three forms of the name of 52 that are consequently transmitted from the *yesod* of *zeir* into the *yesod* of *nuqvah* and that serve as a vehicle to carry the female waters up to *binah*, derive ontologically from these more primordial three names of 72 that are transferred from *abba* to *imma* at the commencement of their first *zivvug*.[86] There he also offers a more lucid visual description of the two "hands" of *binah* (formed by the double letters of מנצפ"ך) that descend to form the vessel in *malkhut* to hold the female waters.[87] He suggests that the two hands are clasped one upon the other and are closed to form a receptacle within which the female waters are gathered:

> And these two hands of *binah* form a receptacle-vessel in *malkhut* for the
> female waters to be inside it, between the right and left hands, which are
> one upon the other and within them are the female waters.[88]

---

83 See *ShK, Derushei ha-Laylah*, ch. 3 and *PEH, Shaar Rosh HaShanah*, ch. 3. For a more detailed explication of the divine-name dynamics of these five doubled letters, see *ShK, Inyan Keriyat Shema*, ch. 6, 147.

84 The name of 52 is spelled like this: יוד הה וו הה

85 See *EH, Heychal* 6, gate 39, ch. 1 and see my discussion of this above, page 75 note 65.

86 See *Olat Tamid*, 116–119 and above, page 75 note 65.

87 See page 73 note 62.

88 *Olat Tamid*, 119:

ואלו הב' ידים של בינה נעשים במלכות כלי בית קיבול להיות בתוכו המ"ן בין יד הימנית ליד שמאלית שהם זו
ע"ג זו ובתוכם המ"ן.

In another text, Vital outlines that there are actually five different "hands" that constitute the vessel of *malkhut*; two each from *zeir* and *nuqvah* and one from *binah* which is ultimately derived from the single hand of *arikh anpin*.[89] This "single" hand of *arikh anpin* is nondual in nature in that it is comprised of two hands unified as one; the left included in the right and the right included in the left.[90] The/se hand/s of *arikh anpin* then descend into the womb of *binah* as the double letters of מנצפ"ך and from there further descend into *malkhut* and form the receptacle for her female waters.[91]

SWAPPING SOUL-PARTS

If we return to our original discussion, we can now understand what Vital meant when he wrote that a person can "deposit his *nefesh* in the upper well in the secret of the female waters." As we explained above, when a person has completely restored his *nefesh* and wants to acquire higher levels of soul during his lifetime he can perform a specific *kavvanah* in order to achieve his goal. This *kavvanah* seeks to keep the soul-part that ascended to the upper well at night in the heavenly realm so that a higher level of soul may then descend to inhabit the body of the sleeper in the morning. The proper execution of this exercise is described by Vital in the following passage:

> This *tiqun* is alluded to in the verse "My *nefesh* desires You at night, with my *ruah* within me I seek You" [Isaiah 26:9]. The interpretation [is as follows]: My aspect [of soul called] *nefesh*, when it has been completely purified and is able to cleave to You, in the secret of "And you shall cleave to Him" [Deut. 11:22], then it "desires You" and I yearn so much to cleave to you. This desire and longing is "at night," at the time when

---

89 See *EH*, part 2, *Sha'ar He-arat ha-Mohin*, ch. 7.

90 See ibid.: "And behold the two hands of *arikh anpin* are both the equivalent of one and are called one hand ... the right integrated into the left and the left integrated into the right":

והנה ב' ידות דא"א תרווייהו שקילי כחדא ונקרא יד אחד ... ימין כלולה בשמאל ושמאל בימין

91 Vital connects this with the three reincarnations of Moses as the embodiment of *yesod* of *abba*. The three incarnations of Moses are based on the acronym cipher of משה as משה שת הבל. See ibid. Also see *ShP, Parshat Shemot*. On the מנצפ"ך in general, also see *ShK, Kavvanat ha-Amidah*, ch. 5, 225; *ShK, Inyan Derushei ha-Laylah*, Derush 10; *PEH, Sha'ar Keriyat Shema she-al ha-Mitah*, chs. 7 and 12; *Sha'ar ha-Yare'ach*, ch. 3; *Sha'ar M"N M"D*, ch. 11, *Kellal* 15; *ShK, Inyan Tefilat ha-Shachar*, 115b; *ShK, Inyan ha-Tzitzit*, ch. 1.

souls ascend there and are deposited in the secret of female waters in order to arouse the upper unification. Through the power of this desire and her ability—since she is purified—to cleave there in a complete cleaving, she [i.e. the *nefesh*] remains there and does not descend. Then when the morning comes—the time when the souls descend—she does not descend. Rather, my *ruah* descends and enters into me in the morning. Therefore, I do not "seek You" [referring to the second half of Isaiah 26:9] with my *nefesh*, but rather with my *ruah*, which has entered me to be restored as we have mentioned above.[92] Therefore the first letters of the words "At night with my *ruah*" בלילה אף רוחי spell "well" באר, alluding to that which we mentioned earlier; namely, that "My *nefesh* desires" to ascend to the upper well as we mentioned. Indeed, it is proper for the man who knows for himself that he has completed his *nefesh* to recite this verse, "My *nefesh* desires You at night, etc." with the *kavvanah* that we have just mentioned when he lies down on his bed [to go to sleep]. Through this he shall attain the secret of the *ruah*, and then the *neshama*, and he will not need any other *gilgulim*. Understand this unknown secret and be careful with it.[93]

---

92 Vital seems to be alluding to a pun: the Hebrew word for "I seek You" is אשחרך, a word that shares the same root letters as the word for "dawn," שחר. Understood this way, the verse could be translated as: "My *nefesh* desires You in the night, and my *ruah* enters into me at dawn."

93 *ShG*, ch. 3, 19:

> והנה ענין התיקון הזה נרמז בפסוק נפשי אויתיך בלילה אף רוחי בקרבי אשחרך. פירוש כי הנה בחינת הנפש שלי כאשר נזדככה בתכלית הזיכוך עד שתוכל להתדבק עמך בסוד ולדבקה בו אז אויתיך ונשתוקקתי מאד לדבקה בך וענין תאוה וחשק הזה הוא בלילה בעת פקדון הנפשות שעולות שם בסוד מיין נוקבים לעורר זווג עליון. ומכח תאוה זו כיון שהיא מזוככת ויכולה להתדבק שם דבוק גמור נשארת שם ואינה יורדת. וכאשר הגיע השחר עת ירידת הנפשות היא אינה יורדת אלא רוחי ירד ונכנס בקרבי אז בשחה. ולכן לא אשחרך בבחי' נפשי אלא בבחי' רוחי הנכנס אז בקרבי להתקן כנזכה. ולכן ר"ת של תיבות בלילה אף רוחי הוא באר הוא לרמוז אל הנ"ל כי נפשי אויתיך לעלות אל בא"ר העליון כנזכה. ואמנם האדם היודע בעצמו שהשלים בחינת נפשו נכון הוא לו שיאמר פסוק זה של נפשי אויתיך בלילה וגו' בכל הכונה הנז"ל כשישכב על מטתו ועי"כ ישיג אל סוד הרוח וכן אל נשמה ולא יזטרך עוד לגלגולים אחרים והבן זה סוד הנעלם והזהר בו.

Alternate versions this text can be found in *ShG*, ch. 7, 29 and in *PEH*, *Sha'ar Keriyat Shema She'al HaMittah*, ch. 11, 333–338. However, the most complete version of this practice is found in *ShK*, *Inyan Derushei ha-Laylah*, ch. 10, 372–373. There Vital testifies that Luria told him that someone who knows that they have perfected one of their soul-levels and wishes to expedite the liberation process should perform this complete series of *kavvanot* every night. For a detailed outline and translation of the full practice as articulated in this text, see the appendix.

The man whose *nefesh* has been completely purified can shorten the number of *gilgulim* he must undergo by meditating on the verse from Isaiah 26:9 when he goes to sleep at night. Concentrating on this verse at night capitalizes on the strong desire already prominent at that hour for souls to bind themselves to the upper world.

As we saw above, pious souls in Luria's circle already engaged in specific contemplative exercises designed to guide the soul to its proper place within *nuqvah's* "well'; a journey that not only served to renew the soul before it descended in the morning, but also helped consecrate the sacred marriage of *zeir* and *nuqvah*. In those meditations ("Into Your hand, etc.") the soul itself became the very essence of desire and longing, acting as a cosmic aphrodisiac—the female waters—to arouse and stimulate the male energies. However, while these *kavvanot* have the capacity to bind the soul above and initiate cosmic union, they do not have the potential to keep the soul there past the night hours. Immediately after the above passage Vital continues:

> Indeed, [the *kavvanot*] that we say on the verse "Into Your hand I deposit my spirit, etc." is not useful for that which we mentioned above, because our intention with it is only that our souls ascend there as a deposit only, and they will return and descend in the morning. But the verse, "My *nefesh* desires You at night" is [used] to keep the *nefesh* above and bring down the *ruah* or the *neshama*, as we have said above.[94]

In the meditation on "My *nefesh* desires You at night," the mystic focuses on the powerful desire and longing that the soul experiences as it cleaves to its place in the upper well at night. A *nefesh* that is completely purified is by its very nature more suited to attach itself to divine matter. Thus, when the pious adept who has completely purified his *nefesh* invokes this verse at the moment of nightly union, the powers of desire are intensified to the degree that his *nefesh* binds itself to *nuqvah* in a way that precludes it from returning to the earthly realm in the morning. In its stead his *ruah* (or *neshama*, if he has purified his *ruah*) descends and inhabits his body while his *nefesh* remains above. His *nefesh* will return to his body only once his *ruah* has been completely restored.

---

94 *ShG*, ch. 3, 19:

ואמנם מה שאנו אומרים פסוק בידך אפקיד רוחי וגו' איננו מועיל אל הנזכר כי אין כונתינו בו רק שיעלו נפשותינו בבח' פקדון לבד ויחזרו לירד בבקה. אבל פסוק נפשי אויתיך הוא להשאיר הנפש למעלה ולהוריד הרוח או הנשמה כנז"ל.

The problem with this sequence is obvious: How can the *ruaḥ* inhabit the body without a *nefesh*? Vital solves this problem by explaining that while his true *nefesh* remains above a different *nefesh*—namely, that of a convert—enters into the body to serve as a "chariot" for the newly acquired *ruaḥ*. Then, once his *ruaḥ* is restored the *nefesh* of the convert leaves and his original *nefesh* returns to his body from above. The same process occurs once he restores his *ruaḥ*: his *nefesh* and *ruaḥ* ascend and remain above while his fresh *neshama* descends into his body, at which point a different *nefesh* and *ruaḥ* (of converts) enter in order to serve as a "chariot" for his *neshama*. This process repeats itself until all three parts of soul are united together in his body.[95]

It is important to note that the one who seeks to receive higher levels of soul at night must still perform the regular regimen of nightly *kavvanot* that accompany the recitation of the bedtime *shema*. This long and complex series of meditations sets the groundwork for the final ascent of the soul that occurs as the body falls asleep.[96] Meditating on the verse "Into Your hand I deposit my spirit" is typically the final step in this nightly mystical process. Concentrating on the cosmic dynamics initiated by reciting this verse ensures that the adept's soul ascend safely to the upper well and fill it in the secret of the female waters, a move that is necessary to catalyze the sacred marriage of male and female in the cosmic realms.

---

95 See *ShG*, ch. 7, 29. The notion that different parts of converts' souls can serve as substitutes for one's true *nefesh* or *ruaḥ* in times of need is expressed repeatedly and in different forms throughout *Sha'ar ha-Gilgulim*. See, for example, chs. 1, 2, 4, and 7 and many other places. Furthermore, according to Luria the souls of converts are of the lowest possible order. See, e.g., *ShG*, ch. 12, 43–44. On the soul construction of converts, see *ShMRSh*, fol. 21d (on *Zohar* II: 167a) and *ShK, Inyan Tzitzit*, ch. 1. Kallus suggests that the term "souls of converts" that appears throughout Lurianic literature is used metaphorically. However, it is not clear if Kallus means that the term refers to the righteous souls that engage in specific theurgic practices (namely, the *kavvanot* of *nefilat apayim* to redeem the trapped souls in the *qelipot*), or, if the term is a metaphoric reference to the actual souls that are trapped in the *qelipot* and subsequently elevated into the *shekhinah* (as a result of the aforementioned *kavvanot*) in order to gestate there and then waylay in *gan eden* until they descend again into human bodies. See Kallus, "Theurgy," 284–285n3.2. Kallus's source for this supposed metaphoric usage is a section from *Sha'ar ha-Gilgulim* that either does not exist, is a misprint, or refers to an edition that I am not aware of. His citation to 267–268 of *ShG* deviates from the format of all other citations to this text in his dissertation, which reference the standard sectional categorizations found in all printed editions. Furthermore, he cites *ShMRsh*, fol. 39b for a statement of Luria himself regarding the souls of *gerim*, but I could not find any such reference on that page. See Kallus, "Theurgy," 285 and *ShMRsh*, fol. 39b. Also see Kallus, "Theurgy," 290.

96 See *ShK, Inyan Derushei ha-Laylah*, chs. 1–10 and *PEH, Sha'ar Keriyat Shema She'al ha-Mittah*, chs. 1–11, where Vital describes the various *kavvanot* that must be performed before the *kavvanah* on "With my *nefesh* I desire You" can work properly.

However, if the mystic falls asleep while meditating on this verse, his soul will not remain above in *nuqvah*'s well but rather will return to his body in the morning. Therefore, when a person wants his *nefesh* or *ruaḥ* to remain above so that a higher level of soul can descend, he must first complete the regular series of *kavvanot* that accompany the bedtime *shema*, followed by the *kavvanah* on the verse "Into Your hand, etc." Then, before he falls asleep, he should focus his attention on the verse "My *nefesh* desires You at night, etc." with the intention of binding his soul—in the heat of the hour—to *nuqvah*, so that it remain tightly bound up with her, not to return to his body until his next level of soul is completely restored.[97]

Although Luria's students took these meditations seriously, these esoteric practices were not widespread. In the following passage, Vital laments the fact that some completely righteous people do not know how to perform the *kavvanot* on the verse "My *nefesh* desires You" and therefore must suffer the consequences:

> This is the wondrous reason why some completely righteous people die at a young age: While they restore their *nefesh* in a small number of years, they still do not know how to draw down their *ruaḥ* and send [up] their *nefesh* with the aforementioned *kavvanah* [i.e. on the verse "My *nefesh* desires You at night"]. Therefore, they die at a young age, since their *nefesh* does not want to be held back in this world, but rather the opposite, it wants to die, so that their *ruaḥ* can come afterwards in another body until it too is restored. This is also true of righteous people that merited to restore their *nefesh* and *ruaḥ*, but did not know how to send them [up] and draw down their *neshama*, as we have mentioned. This is the secret of the verse "They die; for they are without wisdom" (Job 4:21). Because sometimes a person will die due to a lack of wisdom, in that they did not know how to draw down their *ruaḥ* or *neshama*, as we have mentioned.[98]

---

97 In order for this practice to succeed, the practitioner must perform the alternate version of the "Into my hand I deposit my spirit" meditation that transports the completed soul-part into the *yesod* of *leah*, not *raḥel* as it typically done, as I discuss above. In addition, the complete form of the specialized *gilgul*-liberation *kavvanah* must also be performed to ensure success. See the appendix for the complete version of this practice.

98 *ShG*, ch. 7, 29:

וזהו הטעם נפלא לקצת צדיקים גמורים שמתים בקצרות שנים כי להיות שתקנו נפשם בתכלית השלמות בשנים מועטות וכיון שאינם יודעים להמשיך רוח ולשלח נפשם בכונה הנזכרת הם מתים בקצרות שנים כי אין נפשם צריכה להתעכב בעה"ז ואדרבא ימות כדי שיבא אח"כ הרוח בגוף שני ויתוקן גם הוא. וכן עד"ז בצדיקים שזכו לנפש ורוח בתכלית התקון ולא ידעו לשלחם ולהמשיך הנשמה כנזכר. ח"ס פסוק ימותו ולא בחכמה כי לפעמים ימותו בני אדם לחסרון חכמה שלא ידעו להמשיך רוח או נשמתם כנזכר.

In this passage, Vital makes it explicitly clear how ignorance of these *kavvanot* can result in an untimely death. However, even should an adept have knowledge of these practices, there are other dangers associated with their incorrect performance. In the sections of that outline the dangers inherent in the contemplative death practices of *nefilat apayim* that we will explore in the next part of this book, Vital suggests that the same dangers also exist in the performance of the sleep-time *kavvanot* of the bedtime *shema*:

> And so really in this manner is it also actually the case when a person goes to sleep at night, which is also in the secret of death since his soul descends to the level of the tree of death in the locus of the *qelipah*. … And there are some who are able to select and collect souls [from there] and raise them up … and there are those who only [re]ascend [from the *qelipah*] alone and there are those who remain there in the *qelipah* and do not ascend altogether.[99]

Here Vital makes clear that these practices are not intended for the spiritual dilatant, but rather for the truly righteous and properly qualified. Since these sleep time journeys entail some degree of exposure to the realms of the *qelipot*, there is always the risk that certain unlucky or incompetent practitioners will descend and not ascend, eternally binding their souls to the nether realms of darkness.[100]

Like other mystical traditions, Lurianic Kabbalah is especially concerned with expediting the often-interminable cycle of rebirth. For Luria, typically this goal of liberation can only be accomplished once the individual has succeeded in restoring or purifying each of his three primary levels of soul, and has suffered the death of the physical body in-between each of these accomplishments. However, by means of specific meditations, certain souls can immeasurably

---

99 *ShK, Inyan Nefilat Apayim*, ch. 2, 304:

וכן ממש עד"ז הוה ממש בענין שינת האדם בלילה אשר גם היא בסוד המיתה כי נפשו יורדת אל דרגא דאלנא דמותא במקום הקליפה ... ויש מי שיכול לברר וללקוט נשמות ולהעלותם ... ויש מי שעולה הוא לבדו ויש מי שנשאר .שם בקליפה ואינו עולה כלל.

100 On the distinguishing features of the sleep and death practices and their relationship to the demonic realms, see my discussion below on page 112ff.

shorten the duration of this often long and painful process. Since the return of all human souls to their source above is a central goal in Luria's mythology, the *kavvanot* designed to hasten the process of *gilgul* must be seen as an essential element in his system, and one worthy of more detailed study. In the above sections, I have attempted to bring to light the practical meditative techniques taught by Luria to help the mystic achieve in one lifetime what would ordinarily require many.

These practices reflect the landscape of specific regions of Lurianic metaphysics, in which the act of sleep provides the mechanism through which *zeir* and *nuqvah*, the primary actors in the cosmic drama, can reach their full developmental potential. In particular, the deep sleep of *zeir* allows for his consciousness (*moḥin*) to ascend into the more primitive recesses of the cosmos, leaving his body anesthetized. In this condition *zeir*'s body is dismembered and *nuqvah* is established as an autonomous divine entity. This separation-individuation process is necessary for the full maturation of *nuqvah* and consequently offers *zeir* and *nuqvah* the possibility of reunification in the more symmetrical position of face-to-face coitus.

This metaphysical process is rehearsed in the human realm through the theurgic activity of the Lurianic *mekhaven*. By reciting the liturgical script of the bedtime *shema* with the appropriate contemplative gestures, upon falling asleep the performer's soul is deposited above. In this vein, human sleep is not simply a biological process of cellular renewal; rather, it provides an opportunity for the practitioner to contemplatively penetrate the cosmic realms by stimulating inter-divine sex, thereby bringing both renewal to the individual's soul as well as harmony to the supernal and earthly dimensions.

As with *zeir* in the primordial scene, the human sleeper's soul is dislocated from the body. In this de-cathected condition, the soul has more freedom to substitute one soul-part for another before returning to its corporeal habitat. The occasion of sleep thus offers Luria a suitable means through which the adept can manipulate the process of rebirth. By executing specialized meditative practices, the adept who meets the appropriate developmental criteria can permanently lodge one soul-part above during sleep and exchange it for another, thereby avoiding the need for physical death and expediting the *gilgul* process.

Furthermore, just as *zeir*'s deep sleep facilitates the dismemberment of his body and the bifurcation of his androgynous sexual condition into two separate anatomical *loci*, so too, while asleep, the human body, defined by its sex, becomes vulnerable to the somatic processes of separation and integration.

This deconstruction of the soul's anatomical structure into dislocated parts expresses the excessive limits of the Lurianic preference towards fragmentation and dismemberment on the mystical path. It is only through fracture (of both the cosmos and the soul) that the unification of opposites is possible.

The ultimate realization of the Lurianic mystical vision therefore paradoxically lies in the reconstruction of the physical body at the resurrection of the dead and the commensurate deconstruction of the cosmic hierarchy. That is, the mythical fulfillment of the human body's dismemberment and reintegration must occur first through death and second, through the ultimate redemptive phenomenon of the resurrection of the physical body. These two themes of death and resurrection (and their dialectical implications for a monistic metaphysics) will be the subject matter of chapter two.

CHAPTER 2

Death and Resurrection

In a sense, the corpse is the most complete affirmation of the spirit.
　　　　　　　　　　　　—George Bataille, *Theory of Religion*

The theme of death—both spiritual and physical—constitutes one of the most central and potent dimensions of Isaac Luria's vast contemplative system. This is evident both in the content of his metaphysical teachings as well as in the practical methods of the *kavvanot* of prayer, the practice of the *yiḥudim*, and in the personal and communal expressions of his interactions with his students.[1] Considering Luria's fascination and preoccupation with the dynamics of death (and, as we shall see, of rebirth), it is interesting that very little has ever been written on this subject.[2]

The idealization and ritualization of death displays itself in particularly radical ways in the complex array of *kavvanot* that shape the daily prayer service, in particular in the *kavannot* for *nefilat apayim* and *keriyat shema*. As we saw in chapter one, Luria incorporated into the standard liturgical regimen intricate techniques of cosmic exploitation that not only bring sexual fulfillment and harmony to the supernal realms, but that also have a commensurate impact on the soul of the practitioner.

1　On the importance of the theme of ritualistic death in the Lurianic *kavvanot* of prayer, see Kallus, "Theurgy," 263 and my discussion of Kallus's approach below, page 101 note 16. On contemplative death in general in Lurianic Kabbalah, see Michael Fishbane, *The Kiss of God* (Seattle and London: University of Washington Press, 1994) 110–116 and Lawrence Fine, "Contemplative Death in Jewish Mystical Tradition," in *Sacrificing the Self: Perspectives on Martyrdom and Religion*, ed. Margaret Cormack (New York: Oxford University Press, 2002), 95–99. On the relationship between death and the practice of *yiḥudim*, see Fine, "The Contemplative Practice of *Yehudim* in Lurianic Kabbalah" and also Fine, *Physician of the Soul*, 259–299, especially 267. Also, see his discussion of the significance of death in the life of his fellowship in ibid., 300–358.

2　The only substantive treatments of the topic are found in Lawrence Fine's chapter in *Physician of the Soul* (see the previous note), in his four-page synopsis of the topic in his article "Contemplative Death in Jewish Mystical Tradition," and in Fishbane's brief discussion of the *kavvanot* of *nefilat apayim* and *keriyat shema* in *The Kiss of God*, 110–116. Kallus's "Theurgy" discusses it briefly in several footnotes located between 261–263, in the context of his presentation of the *kavvanot* for *keriyat shema*.

In the case of the *kavvanot* of the bedtime *shema*, sleep is utilized as an occasion for spiritual dismemberment: that is, the adept intentionally splits his soul in order to expedite the process of rebirth. Alternatively, during the recitation of the prayer *nefilat apayim*, Luria capitalizes on the contemplatively simulated experience of death in order to allow for a similar process of dismemberment and the hoped-for acceleration of the *gilgul* journey. As sleep is considered to be "one sixtieth of death,"[3] it makes sense that these two phenomena would occupy Luria's attention in related ways. However, the theoretical and experiential elements of the practice of "contemplative death" present us with a different set of questions and considerations that were not apparent in our exploration into the phenomenon of contemplative sleep.

In the following sections I will continue our inquiry into Lurianic techniques of *gilgul* expedition by examining the metaphysical, procedural, and contemplative elements of this fascinating dimension of Lurianic practice. Similar to the *kavvanot* that pertain to sleep, these practices are best understood as part and parcel of Luria's larger metaphysical framework. As such, the specific mechanics of these death simulations can only be appreciated against the backdrop of the parallel inter and intra-divine dynamics that play out on the cosmic stage. By examining these practices in light of their broader metaphysical context we will gain a deeper and more comprehensive appreciation for Luria's radical understanding of the fluid and composite dimensions of the individual human soul, as well as to the experiential practices that take advantage of these properties for the fulfillment of teleological goals.

In particular, I will argue that in formulating these techniques of simulated death, Luria is putting into practice a more fundamental theoretical position that blurs the distinction between the conventional categories of life and death. As such, these practices set the stage for a more radical and thoroughgoing vision of the unity of body and soul, expressed most explicitly in his interpretation of the classical rabbinic doctrine of the resurrection of the dead. For Luria, resurrection represents the final act in a far-reaching process of cosmic redemption that ultimately dissolves all hierarchical structure in the ontological constitution of the cosmos. In this sense, Luria posits a mystical metaphysics that simultaneously includes both dual and nondual perspectives, representing a far-reaching vision of total inclusivity that ultimately seeks to dissolve all hierarchical structure in the ontological constitution of the cosmos.

---

3 *BT Berakhot* 57b.

THE METAPHYSICS OF DEATH

While the theme of mystical death has a rich history in Jewish literature in general, the particular way that Luria approaches the subject develops themes that first appear in the Zohar and in other pre-Lurianic texts from the sixteenth century.[4] An exploration of how these themes developed historically constitutes the central focus of Michael Fishbane's important study *The Kiss of God: Spiritual and Mystical Death in Judaism*. In particular, Fishbane focuses on various forms of ritual and mental simulation of death that emerge in the Jewish religious imagination that seek to empower the aspirant to engage in "spiritual" or "mystical" death as a substitution for physical termination itself or as a proxy for the injunction to sanctify the divine name through actual martyrdom. In the course of his study, he also notes the repeated use of the Hebrew term "כאילו" ("like" or "as it were") in texts that deal with this theme in order to highlight the primary orientation of simulation and substitution when it comes to martyrdom in a contemplative context, lest we misconstrue such traditions to be suggesting some sort of ritual suicide in actuality.

However, in his treatment of the Zohar's expression of this theme, he correctly points out that the Zohar's language betrays some ambiguity as to whether or not one should intend in certain liturgical performances to die in actuality or only in the spirit of "as it were" (כאילו). In his analysis of this apparently ambiguous and contradictory position of the Zohar, he takes the stance of situating the Zohar squarely on the side of simulation, downplaying the Zohar's emphasis of actual ritual martyrdom. He writes:

> In some of the previous texts, the *Zohar* employs a double locution to indicate the status of the ritual action performed. On the one hand, the death simulation is marked by the term *ke'ilu*. This serves notice that the ritual is merely "like" the death of the worshipper; it is only "as if" the performer died in the rite. On the other hand, the action is termed *vada'i*; that is, something "actual"—a veritable deed, "indeed." At the semantic level, such a combination of verisimilitude and actuality is an oxymoron. But as ritual denotations, this paradox finely expresses the double dimension of ritual performance: mimetic substitutes for actions "in the world" are believed to effect changes in this or otherworldly realms, "as if" those (conscious)

---

4 See, e.g., *Zohar* II: 128b–129a; 200b; III: 120b; 120b–121b and Cordovero, *Tefillah le-Moshe*, 107b, 110b–112b. For a review of the Zohar's treatment of this topic, see Fine, "Contemplative Death," 92–94.

imitations were the real thing. Accordingly, it is not necessary to die in fact in order to receive the benefits of death (like expiation); and to be reborn to life on a higher spiritual plane, one must merely (i.e., *actually*—in the ritual) be "as if" dead while the heavenly conjunctions are occurring.[5]

In this passage, Fishbane grapples with the Zohar's paradoxical and contradictory expressions of intentionality that accompany certain liturgical exercises. While a more thorough analysis of these Zoharic sections referred to by Fishbane is beyond the scope of this study, they remain important precursors to the more radical formulations of ritual death that we find in Lurianic literature. Later on, I will argue that these more ambiguous expressions in the Zohar attain greater clarity in the Lurianic development of these themes, with Luria positioning himself more squarely on the side of actual ritual death as the optimal conditions for the eschatological fulfillment of the individual soul.

In order to understand the contemplative death practices that shaped the ritual life of Luria and his fellowship, we must first appreciate the metaphysical framework that informed and supported these exercises. As with the practices performed when going to sleep, so too the *kavvanot* that ritualize death are rooted in, and patterned by, both Lurianic cosmology as well as by the larger system of liturgical intentions that oriented the inner life of the practitioner.

The most important source we have in Lurianic literature for our understanding of the metaphysical meaning of contemplative death is from a short treatise penned by Isaac Luria himself. This text, which Hayyim Vital tells us was copied from Luria's handwritten manuscript, was included by Shmuel Vital in his redaction of the *Shemona She'arim*, in the sections of *Pri Etz Hayyim* (*PEH*) and of *Sha'ar ha-Kavvanot* (*ShK*) that articulate the *kavvanot* of the *nefilat apayim* prayer. Since the version in *PEH* appears to be the more accurate and authentic of the two,[6] I will begin our discussion with a section from this text:

---

5 Fishbane, *The Kiss of God*, 109. Fine takes a less conservative approach and admits that in Lurianic Kabbalah (and in the traditions of other sixteenth-century Safedean kabbalists) we find intimations of physical martyrdom being idealized as the contemplative ideal. He points to statements made by Eleazar Azikri and especially Joseph Karo in which the latter professed a desire to be literally burnt at the stake as an act of martyrdom. See Fine, "Contemplative Death," 98 and *Physician of the Soul*, 246.

6 I am basing this on the conclusion arrived at by Kallus, derived from his comparison of the text from *PEH* with the version found in *ShK*, *Inyan Nefilat Apayim*, ch. 5 and both of them with MS Jerusalem, *Heychal Shlomo* 70a, fol. 140d–142d. Kallus also concludes that in his view this text is in fact authored by Luria himself. See "Theurgy," 260n359. Fine agrees

In the prayer [service] there are two types of giving oneself over to death. When we give ourselves over on the sanctification of the name in the recitation of the *shema*, and with the giving of oneself over to death in *nefilat apayim*, as is known. And the matter is that there are two types of unions in the supernal *atzilut*: One is the union of *ḥokhmah* and *binah*, and the other, the union of *tiferet* and *malkhut*. And neither is possible without female waters.[7]

There are two primary practices in Luria's meditational system of prayer-*kavvanot* that reflect a preoccupation with death and its supernal dynamics. The first are the *kavvanot* performed during the recitation of the *shema* in the morning prayer service and the second are those performed during the ritual of *nefilat apayim*, also during the morning prayer service.[8] As Luria points out in this passage, while both sets of *kavvanot* are necessary for the general task of cosmic maintenance, they each correlate with different theurgic processes. The *kavvanot*

---

with Kallus that this text was authored by Luria, but seems to base his conclusion on Ronit Meroz's comments on 80 and 152 of her dissertation "Torat ha-Geulah." See Fine, *Physician of the Soul*, 244 and 424n71.

7 PEH, Sha'ar Nefilat Apayim, ch. 4, 298:

בתפלה ב' מיני מסירות למיתה עם מה שאנו מוסרים עצמינו על קדוש השם בק"ש ועם מסירה
למיתה בנ"א כנודע והענין כי יש ב' מיני זיווגים באצילות העליון אחד זיוג חו"ב ואחד זיוג ת"ת
ומלכות ואי אפשר לשניהם בלי מ"ן.

8 In his study of mystical death in Judaism, Michael Fishbane bases his short survey of Lurianic Kabbalah on these two *kavvanot* as they are expressed in *ShK* (he ignores the versions in *PEH*). See *Kiss of God*, 112–116 and his notes there. In his analysis, Fishbane literalizes the Lurianic idealization of martyrdom, which in my view should instead be read as a metaphorical reference to contemplative death. Interestingly, Fine's cursory survey of the same topic only references his discussion of *ShK* (and Fishbane's article), ignoring the more authentic record found in *PEH*. See Fine, "Contemplative Death," 95–99 and notes there. Also see Fine's re-treatment of this topic in *Physician of the Soul*, 239–248. While Fishbane does distinguish between certain aspects of these two practices, he conflates the practice of death simulation in each of these *kavvanot*. For example, while he asserts that in the *kavvanot* for *keriyat shema* Luria expects the practitioner to intend physical death, he does not address the crucial point that in the *kavvanot* for *nefilat apayim* the performance of contemplative death is primarily not concerned with simulating physical death at all. Rather, it entails the practitioner entering into the *realm* of death, which is explicitly understood in Lurianic metaphysics to be the realm of the *qelipot*, or the demonic. This makes sense considering that the entire contemplative project of *nefilat apayim* is to redeem the lost souls trapped in the *qelipot*. Furthermore, Fishbane appears to overlook that the technical sense of Luria's usage of the phrase "giving oneself over to the name" refers to the cosmic realm of *binah*. This will be discussed in more detail below.

associated with the *shema* serve to stimulate the higher union of *hokhmah* and *binah* while those performed during *nefilat apayim* act to unify the lower union of *tiferet* and *malkhut*. Note that in the passage just cited, Luria uses the phrase "giving oneself over to death" only with reference to the *kavvanot* for *nefilat apayim* and not for those of the *shema*. This pattern also displays itself as the performative mechanics of each of these *kavvanot* are then outlined by Luria:

> Indeed, the female waters of *malkhut* are the souls of the righteous. When one gives himself over to death it is as if he expires from the world and his soul cleaves above in her [i.e. *malkhut's*] *yesod* in the secret of a "well" and she becomes a well of living water, then the male waters descend from *tiferet* and this holy union is properly accomplished.[9]

Here Luria describes the theurgic process that takes place during the *kavvanot* for *nefilat apayim*, whereby the adept "gives himself over to death" in order to become the female waters of *malkhut*.[10] As the female waters, the soul of the practitioner then stimulates the down-flow of male waters from *tiferet* above, culminating in the sexual union of these two *partzufim*. In order to achieve this, it appears that the *mekhaven* is required to enter into a trance-like state, akin to death, which then permits his soul to adhere to a particular gradation in the cosmic hierarchy. This is the import of his use of the phrase "as if he expires from the world" (כאלו נפטר מן העולם). Later on in the same passage, Luria explains the parallel process in the *kavvanot* of the morning *shema*:

> The blessed female waters of *binah* are the righteous who give themselves on the "sanctification of the name," for she is *binah* who is called "great

---

9 *PEH, Sha'ar Nefilat Apayim*, ch. 4, 298:

אמנם מ"ן דמלכות הם נשמות הצדיקים וכאשר ימסור עצמו למיתה וכאילו נפטר מן העולם ותדבק נשמתו למעלה ביסוד שלה בסוד באר ויעשה באר מים חיים ואז יוצא מ"ד מת"ת חווג זה הקדוש נעשה כתיקונו.

10 Another more radical formulation of this trope is found in *Olat Tamid*, 118, where Vital writes that the *zivvug* of *imma* and *abba* takes place through the practitioner's "giving himself over to murder." One would assume that Vital is referring to the contemplative "self-murder" (that is, suicide) of the *mekhaven*, although it is curious that he does not use the reflexive form of the verb in this case. The trope of murder appears in the *kavvanot* of the bedtime *shema* as well, regarding the adept's charge to intentionally "murder" the bodies of the evil spirits (מזיקין) that formed as a result of improper seminal emissions. See *ShK, Inyan Derushei ha-Laylah*, ch. 7. For examples of even more extreme formulations of intentional death in the writings of post-Lurianic authors, see the passages cited by Fine in *Physician of the Soul*, 425n80.

name." And it is holy for him to ascend from below to above in the secret of the "holy" which is *hokhmah*. However, giving oneself over to death is in the secret of *malkhut*, which is the place of death. And the "sanctification of the name" is above.[11]

In this text, Luria outlines what can be seen as the most central and significant orienting factor to the human role of cosmic maintenance. The contemplative principle of "giving oneself over to death" serves as the directional mantra that describes the adept's shamanic journey into the ethereal realms.[12] But what Luria means by the term "death" turns out to be more complex than first meets the eye. In fact, there are two different processes at play here that fit the category of "giving oneself over to death": one pertains to *nefilat apayim*, the other to the morning *shema*.

Regarding the *kavvanot* for *nefilat apayim*, the attempt to contemplatively attach one's soul to *malkhut* in order to serve as her female waters is termed by Luria "giving oneself over to death" because the term "death" is one of the technical terms that refer to *malkhut*.[13] Thus, when Luria uses the phrase "gives himself over to death," he is not primarily encouraging the practitioner to invite physical death, but rather to attach his soul to the hypostatic gradation of *malkhut* (that is, "death") in order to accomplish specific theurgic goals.

This also explains why in this passage Luria does not utilize the phrase "gives himself over to death" when discussing the *kavvanah* of *keriyat shema*. In this case Luria's terminology is clear: the task of the practitioner is to "give oneself over on the sanctification of the name," not "to death."[14] This is because the

---

11 *PEH, Sha'ar Nefilat Apayim*, ch. 4, 298:

ומ"ן דבינה המשובחים הם הצדיקים המוסרין עצמו על ק"ה שהיא הבינה הנקראת שם גדול וקדוש הוא לעלות ממטה למעלה בסוד הקדוש שהוא חכמה אבל מסירות עצמו למיתה הוא בסוד מלכות שהוא אתר דמותא וקידוש השם למעלה.

12 On the "shamanic" nature of Luria's intention to "give oneself over to death," see Fine, "Contemplative Death," 98–99. For broader context on shamanic expressions in Kabbalah (and especially in Hasidism), see Jonathan Garb, *Shamanic Trance in Modern Kabbalah* (Chicago: University of Chicago Press, 2011).

13 See, e.g., *Zohar* I: 148a. The close association in the Zohar between the *sefirah* of *malkhut* and the *sitra ahra* (the demonic realm) sets up the double locution in the Lurianic texts that apply the technical term "death" both to *malkhut* and to the realm of the *qelipot*. This will be discussed more below.

14 Luria is consistent in his usage (or lack of usage) of the term "death" throughout this entire text, which suggests that its omission in this passage was not an editorial oversight, but a reflection of a clearly thought out metaphysical perspective. The term "death" appears when

"place" within the supernal realms that is inhabited through the performance of this practice is *binah*, whose terminological reference is the word "name," not "death."[15]

While in the performance of the *kavvanot* for *keriyat shema* the contemplative function is to enter into the lofty feminine sphere of *binah* in the cosmic hierarchy, in the *kavvanot* for *nefilat apayim* the phrase of "giving oneself over to death" is used to refer to placing one's soul squarely inside the realm of *malkhut*. As we shall see in our discussion of the *nefilat apayim kavvanot*, this term not only points to an inner journey into the *yesod* of *malkhut*, but more poignantly into the realm of the *qelipot*, or the demonic. Thus, while both *kavvanot* share the emphasis on "giving oneself over to death," what that means on an experiential and metaphysical level is quite different in each of these practices. A proper understanding of this distinction is thus vital to appreciate the nuances implicit in these doctrines.

While the technical use of the term "death" is reserved for pneumatic entry into the sphere of *malkhut* (or the *qelipot*), this passage still betrays a double locution in terms of the inner journey. That is, whether or not one attaches his soul to *malkhut* ("death") or *binah* ("the name"), both still require the contemplative posture of "as if one is expiring from the world." This is not death in a technical sense but is best understood as an orientation to one's journey and experience that mimics certain features of death; namely, it provides a mechanism through which the practitioner can transcend the ordinary limitations of perception defined by an identification with the physical body. This transcendence then allows for trans-dimensional travel into the ethereal realms that comprise the topography of the kabbalistic worlds. That is, the contemplative principle of "giving oneself over to death" serves as a directional mantra that describes the adept's inner journey into the transcendent realms. This orienting principle is perhaps the most central and significant factor that defines the human role of cosmic maintenance in Lurianic practice.

---

he discusses the *kavvanot* of *nefilat apayim*, but not when he discusses those of *keriyat shema*. While this is true for the version in *PEH*, in *ShK* the text occasionally uses the phrase "give oneself over to death" when discussing the *kavvanot* of *keriyat shema*. This terminological inconsistency suggests that the version found in *ShK* is less authoritative than that found in *PEH*, which remains consistent in its usage throughout. This is one of the factors that leads me to agree with Kallus in his assertion that the *PEH* text is the more authentic record of Luria's original manuscript. See my comments above, page 96 note 6.

15 According to Cordovero, the association of the technical term "name" as a reference to the *sefirah* of *binah* has its roots in the Zohar. See Cordovero, *Pardes Rimonim, Sha'ar Erchei ha-Kinuyim*, 42a and also see *Tiqunei Zohar Chadash*, 129b.

However, while here we see an emphasis on the intention towards death as a gesture of transcendence vis-a-vis the physical body, the mature development of this theme in Vital's writings takes us closer to a more radical understanding of this contemplative process. This more far-reaching possibility, which entails the practitioner giving up his physical body to the realm of death, will be explicated in the following sections.

DEATH AND REBIRTH

The central practice used by Luria to intentionally dismember the soul for the sake of expediting its liberation from the reincarnation process is to be performed during the day, at the *nefilat apayim* prayer that immediately follows the *amidah* in the morning service.[16] The criteria that determine who may perform

---

16 For other texts that deal with this topic, see: *EH, Hechal* 6, gate 39, chs. 1–4; *ShK, Inyan Nefilat Apayim*, chs. 1–5; *Inyan Tefillat ha-Shachar*, ch. 1; *ShK, Inyan Kavvanat Keriyat Shema*, ch. 6; *ShG*, sections 3, 19, inter alia. On the history of the *nefilat apayim* prayer, see Fishbane, *The Kiss of God*, 104–105, and his sources on 147n34; Fine, "Contemplative Death," 92–93 and 104n1, and in Fine, *Physician of the Soul*, 423n60 and the sources listed there. Kallus only devotes several footnotes to the topic of contemplative death in his dissertation, although he admits that this "motif empowers what constitutes the central Yihud practice of the Lurianic Kabbalah; for it is applied whenever one's intention is to effect a new zivvug of 'Ab'a v'Im'a" (see Kallus, "Theurgy," 263n361). In an earlier note Kallus argues that Luria's intention is not literal martyrdom, although he admits that there are passages that imply a literalist reading of actual martyrdom (see especially Kallus, "Theurgy," 261). He cites the passage in *ShHY*, fol. 4a: "Indeed, the Feminine Waters of Malkhut are the souls of the Zadykim; and when the person shall give himself over to death, it is as if he passes from this world; so that his Neshamah cleaves above in the Wellspring of the Yesod. And this becomes a Wellspring of Living Water" and compares it with *Likkutei Torah*, fol. 58a, where Vital states that to effect the zivvug of Abba and Imma, actual martyrdom is required. However, Kallus hedges the import of this text by suggesting that "the context there may suggest that this is the case only with sinners who have incurred the penalty of Karet." See Kallus "Theurgy," 261. He does, however, point to several other important texts that state explicitly that what is required is "martyrdom-in-potential" (*ShMRzl*, fol. 6b; *EH*, gate 39, ch. 11, 16; *Likkutei Torah*, fol. 121a). However, cf. with *ShG*, 385, where Luria is reported to have stated on his deathbed that had there been one *tzaddik* among his disciples he would not have had to die prematurely. On this question Fine is more ambivalent, simply concluding that for Luria, "martyrdom—be it actual physical death or imagined death—along with the recitation of the *shema* prayer, has the enormous power to generate the dynamic processes of divine unification and cosmic mending." See Fine, "Contemplative Death," 98. In his book *Physician of the Soul*, Fine revisits the same material that he treats in his earlier article, and while he goes into more detail in his analysis of the topic he nevertheless maintains the same fundamental position outlined in his essay "Contemplative Death" devoted to this topic. See Fine, *Physician of the Soul*, 239–248. On the relationship between contemplative death and the practice

this *kavvanah* are different than the ones we saw above for deconstructing the soul when going to sleep. Unlike the sleep practices explored in chapter one, in order to perform the *nefilat apayim* practice, the soul must originate from a loftier stratum in the cosmic hierarchy. This is because the main function of this practice is to facilitate the ascent of the soul, or rather parts of the soul, to its cosmic source. Therefore, if the root of the soul originates in a lower realm, then this exercise will prove inefficacious; the nocturnal *kavvanot* described above would be more appropriate in such a case.[17]

---

of *yihudim*, particularly the *yichud ha-hishtatchut* (the practice of communion with the souls of dead *tzaddikim*), see Kallus, "Theurgy," 262 and the texts quoted there (*ShRhK* 1, fol. 28a and especially 43a-b, and *ShRhK* 2, 579ff). Also see his argument for the gender-dimorphism of Lurianic Kabbalah (and he notes here his disagreement with Elliot Wolfson's claim of the "assimilation of the feminine by the masculine") based on the principle that the *tzaddik* becomes a conduit both for the feminine waters as well as for the male waters when they attain the level of *ruah* of *aztilut* (i.e. they embody both aspects of Joseph and Binyamin). See Kallus, "Theurgy," 263. On the related *kavvanot* associated with the verse *Or Zarua L'Zaddik*, see Kallus, "Theurgy," 282. For an example of how Luria connects the kavvanah of *Or Zaruah L'Zaddik* with the process of reincarnation, see *ShG*, ch. 18.

17 See the passage in *EH*, gate 39:4 where Vital states that all souls, regardless of level of origination, may ascend to higher levels with unlimited potential:

שכל הנשמות יכולין לעלות לעלות ממדרגה למדרגה עד אין קץ אלא שהעליון הרוצה לחזור על שורשו עולה ביום בנפילת אפים והתחתון הרוצה לעלות למעלה ממדרגתו אינו אלה בלילה.

(All souls are able to ascend from level to level *ad infinitum*; however, the more lofty [soul] who wants to return to his root ascends during the day with *nefilat apayim* and the lower [soul] who wants to ascend above his level can only do it at night.)

This passage seems to contradict what he writes later on in this very same chapter in *EH* as well as in numerous passages in *ShG*, that only certain categories of soul can benefit from the performance of the *kavvanah* of בידך אפקיד רוחי. See my discussion above in chapter one, and also see *ShG*, chs. 3, 4, 6, 7, and 19, inter alia. It therefore seems to me that his statement about all souls having the capacity to ascend only applies to all souls from the "new souls" category. However, at first glance there appears to be an even greater self-contradiction in Vital's writings regarding this matter. In *ShG*, ch. 7, he explicitly states the opposite of what he writes in the passage in *EH* cited above. In this section of *ShG*, he first explains that it is only those souls who descend from Cain and Abel (that is, from the category of "new souls" that I discuss above in chapter one) that are able to liberate themselves from rebirth in a single lifetime through the performance of the kavvanah of בידך אפקיד רוחי. Then he proceeds to outline how it is possible for souls of a lower order (that is, from the category of "old souls") to free themselves from rebirth in a single lifetime through the performance of the specialized *kavvanot* for *nefilat apayim* (*ShG*, ch. 7):

אבל הנצוצות המדרגה השלישית יש להם כח באופן אחר והוא כי אף שאינם יכולים בבת אחת כל חלקיהם הנה יש להם תיקון ע"י כונתם בעת נפילת אפים בתפלה וגו'.

The theurgic elements of each of these practices are also different: for the *nefilat apayim* practice, the ascendant soul attaches itself to the *zivvug* of Jacob and Rachel which is a diurnal coupling that is especially potent during the morning prayer service, so that the soul is renewed and can ascend to the locus of its origination.[18] However, for the soul of a lower order of origination, this

(But the sparks of the third category have a power through a different mechanism and that is that even if they cannot [liberate all their soul parts] in a single instant, they still have a rectification through their performance of the *kavvanot* during *nefilat apayim*.)

This passage seems to be in direct contradiction with the passage from *EH* quoted above that states it is only the higher souls that can benefit from the *kavvanah* of *nefilat apayim*. This apparent contradiction may be resolved by closely comparing this section from *ShG*, ch. 7 with another passage in *ShG*, ch. 19. In the section from ch. 7, the key phrase to note is: "even if they cannot liberate [all their soul parts] in a single instant." That is to say that a person from a lower soul-origin is able to utilize the *kavvanah* of *nefilat apayim* as a means of expediting rebirth only up to a certain point. That point is determined by the person's exact soul root. If his soul comes from the world of *yetzirah* (corresponding with the soul-level of *ruaḥ*), then he will only be able to use *nefilat apayim* in order to descend into the *qelipot* and redeem his *nefesh* level of soul. Beyond that he will be required to use the sleep-time *kavvanah* of the bedtime *shema* in order to draw down the other parts of his soul (and he can only do so if he is from the "new soul" category). For those whose souls originate from a lower world and are also not in the category of "new soul," while they can benefit from the *nefilat apayim* practice, it will nonetheless be impossible for them to self-liberate from the cycle of rebirth "in an instant"; that is, without first dying and being reborn. These discriminations seem contradictory in Vital's writings because in each passage he is referring to different categories of souls and different loci of soul origin without always making it clear to which he is referring.

18 In *ShK, Inyan Tefilat ha-Shachar*, ch. 1, Vital explains that the contemplative mission of the prayer-practitioner over the course of the morning prayer service is to progressively gather the trapped sparks and souls in each of the worlds and elevate the sparks of each respective world into *atzilut*. After the *amidah* prayer the time is ripe to transform these fallen sparks into the aphrodisiacal chemicals that will arouse Jacob and Rachel towards coitus (all this transpires in the realm of *atzilut*). Then, during the prayer of *nefilat apayim*, the most stubborn soul sparks that are trapped deep inside the realm of *asiyah* require redemption and elevation by extraordinary means, ultimately in the death of the physical body. This sacrificial act serves as a powerful catalyst for the extraction and elevation of the most ensnared sparks. These sparks are then converted into female waters that ascend to the womb of *nuqvah* (as Rachel) and there act as erotic stimulants for *zeir* (as Jacob) to inseminate her with his male waters. Therefore, *nefilat apayim* serves as both the culmination of the diurnal cosmic drama that allows the *zivvug* of Jacob and Rachel to ultimately take place as well as the mechanism through which the theurgic act of contemplative death is rehearsed and acted out in the realms of the *qelipot*. I will discuss this later on in chapter two. Indeed, in one place Vital states explicitly that death is required for this *kavvanah* because the *qelipot* are embedded inside the realms of death. See *EH*, part 2, *Sha'ar Mayin Nukvin u'Dekorin, Sha'ar* 39, ch. 1; see *ShK, Inyan Nefilat Apayim*, ch. 5.

mechanism will not work; in order for them to ascend to a cosmic rung above that of their soul-root, they must attach themselves to the *zivvug* of Jacob and Leah that is operative at night.[19]

As a result of this practice, the soul is capable of ascending to an even higher rung than its generative source, thereby freeing itself from the need for future incarnations:

> A soul whose root is in *atzilut* that descends into *asiyah* as a result of blem-ish, if he exits *asiyah* he is certainly able to be rectified during the course of his lifetime, and ascend from level to level until he enters the union of *atzilut*[20] which is where his soul's root is from, and he is re-integrated into that place. And he will [then] not need to reincarnate. This secret is the matter of *nefilat apayim* [recited during the] weekday.[21]

The underlying metaphysical principle that informs this *kavvanah* relates to the larger process of integration that transpires in the morning prayer service, whereby the four worlds are theurgically inculcated into the highest realm of *atzilut*.[22] Following the successful encapsulation of the cosmic totality into this

---

19 Vital specifies that souls of a lower order who wish to ascend above the level of its root must do so by way of its "deeds." Vital is either referring to the *mitzvot* that the practitioner has performed in his lifetime that grants his soul the capacity to ascend to a locus that transcends his soul-root, or he could be referring to the act of performing the appropriate *kavvanah* to facilitate the ascension. See *ShG*, ch. 19 for a more thorough discussion of the place of "deeds" in this process. On the particular dynamics of the *zivvug* of Jacob and Leah, see *EH*, *Heichal Nuqvah de-Zeir Anpin*, gate 37:4, chs. 1–5. Also see Fine's overview of the different categories of *zivvugim* that take place between the *partzufim* and the corresponding prayers that effect each respective unification (*Physician of the Soul*, 237–239).

20 The phrase Vital uses is: עד שיבא בזיווג דאצילות. In an alternate manuscript of this text, noted in the gloss by Menachem Menkin Halperin (*EH* [Warsaw: n.p., 1890], 140, it reads, "Until the time that the union of *atzilut* comes," עד שיבא עת זיווג דאצילות.

21 *EH*, *Sha'ar M"N*, ch. 39:4:

> הנשמה ששורשה באצילות ואח"כ ע"י הפגם ירדה בעשיה ויצאה מעשיה זו ודאי יכולה
> להתתקן בחייו חיותה ולעלות מדרגה אחר מדרגה עד שיבא בזווג דאצילות שמשם היה
> שרשה ויוכלל עד שם ולא יצטרך להתגלגל וסוד זה ענין נפילת אפים בחול.

Vital explains later on in this section that as a result of this practice a "new creation" is formed ("ויצא משם בריאה חדשה עד שעולה עד שרשו"). It is not clear if he means that the soul itself emerges as a new creation or if an ontologically different life-form emerges as a result of this practice. Cf. *Olat Tamid*, 118. On the creation of new souls as a result of the *nefilat apayim* prayer, also see *ShK*, *Inyan Nefilat Apayim*, ch. 2, 304.

22 The contemplative act of integrating the four worlds into *atzilut* can only be accomplished during the morning prayer service because it requires the attribute of *hesed* to be dominant,

recondite realm, the particular *zivvug* that is scheduled for sacred union at that hour is ready to be activated by the practitioner's contemplation.[23] In this case as well, the divine coupling requires the assistance of the adept in raising up the female waters; in fact, the human soul (and in some cases, as we will see below, the physical body) absorbed in contemplation is *itself* the female waters that stimulates the appropriate *zivvug*.[24]

More specifically, during the time of the recitation of *nefilat apayim*, the *ḥasadim* (that constitute the male waters) descend from the *partzuf* of

---

which only occurs during the hours allotted to the morning prayers. See *ShK, Inyan Nefilat Apayim*, ch. 1.

23 Each part of the morning prayer service serves to elevate one of the three lower worlds of *asiyah, yetsirah,* and *beriyah,* into the highest world of *atzilut*. Only when all the upper worlds are unified in *atzilut* can the appropriate *zivvug* take place. At the conclusion of the *amidah* prayer, the integration of all the worlds into *atzilut* is nearly complete, and all that is needed to effect the required *zivvug* is the participation of the theurgist in raising up the female waters into the womb of *nuqvah*. This is the function of *nefilat apayim*. Vital notes that this *zivvug* between Jacob and Rachel that is affected by the *kavvanah* of *nefilat apayim* during the morning prayer service occurs in the aspect of "face-to-face," while the *zivvugim* of the afternoon and evening services all occur in the aspect of "back-to-back." The "back-to-back" union is actually not a union at all but a defensive posture that these *partzufim* assume in order to protect themselves from the influence of the *sitra aḥra*. In order for their union to properly take place they must first ascend into *abba v'imma* where they are safe from demonic influence and only then can they turn towards each other and unite in a face-to-face *zivvug*. See *EH, Heychal Nuqvah DeZeir Anpin*, gate 6:39, ch. 1: לכל המקמות שנזכר ענין זווג אחור באחור שאין הענין כפשוטו אלה על דרך הנ"ל, (Everywhere the matter of back-to-back union is mentioned, the matter is not in accordance with the obvious meaning, but rather [must be understood] by way of what we have [explained] earlier). See Vital's explanation in the text there, and also see the gloss published in *ShK, Inyan Keriyat Shema*, ch. 1, note 3, 120.

24 See, e.g., *EH*, gate 6:39, ch. 1, 2; *ShK, Inyan Nefilat Apayim*, ch. 5 and in many other places throughout the Lurianic corpus. Generally speaking, the female waters are understood to be the souls that are redeemed from the *qelipot*. See, e.g. *ShMRsh*, 167: בחינת מים נוקבין הם מציאות הנשמות של בני אדם התחתונים עצמם והבן זה היטב וזכרהו כי הוא כלל גדול (The aspect of female waters is the existence of the souls of terrestrial human beings themselves, and understand this well and remember it, for it is a great principle). Also see *EH*, gate 39, ch. 1: נשמות הקדושות הם ממש מ"ן (The holy souls are the female waters in actuality [*mamash*]). On the rabbinic origin of the concept of male and female waters, see *PT Berakhot* 9:3; 14b and Fine, *Physician of the Soul*, 396n41. On the differences between the female waters of *nuqvah* and those of *imma*, see *EH*, gate 39, ch. 1. Fine seems to have misunderstood the Lurianic position on this matter, as in his synopsis of the *kavvanah* of *nefilat apayim* he describes the adept as descending into the realms below and there "he concentrates on gathering the 'female waters'" (Fine, "Contemplative Death," 95). However, as I demonstrate above, the souls of the adepts themselves *are* the female waters, they do not gather them from anyplace external to themselves.

Jacob into Rachel.[25] The task of the kabbalist at this point in the prayer service is therefore to contemplatively enter into Rachel and infuse her with
female waters so that she can properly receive the male waters from above.[26]
He does this by intentionally plunging the *nefesh* level of his soul into the
depths of the *qelipot* that are located in the darkest recesses of the world of
asiyah, thus gaining access to the most hidden sparks in need of redemption.[27] From there he is able to progressively ascend through each of the
higher worlds (namely, *yetzirah* and *beriyah*), extracting the sparks from the
qelipot along the way, until he reaches his destination in *yesod* of *nuqvah* in
the world of *atzilut*.

---

25 Immediately preceding *nefilat apayim* is the "confession" prayer (ודוי), whose theurgic function is to draw down the *ḥasadim* from the hidden cavity of the chest of *zeir* to the "revealed"
place in his heart. After this is accomplished, the *zivvug* between Israel and Leah can take
place from the chest and above by means of the prayer *vaya'avor*. Then, at the time of *nefilat
apayim* the "drops" of *ḥasadim* descend into the *yesod* of *zeir anpin* where they are expunged
into the *da'at* of Jacob, which is correlated with the *yesod* of *zeir anpin*. These *ḥasadim* then
are able to descend into the *yesod* of Jacob and be transmitted to Rachel through the act of
divine coitus. This descent of the *ḥasadim* into the *zivvug* of Jacob and Rachel is facilitated
through the pathway of Leah's feet. See *ShK, Inyan Nefilat Apayim*, ch. 2. For a description
of the pathway through the feet of Leah, and of the function and mechanism of the descent
of the *ḥasadim* within the *partzufim* in general, see *Magid, Metaphysics*, 26–29. Vital correlates the descent of the *ḥasadim* with the postural movement of the falling on the face (the
literal meaning of *nefilat apayim*). See *ShK, Nefilat Apayim*, ch. 2. For a more detailed discussion of the contemplative features of anatomical posture in the *kavvanah* of *nefilat apayim*,
see the following section.

26 The establishment of the female waters must precede the flow of male waters from above.
See *ShK, Nefilat Apayim*, ch. 2: צריך להקדים להעלות מ"ן כדי לקבל אח"כ מ"ד (He must first raise
up the female waters in order that he may afterwards receive the male waters). As a proof
for this, Vital quotes from the Talmudic statement that a male child is born only when the
female reaches orgasm before the male (*BT Berakhot* 60a; *BT Niddah* 31a; also see Rashi's
comment on Gen. 46:15). The anatomical locus for the placement of the female waters by
the adept is in *yesod* of *nuqvah de-zeir* (i.e. Rachel), which is correlated with her vaginal cavity. See *Magid, Metaphysics*, 28.

27 See *ShK, Inyan Nefilat Apayim*, ch. 2: מפילים עצמנו מלמעלה מן עולם האצילות עד למטה בסוף עולם
העשיה כאדם המפיל עצמו מראש הגג עד למטה בקרקע (We cast ourselves from above in the world
of *atzilut* to below in the end of the world of *asiyah*, as a person who throws himself from a
rooftop down to the earth below). Fine notes the erotic implications of this passage: "The
erotic nature of this ritual is thinly veiled. The devotee's ecstatic descent constitutes an orgasmic release that results in utter exhaustion and a depletion of energy akin to death." See *Physician of the Soul*, 241.

ANATOMICAL EMBODIMENT

One of the key features in the performance of the contemplative death practices of *nefilat apayim* is its anatomical requirements. To be sure, Vital articulates a double-inversed locution of the postural significance of the ritual of "falling of the face," the literal translation of the term *nefilat apayim*. On the one hand, the adept must drop his face down onto his forearm as a way to shield his eyes from gazing upon the union of *zeir* and *nuqvah*; on the other hand, the gesture of falling on one's face is designed to separate himself from the presence of the king and queen (i.e. *zeir* and *nuqvah*).[28] What is interesting is that while the former act is intended to prevent the incurring of the death penalty, the latter is intended to invite it:

> He must fall on his face, for it is the time of the union of the king and queen, and it is not fitting to gaze upon them, for one who gazes is liable for the death penalty. Therefore, he must fall on his face and give himself over to death since he is removed from the company of the king and queen, for "In the light of king's countenance is life" (Proverbs 16:15). And now this [causes him to] depart from the presence of the king, and it is as if he is liable death in separating from him. Therefore, he falls on his face and gives himself over to death.[29]

Why the death penalty caused by the illicit voyeurism of the king and queen is to be avoided while the death penalty caused by cutting oneself off from the king's presence is to be encouraged is unclear from this text. However, it may have something to do with the centrality of the eyes in the physiological expression of this particular mystical journey. This postural element of this process is explicated later on in this same pericope:

---

28 On the topic of bodily postures and gestures as modes of worship in pre-Lurianic Kabbalah, see Seth Brody, "Human Hands Dwell in Heavenly Heights: Contemplative Ascent and Theurgic Power in Thirteenth Century Kabbalah," *Mystics of the Book: Themes Topics and Typologies*, ed. R. Herrera (New York: Peter Lang, 1993), 123–158, and Maurizio Mottolese, *Bodily rituals in Jewish Mysticism: The Intensification of Cultic Hand Gestures by Medieval Kabbalists* (Los Angeles: Cherub Press, 2016).

29 *PEH, Sha'ar Nefilat Apayim,* ch. 2:

צריך ליפול על פניו לפי שהוא עת זיווג מלך והמלכה ואין ראוי להסתכל בהם כי כל המסתכל חייב מיתה לפי שהוא נסתלק מחברת מלך והמלכה כי באור פני מלך חיים ועתה זה יצא מלפני המלך וכאלו נתחייב מיתה בהפרדו ממנו לכן יפול על פניו וימסור למיתה

And he should shut his eyes and place his hands upon them to make himself appear as if dead and as one who has no arms or legs and who has left the earth. And he should give himself over and place his soul with the righteous who have died. And he must intend to make himself in this death [into] female waters ... and in each world he should make himself dead among the righteous in each world.[30]

Here, keeping one's eyes closed invokes an inner experience of giving oneself over to death and the subsequent cleaving to the souls of the righteous that inhabit the hidden worlds.[31] The functional purpose of this journey is ultimately to enable the practitioner's soul to transform into the female waters which serve as the aphrodisiacal chemicals for the supernal union of *zeir* and *nuqvah*.[32] But how and why does closing one's eyes enable the soul to transmute itself into female waters?

An answer to this question may be found by examining a similar relationship between the eyes and the alchemy of the soul articulated by Vital in his exposition of the *kavvanot* for the recitation of the morning *shema*. In this comparison, we will also uncover a possible resolution to the apparent contradiction in the passage cited above, where the death penalty for gazing at the union of the king and queen is discouraged while that of withdrawing from the presence of the king is promoted:

Also, when you recite the *shema* you should close your eyes with your right hand as it says in [the section of the Zohar known as] *Saba DeMishpatim*: "The beautiful maiden without eyes." [This] refers to Rachel who is now ascending in the secret of female waters.[33]

---

30 Ibid.:

ולסתום עיניו וישים ידו עליהם להראות עצמו כמת וכמי שאין לו ידים ורגלים ועזב את הארץ וימסור וישיב נפשו עם הצדיקים שמתו וצריך לכוין לעשות עצמו במיתה זו מ"נ לזיוג זו"נ ... ובכל עולם יעשה עצמו מת בין הצדיקים שבכל עולם

31 Vital's description of the contemplative function of sensory deprivation echoes the practice of Hesychasm in certain Eastern Orthodox monastic traditions. See *The Blackwell Companion to Eastern Christianity*, ed. Ken Parry (Oxford: John Wiley and Sons, 2010), 91ff.

32 This is because, as we have seen above in chapter one, the souls of the righteous are the female waters themselves. See page 79 note 74 and page 105 note 24.

33 *PEH, Sha'ar Keriyat Shema*, ch. 6:

גם כשתאמר שמ"ע תסגור עיניך ביד ימינך כמ"ש בסבא דמשפטים עולימתא שפירתא דלית לה עיינין הנאמר על רחל שהיא העולה עתה בסוד מ"נ.

In this passage, Vital makes an explicit correlation between the gesture of closing one's eyes and the transmutation of the soul into the lubricating fluids of Rachel's (that is, *nuqvah*) erotic union with *zeir*. In our exploration of the *kavvanot* for the bedtime *shema* in chapter one, we saw how the practitioner is urged to "be like *zeir anpin*" in his contemplative engagement with sleep.[34] Here, in the recitation of the morning *shema*, the adept becomes like *nuqvah*, the "beautiful maiden without eyes," embodying the anatomical posture of covering his eyes. Just as *nuqvah* has no eyes, so too the *mekhaven*, by negating the functionality of his eyes, becomes (like) *nuqvah*.[35] This process of transformational similitude permits the contemplative to assume the ontological stature of *nuqvah* and transfigure into her vaginal fluids.

The mechanics of this process also reveal why in the passage cited above, Vital seemingly contradicts himself in advocating a succumbing to death for separating from the king's presence but not for gazing at the king and queen. To recount, during the performance of *nefilat apayim* the adept covers his eyes with his arm so as not to gaze at the union and be liable for the death penalty. Yet, at the same time he intentionally solicits death by removing himself from the presence of the king.

Based on the above analysis, it makes sense why in his explanation of the *kavvanah* for *nefilat apayim* Vital specifies that the practitioner enters into "death" as a result of separating from the king, not the queen. That is, by removing himself from the king and simultaneously covering his eyes with his arm, he somatically embodies the queen, or *nuqvah*, the "beautiful maiden without eyes." This serves as another example of how Luria persuades the *mekhaven* to embody the ontological station of one of the *partzufim*, thereby further bridging the anatomical gap separating human and divine.

The performative features of the *kavvanah* to expedite *gilgul* associated with the prayer *nefilat apayim* involves—in addition to the inner (and outer) posture of contemplative death—the proper use of the divine names. Such linguistic manipulations provide the mechanism of extracting the trapped sparks as well as serving as the vehicle of their ascent into the more illuminated dimensions of the Godhead. This is largely accomplished by focusing

---

For the reference to this Zohar passage, see *Zohar* II: 94b. For more on this, see Elliot Wolfson, "Beautiful Maiden Without Eyes: Peshat and Sod in Zoharic Hermeneutics," in *The Midrashic Imagination*, ed. Michael Fishbane (Albany: SUNY Press, 1993).

34 See page 61 note 24.

35 On this imitational gesture, see Fine, *Physician of the Soul*, 229.

on the expanded form of YHVH that has the numerical value of 52, and the linguistic correspondences to this divine name that appear throughout Psalms 25:1.[36] This particular version of the divine name thus serves as a binding agent and vehicle, attaching the sparks to the specific level of his soul that correlates with each respective world, and transporting them above to the world of *atzilut*. Thus, his *nefesh* collects the sparks trapped in *asiyah*; his *ruaḥ* collects those in *yetzirah*; and his *neshama* collects those from *beriyah*. Then, along with the soul parts, all the sparks are gathered and deposited as female waters in the *yesod* of *nuqvah*.[37]

However, the primary contemplative element underscored by Vital in his outline of the performance of this *kavvanah* relates to the practice of intentional death. This inner posture as well as the proper use of the divine name both echo the classical Lurianic trope of a shamanic descent into the realms of evil in order to redeem trapped sparks of light.[38] But more poignantly, in this case it is the inner intention of death that allows the practitioner to overcome the limitations of body-identification that ordinarily prevent her from entering into the hidden realms of spirit. As it is central to our exploration, I will now examine in more detail this complex and paradoxical dimension of the practice.

---

36   For descriptions of this *kavanah*, see ShK, *Inyan Nefilat Apayim*, chs. 3–4 and PEH, *Sha'ar Nefilat Apayim*, ch. 2.

37   Vital notes that this is the only way that the sparks can be elevated to *nuqvah* and effect the proper *zivvug*. See ShK, *Nefilat Apayim*, ch. 2: ודע שאותם נצוצות המתבררות אינם יכולות לעלות .מעצמם עם לא ע"י שיכוין האדם לשתף נפש רוח נשמה שלו עמהם "And know that those selected sparks cannot ascend on their own without the person intending to attach his *nefesh*, *ruaḥ*, and *neshama* to them." Regarding the efficacy of the divine name of 52 in this process, see ShK, *Nefilat Apayim*, ch. 3: "Since all aspects of female waters is through the [version of the] tetragrammaton [that has the numerical equivalency of] 52." In order to effect the ascent from each of the three lower worlds (*beriyah*, *yetzirah*, and *asiyah*), the corresponding levels of soul (*neshama*, *ruaḥ*, and *nefesh*) must bind to three different instantiations of the "full" form of the YHVH, known as the "name of 52." Vital explains that the first instance of this name is derived from the numerical value of the first letters in each of the first four words of Ps. 25:1: אליך ה' נפשי אשא, but he does not account for the mathematical discrepancy in that these letters actually add up to sixty-two. See PEH, *Sha'ar Nefilat Apayim*, ch. 2.

38   On the "shamanic" nature of the *kavvanot* of *nefilat apayim*, see Fine, *Physician of the Soul*, 247. On the gnostic character of this theme in Lurianic Kabbalah in general, see Scholem, *MTJM*, 267–268 and Fine, *Physician of the Soul*, 144–149. On shamanic dimensions of kabbalah more broadly, see Garb, *Shamanic Trance in Modern Kabbalah*.

THE RADICAL UNITY OF BODY AND SOUL

Vital describes the theurgic features of the first element of *nefilat apayim*, the "intention unto death," in the following way:

> The matter is that real death is the locus of the husks, in the secret of "and her feet descend to death" (Proverbs 5:5). And it is required that the person give himself to death, and intend to plunge his soul unto the place of death, which are the husks. And he should intend through the power of the merit of his prayer to extract from there those selections (ברורים; i.e. trapped sparks).[39]

Once the theurgist has successfully entered into the subterranean dimension of the *qelipot*, he must then collect the sparks of light that are bound there as a result of the breaking of the vessels. He does this by binding these sparks to his soul substance and contemplatively clambering toward more elevated realms with the gathered sparks of light in tow. Each level of the soul thus serves both as an attachment-site for the sparks of each corresponding world, as well as a vehicle for their ascension:

> And this [i.e. the collection of the sparks trapped in the world of *asiyah*] will be through his *nefesh*, which is from *asiyah*. They [i.e. the sparks] will attach themselves to her [i.e. the practitioner's *nefesh*] and ascend from there with her to the world of *yetzirah*. From there, by means of his *ruaḥ*, which is from *yetzirah*, he shall intend to also collect the selections that are in the world of *yetzirah*. He shall ascend from there to *beriyah*, and by way of his *neshama* which is from *beriyah*, he shall intend to also collect the selections that are in the world of *beriyah*. And he shall ascend from there with all these three types of selections, to the world of *atzilut*.[40]

---

39 *ShK, Inyan Nefilat Apayim,* ch. 2:

> והענין הוא שהנה בחי' מיתה האמיתית הוא מקום הקליפה בסוד רגליה יורדות מות וצריך שהאדם
> ימסור עצמו למיתה ויכוין להוריד נפשו עד מקום המיתה שהם ו,קל'עות ולפזין שיוציא מזיח ררח
> זכות תפילתו אותם הבירורין אשר שם.

40 Ibid:

> חה יהיה ע"י נפשו שהיא מן העשיה ויחברם עמה ויעלו משם עמה אל עולם היצירה ושם ע"י רוחו
> שהיא מן היצירה יכוין לברר ג"כ הבירורים שבעולם היצירה ויעלם משם עד הבריאה ושם ע"י
> נשמתו שהיא מן הבריאה יכוין לברר ג"כ הבירורין שבעולם הבריאה ויעלם משם עם כל אלו ג' מיני
> בירורין עד עולם האצילות.

This text displays the soul's division into independently functioning parts. Once the individual accesses the cosmic realms through the pneumatic strategy of "intention unto death," each soul-part then performs its theurgic duty of spark collection within its supernal sphere of activity.[41] Then, these three levels of soul along with their haul of liberated sparks are successfully gathered into the *yesod* of *nuqvah* in the highest world of *atzilut* and the sacred goal of the *kavvanah* has been accomplished:

> And he should intend to bind together his *nefesh, ruah,* and *neshama* and insert all of them, along with these three categories of selections, into the *yesod* of *nuqvah* of *zeir anpin* of *atzilut.* Then the male waters will descend from above from the *yesod* of the male, and then a great light and efflux will also descend within those male waters into the *nefesh, ruah,* and *neshama* of this person who is performing *nefilat apayim.*[42]

After outlining the spiritual boons bestowed on the successful performer of these heroic feats,[43] Vital warns his readers about the many dangers inherent in such a risky operation. Giving oneself over to death is not a simple or casual

---

41 Luria's interest in the connection between contemplative death and the *nefilat apayim* prayer (especially as it relates to the death of the ten martyrs, as we will see later on) is influenced by the Zohar's understanding of this prayer which also correlates the two. See *Zohar* II: 129a, 142a, and *Zohar Chadash, Terumah,* 42a. Also see Zak, *Bisha'arei,* ch. 9, esp. 234–235 and note 15 where she suggests that these Zoharic passages serve as the basis for these Lurianic *kavvanot.* On the role of martyrdom in pre-zoharic kabbalah, see Haviva Pedaya, *Name and Sanctuary in the Teachings of R. Isaac the Blind* [Hebrew] (Jerusalem: Magnes Press, 2001), 201 and note 14. And see Kallus, "Theurgy," 260 for these and other sources, particularly the mention of contemplative death in reference to *keriyat shema* in the works of Meir ibn Gabbay, Joseph Karo, and Moses Cordovero.

42 *ShK, Inyan Nefilat Apayim,* ch. 2:

ויכוין לשתף שם נר"ן שלו עם ג' חלקי הבירורין האלו ויכניס הכל תוך היסוד דנוקבא דז"א דאצילות ואז ירדו מ"ד מלמעלה מיסוד הזכר ואז ירד ג"כ שפע ואור גדול באותן המ"ד אל נר"ן של האדם הזה שעושה בנ"א

43 Cf. with the descriptions of light and soul renewal outlined in *ShK, Inyan Nefilat Apayim,* ch. 2, 304:

העושה מצוה רבה זו למסור עצמו למיתה בכל שלשה עולמות הנזכר כדי לברר אותם הנשמות ולגרום זווג זו"ן בלי ספק ששכרו עצום מאוד ... יורדין בתחלה מ"ד עלאין לצורך האדם הזה שעושה נפילת אפים ואותו האור מתעבר בנפשו אשר נכנסת שם ומתחדשת נפשו שם ומתתקנת בתכלית השלימות.

(The one who performs this great *mitzvah* to give himself over to death in all three worlds as mentioned in order to collect those souls and cause the union of *zeir* and *nuqvah,* there is no doubt that his reward is very great ... first the supernal male waters descend for the good of this person who

process. In fact, in order to successfully engage these exercises, one must be nothing less than a *tzaddik gamur*, a completely righteous person. Furthermore, the *kavvanot* must be performed without omission or error from beginning to end. If these two conditions are not met, then either the adept will descend into the *qelipot* and be unable to re-ascend, remaining trapped in the realm of evil forever, or, if he has sufficient merit to ascend, he will only do so without carrying the load of the redeemed sparks with him.[44]

In this context, Vital provides us with a fascinating explanation for why sometimes people undergo sudden and unexpected changes in character. In particular, he is interested in the soul-dynamics of dismemberment that underlie the transformation from righteousness to wickedness:

> And through this you will understand a great secret [concerning] a surprising thing that we have found and seen: That sometimes a person will be completely righteous and then he changes into a different person and becomes a complete villain. ... The matter is that when a person gives his soul over to death in *nefilat apayim* into the place of the *qelipah*, and due to a certain sin that he has committed his soul is unable to ascend from there, and the *qelipah* snatches him and he remains there forever. Then they give him a different soul, a wicked one from the side of the *qelipah*.[45]

This passage offers us another glimpse into the dynamics of soul-swapping that occupied our attention in our discussion of the *kavvanot* for the bedtime *shema* in chapter one. However, unlike with the *kavvanot* performed before sleep, in this case the splitting and substitution of soul-parts is unintentional. To

performed *nefilat apayim* and that very light impregnates [itself] in his *nefesh* that enters there and it renews his soul there and rectifies it completely.)

44 See *ShK, Inyan Nefilat Apayim*, ch. 2, 304.

45 Vital also notes that these same dangers also exist in the performance of the sleep-time *kavvanot* discussed above in chapter one. See *ShK, Inyan Nefilat Apayim*, ch. 2, 304.

וְכֵן מַמָּשׁ עַד"ז הוה ממש בענין שינת האדם בלילה אשר גם היא בסוד המיתה כי נפשו יורדת אל דרגא דאילנא דמותא במקום הקליפה ... ויש מי שיכול לברר וללקוט נשמות ולהעלותם ... וייש מי שעולה הוא לבדו ויש מי שנשאר שם בקליפה ואינו עולה כלל.

(And so really in this manner is it also actually the case when a person goes to sleep at night, which is also in the secret of death since his soul descends to the level of the tree of death in the locus of the *qelipah*. ... And there are some who are able to select and collect souls [from there] and raise them up ... and there are those who only [re]ascend [from the *qelipah*] alone and there are those who remain there in the *qelipah* and do not ascend altogether.)

be sure, the possibility of unintended consequences in a practice of this nature is to be expected, due to the inner instability engendered by the intentional dislocation of parts of the soul from the body.[46]

Furthermore, as we saw with the sleep-time *kavvanot,* in the contemplative performance of *nefilat apayim* the potential of soul dismemberment is leveraged towards expediting the journey of rebirth. However, as we see in the following passage, this feat is only accomplished by certain categories of souls whose onto-logical makeup allows for such a radical process of shamanic soul-swapping:

> The sparks of the third category [of souls] have a power through a different method. And that is, that even if they cannot attain all their [soul] parts in an instant, they nevertheless have a rectification through their [perfor-mance of the] *kavvanah* during the prayer *nefilat apayim,* whereby they extract their *ruah* from the depths of the *qelipot* even though they have not yet completed the rectification of their *nefesh.* [They do this] through the secret of the ascent of female waters through the verse "To You God I lift up my *nefesh*" (Psalms 25:1), etc.[47]

The third category of souls refers to those soul-sparks that descend from *adam ha-rishon's* third son, Seth. These souls are of a lower order in Luria's pneumatic hierarchy and thus are prevented from the efficiencies offered to those souls of higher progeny.[48] The second category of souls that descend from Cain and Abel, for instance, are capable of attaining liberation from rebirth in a sin-gle lifetime by taking advantage of the *kavvanot* for the bedtime *shema,* as

---

46 It is interesting to consider these dangers articulated by Luria in light of recent literary tropes in contemporary fiction. For example, in the popular *Harry Potter* series of books written by J. K. Rowling, the villain Voldemort intentionally splits off parts of his soul and dislocates them from his body, lodging these soul-fragments in various physical objects called "hor-cruxes." See, e.g., J. K. Rowling, *Harry Potter and the Half-Blood Prince* (London: Blooms-bury, 2014), 492–512. Since it is highly unlikely that Rowling has read Lurianic literature, it is fair to assume that Luria is not a direct source. However, it remains a curious question as to whether or not there were possible lines of transmission for this lore, perhaps through cer-tain occult traditions influenced by Kabbalah in general, and by Lurianic tropes specifically.

47 *ShG,* ch. 7:

> אבל הנצוצות המדרגה השלישית יש להם כח באופן אחר והוא כי אף שאינם יכולים להשיג בבת אחת כל
> חלקיהם הנה יש להם תיקון על ידי כונתם בעת נפילת אפים בתפילה להוציא את הרוח שלהם מעמקי הקליפות
> אע"פ שלא חשלים הנפש תקון הנפש בסוד עליית מיין נוקבין בפסוק אליך ה' נפשי אשא וכו'.

48 See *ShG,* ch. 7, 30 and my discussion of this category of souls in chapter one.

Here Vital emphasizes that in contradistinction to the second category of souls, the third category is not privy to the potential for complete liberation from rebirth in a single lifetime.

However, these lower souls are able to take advantage of the transformative potential latent in the *nefilat apayim* practice in order to free their *ruaḥ* from the *qelipot* and deposit it in the body of another person. Remarkably, the adept is able to do this even if he has not yet completed his *nefesh* level of soul. This possibility bypasses a fundamental restriction of the *gilgul* process that requires an individual to have first completed the rectification of his *nefesh* prior to acquiring the higher soul strata. With such an efficient strategy in place, the practitioner is then able to potentially rectify both his *nefesh* and *ruaḥ* in a single lifetime, thereby speeding up the overall process of rebirth.

However, souls of this category are still more limited than souls of a higher order in that their *neshama* level of soul cannot be extracted from the *qelipot* utilizing the salvific practices of *nefilat apayim*. Therefore, in order for the *neshama* level of soul to be integrated into the individual's consciousness, he must first die and then be reborn again with the incomplete soul part in its nascent condition:

> And it is required that you know that this rectification is only relevant for the *ruaḥ*. For it is able to exit the *qelipah* by means of the *kavvanah* of *nefilat apayim* before the completion of the rectification of the *nefesh*. However, the *neshama* does not exit the depths of the *qelipah* under any circumstances until the rectification of the *nefesh* and the *ruaḥ* are complete and

---

49 Vital makes this point clear in the following passage from *ShG*, ch. 7:

אי אפשר אל הרוח שלהם לצאת מעמקי הקליפות עד שישתלם תקון נפשם ואח"כ יצא וכיון שכן נמצא שאין
תקון אל הרוח שלו ע"י איש זולתו אלא ע"י עצמו ולכן או ימות האיש הזה ורוחו אם נפשו יבא אח"כ בגוף אחד כנ"ל
או אפשר שהוא בעצמו ע"י הכונות הנ"ל בסוד נפשי אויתיך בלילה אחר תקון תשלום הנפש תצא ויבא בו הרוח לבדו
להתקן כנ"ל וכן הענין הזה בנשמה.

(It is impossible for the *ruaḥ* of the second level of [soul] sparks from Cain and Abel to exit the depth of the husks until the fixing of their *nefesh* is completed. After [it is completed] it [is able to] exit. And since this is so, it is the case that there is no rectification for his *ruaḥ* through another person, but only through himself. Therefore, either the person dies and his *ruaḥ* along with his *nefesh* returns afterward in another body as we mentioned earlier, or it is possible that he himself through [the performance of] the *kavvanot* mentioned earlier, in the secret of "My soul desires you at night," that after the complete fixing of his *nefesh*, it departs, and the *ruaḥ* enters him alone to be fixed. And this matter is also thus with the *neshama*.)

these people, these *nefesh* and *ruaḥ* beings, die, and their *neshama* exits and is reincarnated in order to be rectified.[50]

To be sure, this bypass mechanism only functions properly if the precociously extracted soul part is situated inside a different body, thereby mobilizing a most bizarre dynamic in the life of the individual: while he is yet alive, different parts of his soul are simultaneously abiding in different physical bodies. After describing the redemptive elements of this practice as cited above, Vital writes:

> Then his *ruaḥ* comes while he is still alive and [enters] into the body of another man who is born, riding on the *nefesh* of a convert. And if he merits further, it is possible that he draws her down into his own son who is born to him.[51]

Not only does the soul of the convert as an abode for transient soul-parts once again displays itself, but here Vital articulates an even more radical notion; that is, that a person's redeemed soul-part can incarnate in the body of his own son.[52] The far-reaching implications of this scenario are not lost to Vital. He recognizes that when distinct parts of one soul simultaneously inhabit two different bodies it presents particular challenges for the individual(s):

> Even though in [the performance of] the *kavvanah* of *nefilat apayim* the two of them are able to enter the world in two separate bodies, nevertheless these individuals stand in a very precarious balance.[53]

---

50 *ShG*, ch. 7:

וצריך שתדע כי לא שייך תיקון אל הרוח לבדו כי יכול לצאת מן הקליפה ע"י כונת נפילת אפים קודם
תקון השלמת הנפש אבל הנשמה אינה יוצאה בשום אופן מעמקי הקליפות עד שיושלם תקון הנפש
והרוח וימותו האנשים ההם בעלי הנפש והרוח האלו ואח"כ תצא הנשמה ותבא בגלגול להתקן

51 *ShG*, ch. 7:

ויבא הרוח שלו בחיים חייתו בגוף איזה איש אחר שיולד מורכב בנפש הגר ואם יזכה יותר אפשר שימשיכנה
בבנו עצמו הנולד לו.

52 On the soul of the convert, see my discussion above on pages 85–86ff.

53 *ShG*, ch. 7:

אעפ"י שיכולים לבא שניהם בעולם בשני גופים מחולקים ע"י כונת נפילת אפים ויתוקנו שניהם עכ"ז
עומדים בשיקול גדול האנשים האלה ובכף מאזנים

For Vital, this delicate balance largely concerns the teleological implications regarding the future resurrection of the body. If the soul inhabits two different bodies, which one will return in the flesh to accommodate the doctrine of the resurrection? That is, which body is the soul's true or primary body that will resurrect in the messianic age? On this point, Vital admits his ambivalence:

> Which one of these [two bodies] will prevail over the other? For if the person that takes the majority completes his rectification before the other rectifies his *nefesh*, then it comes out that the one with the *ruaḥ* is primary. And therefore, at the time of the resurrection of the dead both the *ruaḥ* and the *nefesh* together will enter into the body of the one who had the *ruaḥ*. However, if the owner of the *nefesh* completes his rectification first, I do not remember what I heard concerning this. But in my humble opinion I heard that they both enter into the body of the owner of the *nefesh* at the resurrection of the dead since it is primary [in that case].[54]

The relationship between the body and soul is organized by a system of merit. Those souls that advance their evolutionary process more rapidly establish a more enduring relationship with the physical body that they inhabit. Therefore, which physical body will reincarnate with which soul is determined by which body houses the soul-part that "prevails" over the other in terms of the goal of rectification.

In this situation, the thread that binds the soul to the body seems to be one's physical activities, specifically the performance of the commandments of the Torah, which are the primary means for rectifying the various soul-parts in the Lurianic system.[55] That is, through physical action the soul develops in two opposite directions: on the one hand, through one's physical deeds the soul is endowed with transcendental capacities of ascension; on the other, one's

---

54 ShG, ch. 7:

אי זה מהם ינצח לחבירו כי אם ואיש חחוו שלקח הרוב היזרליח חקווו קודם שהאחר תקן את הנפש נמצא שבעל הרוח הוא העיקר ולכן בזמן תחיית המתים יכנסו הרוח והנפש שניהם בגוף בעל הרוח אבל אם בעל הנפש השלים תקונו בתחילה איני זוכר מה ששמעתי בו והנלע"ד ששמעתי כי שניהם יכנסו בגוף בעל הנפש בתחית המתים כי הוא העיקרי.

55 On the commandments as the primary agents for the process of soul rectification through *gilgul* in Lurianic Kabbalah, see Scholem, *MTJM*, 279–280. Also see Matt, "The Mystic and the Mitzwot."

conduct weaves the fabric of the soul into a more solid and enduring union with the physical body.[56]

This bi-directional paradoxical process demonstrates the Lurianic view of the radical unity of body and soul, the full realization of which occurs with the resurrection of the dead. That is to say that while the soul appears to separate from its primary body over the course of its incarnational journey, its soul substance actually remains inextricably wed to the body with which it performed the most commandments. Thus, at the time of resurrection all the individual soul-parts return to, and reintegrate with, their primary physical body; a body which, it turns out, was never completely separated from the soul.[57] In this sense, the ultimate fulfilment of the *gilgul* journey is not realized through the integration of the various soul-parts back into the cosmic soul of *adam ha-rishon*, but rather it is through the reunion of the completed individual soul back into its rightful physical body.

This approach, which sees the physical body as the final locus for cosmic redemption, is counterintuitive to a hierarchical view of cosmic structure. That is, Lurianic metaphysics ultimately holds that there is never a complete separation between the physical body and the soul even as it admits that fragmented parts of the same soul can simultaneously function in different bodies and locations. In this approach, the physical body turns out to be divinized and the soul materialized as the ultimate cap on the process of cosmic *tiqun* comes into fruition. This final stage of the process erases all hierarchy in the cosmic structure, revealing the *partzufim* and the human body to ultimately be one and the same

---

56 The phrase that Vital uses throughout his discussions of the *kavvanah* for *nefilat apayim* is "in accordance with his deeds" (כפי מעשיו). See, e.g., *ShG*, ch. 19: או ביום בסוד נפילת אפים בכונת פסוק אליך ה' נפשי אשא יכולה לעלות ממדרגה למדרגה כפי מעשיו עד שרשו ממש כנזכר (Or during the day in the secret of *nefilat apayim* with the *kavvanah* of the verse "To you God I lift up my soul," he is able to ascend from level to level in accordance with his deeds, until his actual root as was mentioned). Later in the same chapter, a similar chord is echoed by Vital: כלם יכולות ע"י מעשיהם לעלות ממדרגה למדרגה עד אין קץ (All [souls] are able by way of their deeds to ascend from level to level to no end). Also see the passage in *EH*, gate 39, ch. 4: וכל זה אם ישים אליו לבו בכוונה אחר שיהיה לו מעשים טובים ראויים שיוכל לעלות (And all this if he places his heart to it in a different *kavvanah* that he should have good deeds that are fitting for him to be able to ascend). Concerning the import of the phrase "if he places his heart to it," see my discussion below in section Soul Rupture and Cosmic Union.

57 The view that only the body that performs the most *mitzvot* will resurrect along with the split off soul parts explains why Vital is so concerned with the proportions of good and evil that are attributed to each one of the respective physical bodies, and the manner in which good and/or evil is transferred between the two bodies. See *ShG*, ch. 7 for Vital's explanation of this process.

truth. Here we have an integral expression of monistic mysticism that includes within it a functional dualism, thereby expressing a path of soul fragmentation and somatic integration that allows for both dualism and nondualism to simultaneously coexist.[58]

HUMAN SACRIFICE AND INTEGRAL MONISM

This inclusive perspective of integral monism is echoed throughout Lurianic metaphysical teachings, but is easily overlooked if the reader is filtering the material through a dualistic, hierarchical lens.[59] Indeed, Luria (or Vital) intentionally left these more radical allusions more obscure and encoded in cryptic formulations. For example, several times in his articulation of the *kavvanah* for *nefilat apayim*, both in *ShK* and *EH*, Vital mentions that the success of this practice is contingent upon the adept attending to the secret of putting "his heart to it," but offers no explanation for what this means. Only by scouring the totality of the Lurianic corpus and putting the scattered puzzle pieces together is it possible for a reader to begin to make sense out of this allusion.

Let us begin by examining one example of such a cryptic passage. In Vital's discussion of the two practices of expediting release from rebirth (namely, the

---

58 The term "nondualism" is applied in the academic study of religion to metaphysical systems that posit that there is no ontological duality inherent to the nature of existence. The prototype for this perspective is the Hindu path of Advaita Vedanta (the Sanskrit word "Advaita" literally means "Nondual"), that claims that the only true existence is the nondual ground of reality, generally referred to with the term "Brahman." In this system, there is no ontological truth to dualism; it is simply an epistemological error and fundamentally illusory (this error is referred to by the term *avidya*, "ignorance"). See, e.g., Deutch's classic *Advaita Vedanta: A Philosophical Reconstruction*. However, Lurianic Kabbalah is not a nondual system in this classic usage of the term, since it does not claim that dualistic ways of perceiving are fundamentally erroneous. It's acceptance of the reality of dualism is expressed through the multiple soul-parts that live and function independently of the others in different loci. This perspective allows Luria to posit his doctrine of multiple soul-parts inhabiting several bodies simultaneously as well as the possibilities of one body housing up to four soul-parts of different individuals. All this can happen in this view without the individual soul ever losing its fundamental integrity as an ontological unity. Thus, Luria views reality and the soul to be simultaneously dual and nondual in nature. This view is closer to the particular form of monism found in the teachings on nondual Shaivite Tantra, or Kashmir Shaivism. Mark S. G. Dyczkowski calls this approach "Integral Monism," and I have adopted his term to describe Lurianic Kabbalah. See Dyczkowski, *The Doctrine of Vibration*. See my comparative discussion of Advaita Vedanta and Kashmir Shaivism below on page 143ff.

59 On my use of the term "Integral Monism," see the previous note.

one performed at night while going to sleep and the other during the day while rehearsing contemplative death during *nefilat apayim*) he states that these practices are only effective:

> If one puts his heart to it [i.e. to perform] a different *kavvanah*, that he should have good deeds that are fitting [and that will] enable him to ascend and in this manner, he will not need to reincarnate after his death.[60]

Which *kavvanah* is Vital referring to? I think there are two plausible answers. The first possibility is that he is referring to the process outlined in *ShG*, chs. 18 and 19, whereby Vital explains how someone can attain higher levels of soul through the performance of *mitzvot* and through engagement with the mystical interpretations of Torah.[61]

However, it is more likely the case that Vital is hinting at an obscure contemplative mechanism taught by Luria based on the following verse from Job 34:14: "If he set his heart upon it, his *ruaḥ* and his *neshama* will be gathered to him." The first part of the verse contains the same Hebrew phrase that Vital uses in the passage from *EH* cited above that states: "If one puts his heart to it," and so forth. Even though in the context of the selection in *EH* Vital seems to be utilizing this phrase to point to a more general orientation of heartfelt intentionality that is required for the success of the relevant *kavvanot* under discussion, his precise use of this biblical formulation must be seen as suggestive.[62]

---

60 *EH*, part 2, *Sha'ar M"N M"D* 39, ch. 4: וכל זה אם ישים אליו לבו בכוונה אחר שיהיה לו מע"ט ראויין Also Cf. *ShG*, ch. 19: אבל הצד השוה שבהם שבכל שיכול לעלות ועי"ז לא יצטרך להתגלגל אחר מותו הנשמות הוא כי כולם יכולות ע"י מעשיהם לעלות ממדרגה למדרגה עד אין קץ וכל זה עם ישים אליו לבו ויכוין לכך.
(But the common denominator among them is that they are all able to ascend from level to level to no end by way of their deed; and all this if he sets his heart to him and intends thus.)

61 Vital explains that each level of soul is acquired through different contemplative means. If a person is diligent in the performance of the *mitzvot* but does so in a superficial manner, only fulfilling the outer forms of the practice, then he will complete his *nefesh* level of soul but it will be like a woman whose husband is in a far-away land; it will be devoid of spirit. The *ruaḥ* level is attained by applying oneself in the study of Torah for its own sake and the *neshama* level is integrated through the study of the mystical secrets of the Torah. These three levels also correspond with the divine names of ה אהי"ה יהו"י אדנ"י respectively. See *ShG*, ch. 18.

62 It is plausible that Luria used this verse in several different hermeneutical ways, one of which interpreted the import of the verse to be pointing to a more general sense of orienting one's heart toward intentional contemplation. This way of applying the verse has roots in the Zohar. See, e.g., *Zohar* I: 155b; *Zohar* II: 162b. However, elsewhere the Zohar interprets the verse in more provocative ways which may serve as the inspiration for Luria's more

The obscure practice based on this verse is explicated by Vital in several fragmented passages scattered throughout the Lurianic corpus.[63] In each locus the context points to some secret regarding the performance of the techniques meant to expedite rebirth that I have been examining in this study. The way the allusion to this practice is strategically placed in the texts suggests that this exercise holds some secret key to the most esoteric dimensions of the process of contemplative *gilgul* expedition. Take, for example, the following pericope:

> But the common denominator among them [i.e. the souls that engage these *kavvanot* to expedite rebirth] is that they are all able to ascend from level to level *ad infinitum* by way of their deeds; and all this if he "sets his heart to it [or to him—אליו]" and intends thus.[64]

Here the intention of setting "his heart to it" is situated by Vital squarely in the center of the entire process of contemplatively expediting rebirth. Indeed, it is stipulated as a condition for its very success. Yet in this section we are not given any further data regarding its meaning or its method of application. The most explicit indications regarding this allusion is found in only a few passages, which we will turn to now.

The first text appears in the context of Luria's teachings on the metaphysical dynamics of *gilgul* itself, and reveals that the secret *kavvanah* for this verse pertains to the enactment of the traditional ritual of *yibum*, or "levirate marriage":[65]

---

innovative approach to this metaphysical principle. See, e.g., *Zohar* III: 177a, and my discussion below on page 142 note 115.

63 See, e.g., *EH*, part 1, *Sha'ar Malachim*, ch. 6; *ShHK*, 259; and in *ShG*, ch. 3, 7, 19; *ShP*, *Ki Teitzei*, *Siman* 25, 200.

64 *ShG*, ch. 19:

> אבל הצד השוה שבהם שבכל הנשמות הוא כי כולם יכולות ע״י מעשיהם לעלות ממדרגה למדרגה עד אין קץ
> וכל זה עם ישים אליו לבו ויכוין לכך.

65 The tradition of *yibum* and its counterpart ritual of *chalitzah* has its roots in the Bible (Deuteronomy 25:5–10) and is developed in the Talmudic Tractate of *Yevamot* which is dedicated to this rite. The basic contours of the practice require the brother-in-law of a childless widow to marry her in order to provide her with offspring. The intricate details of this law make up a huge repository of commentary and discussion in the legal codes. See especially *Shulchan Arukh*, *Eben ha-Ezer*, sections 156; 157; 161; 165; 166 and Maimonides, *Mishneh Torah*, *Hilkhot Yibum v'Chalitzah*.

Also, one who comes through the secret of *yibum*, since he is like a new building, is able to attain the *nefesh*, *ruaḥ* and *neshama*—all three of them together at the same time according to his deeds as mentioned. And this is the secret of the verse "If he puts his heart to it, his *ruaḥ* and *neshama* will gather to him," which is explicated concerning one who comes in the secret of *yibum* in [the section of the Zohar called] *Saba de-Mishpatim*.[66] And its explanation is as stated before, for just as the one who performs the *yibum* has the power to return part of his brother's[67] soul to this world, so too there is the power in the *yibum* itself to return and gather to himself all of the soul; both the *ruaḥ* and *neshama* together. But [only] through good deeds, as it says in the verse, "If he puts his heart to it."[68]

In order to understand this passage, we must first unravel what Vital is referring to by the "secret of *yibum*." Earlier in this section of *ShG*, Vital explains that this lore pertains to the process of rebirth for a man who dies childless:

The reason someone comes in the secret of *yibum* is because he died without children. Behold, it is as if he did not succeed at all and as if he was never in the world. And it is as if his first body never existed. ... So, someone who reincarnates through the secret of *yibum* since his first body is considered as if it never existed as mentioned, therefore when his *nefesh* reincarnates it returns with all of its parts as mentioned and it happens

---

66 I have not been able to find any explicit reference to this verse in the *Saba de-Mishpatim* section of the Zohar II: 94b-114a. The only appearances in the Zohar of this verse are found in Zohar I: 155b; II: 162b; III: 177a, and none of them mention *yibum*. It is also noteworthy to mention that in the published editions of this text the classical commentaries and *hagahot* all ignore this reference to *Saba de-Mishpatim* and do not provide a source, even while they do provide a source for every other reference Vital makes to the Zohar throughout the rest of the text. I believe this mysterious reference is an intentional allusion to a passage from the Zohar III: 177a. See my discussion below concerning this matter on page 142 note 115.

67 The published text actually says אביו, "his father." This is clearly a misprint as it should read אחיו, "his brother."

68 *ShG*, ch. 3:

ולכן גם הבא בסוד היבום שהוא דומה לבנין חדש יכול להשיג שלשתם נר"ן יחד בפעם ההיא כפי מעשיו
כנזכר וח"ס פסוק אם ישים אליו לבו רוח ונשמתו אליו יאסוף הנדרש בענין הבא בסוד היבום בסבא
דמשפטים וביאורו הוא כאמור כי כמו שיש כח ביד היבם להחזיר חלק הנפש של אביו (sic) בעה"ז ע"י היבום
כי יש כח ביבום ההוא להחזיר ולאסיף אליו כל הנפש גם את רוחו ונשמתו יחד ע"י מעשים טובים
כמש"ה אם ישים אליו לבו.

that it is actually a new structure. Therefore, also the *ruaḥ* and *neshama* will reincarnate together with her. However, not all at once but only if he merits it by doing the appropriate *mitzvot*.[69]

From this text it appears that the "secret of *yibum*" points to a loophole in the laws of *gilgul*.[70] Ordinarily, only a "completely new" soul has the possibility of rectifying all three soul parts in a single lifetime without having to go through the hassle of performing complex and dangerous *kavvanot*.[71] Here we have an apparent exception to this rule: a man who dies childless may—through the "secret of *yibum*"—reincarnate with all three soul-parts into a new body and rectify all of them in a single lifetime if his deeds merit such. This is possible because the body and life of a childless man is considered to be fundamentally null and void. Not only that, but all historical and ontological existence of such a man is erased to the point that the body that he inhabited during his childless life will never resurrect.[72] This means that when such a man reincarnates through "the secret of *yibum*" his new body is like a "new structure"—in a sense, like one of the "completely new soul" category—and all three of his soul-parts can then be rectified in a single lifetime.

But this passage still does not provide us with a clear picture of what it means for such a person to reincarnate through the "secret of *yibum*." How does

---

69 *ShG*, ch. 3:

מי שבא בסוד היבום הוא לסבת שמת בלא בנים והרי הוא כאלו לא הצליח כלל ועיקר וכאלו לא היה בעולם וגוף הראשון הוי כלא היה ... כי הנה המתגלגל בסוד יבום כיון שגופו הראשון נחשב כלא היה כלל כנזכר אשר לסיבה זו תבא הנפש בגלגול בכללות חלקיה כנזכר ונמצא כי זהו בנין חדש ממש ולכן יתגלגלו עמה גם הרוח והנשמה שלשתם ביחד אמנם לא בפעם אחת רק כאשר יזכה ויעשה מצות הראויות.

70 On the relationship between *gilgul* and *yibum* in the Zohar, see *Zohar* II: 94b-114a. Also see the discussion in Giller, *Reading the Zohar*, 54–57; Michal Oron, "Lines of Influence in the Doctrine of the Soul and Reincarnation in Thirteenth-Century Kabbala and the Worlds of R. Todros Abulafia" [Hebrew], in *Studies in Jewish Thought*, ed. Sara O. Heller-Wilensky and Moshe Idel (Jerusalem: Magnes, 1989), 277–290; Eitan P. Fishbane, "A Chariot for the Shekhinah: Identity and the Ideal Life in Sixteenth-Century Kabbalah," *Journal of Religious Ethics* 37, no. 3 (2009): 393–394 and Oded Yisraeli, *The Interpretation of Secrets and the Secrets of Interpretation: Midrashic and Hermeneutic Strategies in Sabba de-Mishpatim of the Zohar* [Hebrew] (Los Angeles: Cherub Press, 2005), 113–129.

71 Indeed, the other categories of soul do not have the option of a single incarnation unless they successfully apply either the *kavvanah* of "my soul desires you at night" when going to sleep, or the *kavvanah* of *nefilat apayim*. On the categories of souls and their respective rules regarding *gilgul* see my discussion in the introduction.

72 See *ShG*, ch. 3.

a man who died childless succeed in reincarnating through this mechanism, such that he is reborn with all three soul-parts integrated together and available for rectification in a single lifetime? There are only two passages in the entire Lurianic literature that provide us with clues. The following pericope is the clearer and more complete of the two:

> The secret of *yibum*: As we explained at the beginning, in the first intercourse he makes her into a vessel and places into her one spirit. From this is understood the secret of the *mitzvah* of *yibum*. That is, that behold the brother who died placed inside his wife one spirit, and in intercourse with the living brother, who performs *yibum* with his wife, for he is kin to him, before he copulates with her, also the spirit of this living brother who is the one performing *yibum*, invokes the *neshama* of the dead brother and joins it with his *ruah* that is inside his wife. And this is performed with three preparations: The first is the spirit of the dead brother that is left in his wife. The second, by means of coitus with the one performing *yibum* [i.e. the living brother]. The third, by means of the *kavannah* of the one performing *yibum*, who intends through intercourse with [his dead brother's wife] to bring there the *neshama* of his dead brother. And this is the meaning of the verse, "If he sets his heart to it his *ruah* and *neshama* will be gathered to him" (Job 34:14). This verse intends to say: If the one performing *yibum* "sets his heart" and intention "to him," that is, to his dead brother, [since the Hebrew word אליו can be translated either as "to it" or as "to him"] through this he will cause the *ruah* of the dead [brother] that is inside his wife as well as the *neshama* of the dead [brother] that departed to that [other] world, the two of them shall be gathered together and interpenetrate and be inside this woman who received the one performing *yibum*. And she shall become pregnant and give birth to them [sic], and the dead [brother] will return in a *gilgul* in this world and be rectified.[73]

---

73 *Sha'ar ha-Hakdamot*, 259:

סוד היבום: וכמו שביארנו תחלה כי בביאה ראשונה עושה אותה כלי ומניח בה חד רוחא וממנו יובן
סוד מצות היבום והוא כי הנה אחיו שמת הניח באשתו חד רוחא ובביאת אחיו החי המייבם את אשתו
שהוא קרובו קודם שיבא בה גם רוח האח הזה החי שהוא היבם מקדים נשמת האח המת ומתחבר עם
רוחו שהיה בתוך אשתו וזה נעשה בשלושה הכנות האחת היא רוח האח המת שהשאיר באשתו הב'
ע"י היבם הזה וביאתו הג' ע"י כונת היבם שמתכוין ביאתו ביבמתו להביא שם נשמתו של אחיו המת
חש"ה אם ישים אליו לבו רוחו ונשמתו אליו יאסוף וירצה אם היבם הזה ישים לבו וכונתו אליו רוצה
לומר אל אחיו המת יגרום ע"כ כי רוחו של המת שהיה בגו אתתיה וגם נשמתו של המת שהלכה לה

In this process, the brother of someone who dies childless fulfills the *mitzvah* of *yibum* by having sex with his brother's widow and impregnating her. So far this fits the normative expression of this ritual practice. However, Luria's provocative twist to this tradition is his assertion that the offspring from this act of ritual sex—performed with the *kavannah* of "If he sets his heart to *him*"—is actually the deceased brother himself reincarnating as the child of his widow's and brother's copulation.

The dynamics of this affair are based on the understanding that a part of the deceased brother's soul was deposited inside his wife's womb in their initial act of intercourse and remains there even after his death.[74] Therefore, with the impetus from, and intermingling with, his brother's seed in his post-mortem coition with his sister-in-law, that spirit that was deposited inside her (and is itself a part of the deceased husband's soul) reincarnates anew in the resultant progeny. According to Luria, if a soul reincarnated through such an act, it is privy to the same expeditious benefits as a soul that is of the "completely new" category. That is, it has the potential to acquire all three levels of soul in a single lifetime simply through the proper performance of the commandments.

However, the condition for this outcome is that the proper intention of the verse "If he puts his heart to him" be applied. That is, the living brother must invoke and manifest the soul-parts of his dead brother that have been dislocated from each other as a result of his dying without brood. This is accomplished, Vital tells us, by focusing the contemplative gaze of his heart upon his deceased brother while he has sex with his wife. The result of such concentration is the cathexis of his brother's dislocated parts (i.e. his *neshama*) onto the remnants of his own *ruaḥ* that remain embedded in his wife's body from their very first intercourse. Then these two-reunited soul-parts commingle with the living brother's semen to produce a new physical body—a "new structure"—to house his dead brother's soul.

This process suggests that the spirit that the male inserts inside the female in the first act of mating is the source of the anatomical substance that constitutes one's physical body. To be sure, this is exactly how it is understood in the

---

לאותו עולם שתיהם יאסופו יחד וישתתפו ויהיו תוך האשה היבמה הזאת ותתעבר ותלד אותם ויחזור המת בגלגול בעוה"ז ויתוקן.

Cf. with the second passage found in *EH*, *Sha'ar HaMelachim*, gate 11, ch. 6.

74 See my discussion of the metaphysical template of the "first" and "second" intercourses on page 70 note 55. Also see Kallus, "Theurgy," 248–249.

Lurianic writings.[75] While the physical substance of the body is more directly a development of the second act of coitus, it is the spirit that is deposited inside the female in the first intercourse that is correlated with the Lurianic doctrine of soul garments which serves as the ethereal source for one's anatomical structure.[76]

In this context, it is interesting to consider why the physical body of the brother who dies childless is nullified of its ontological existence (In Vital's words, it is "as if it never existed")[77] and his body will thus not revive at the time of the resurrection of the dead. This means that the production of offspring imparts the endurance of one's physical body-identity beyond death. That is to say, for Luria there is a connection between an individual's resurrection of his or her physical body and the successful production of a genealogical line of progeny. Why is this so? The answer to this question is fundamentally tied up with Luria's understanding of the relationship between the spirit deposited in the first intercourse, the construction of the soul garments, and the cosmological process of impregnation and birth that is intimately intertwined with the principle of the "deposited spirit."[78] As we will see, the soul garments relate directly

---

75 See, e.g., *ShG*, ch. 39, 170:

בענין הלבושים והכלים של הנשמות עצמם הנקראים אורות שמהם נעשה רמ"ח
איברים שהנשמה מתלבשת בהם.

(Regarding the garments and vessels of the souls themselves that are called "lights"; from them are constructed the 248 limbs that the soul is clothed in.) The "garments" referred to in this passage is the "deposited spirit" itself. See, e.g., the statement in *ShP, Vayera*, 49: "From that spirit that is deposited into her by her husband are constructed the garments for all the souls that are created from her from then onwards forever." Also see *EH*, gate 39, ch. 10; *ShK, Inyan Derushei ha-Laylah*, ch. 8, and for a review of this subject and more sources, see page 70 notes 55 and 57, page 75 note 65, and page 79 note 74.

76 As discussed above in chapter one, the *kavvanot* for the bedtime *shema* act as the "first intercourse" that provides the theurgic function of establishing *nuqvah* with a "vessel" that will enable her to receive the fluids from the "second intercourse" that occurs during the *kavvanah* for the morning *shema*. It is the substance from the second intercourse that acts as the material for the physical structure of the gestating organism. See *ShK, Inyan Derushei ha-Laylah*, ch. 8 and see my discussion of this topic above in note 68. On the correspondence of the first intercourse with the soul garments, see *Olat Tamid*, 119; *ShP, Vayera*, 49 and especially *EH*, gate 39, ch. 10. On the soul garments in general, see Fine, *Physician of the Soul*, 308–314. On the "deposited spirit" as the ingredients of the vessel of *nuqvah* and the substance of the female waters, see my discussion and sources above on page 78ff. On the myth of the drops of semen that fell from Joseph's fingernails as the source for the soul garments, see *ShG*, ch. 39.

77 *ShG*, ch. 3: הוי כלא היה

78 See, e.g., the statement in *ShP, Vayera*, 49: "From that spirit that is deposited into her by her husband are constructed the garments for all the souls that are created from her from then onwards forever."

to the resurrection of the dead since they serve as the very material out of which the physical organism is reconstructed.[79]

These associations find their scriptural prototype in the Lurianic myths that provide the esoteric meaning for the biblical tale of the birth of Joseph and Benjamin. As mentioned above, the spirit that is deposited inside *nuqvah* in the first act of cosmic sexual penetration serves as a vessel to hold the seminal fluids received in the second ejaculation. Vital explains that this spirit is called the "*nefesh* of Rachel," since it is what provides her with the life-force that enables her to live. In fact, if it were to depart from her she would literally die.

This explains why the biblical Rachel died at the birth of her youngest son Benjamin. At his birth, the spirit deposited in the first intercourse left her body and became the soul of Benjamin.[80] With the departure of this spirit Rachel physically died, which explains the wording of the verse in Genesis 35:18: "When her *nefesh* went out, she died." However, Rachel does not die when she gives birth to Joseph, since what departed at his birth was the spirit deposited in the second intercourse which does not constitute her life force.[81] Since these female waters are not constitutive of Rachel's life-force, when they departed from her to form the soul of Joseph, she remained alive.[82]

Here we see that the soul garments—and hence the anatomical structure—of one's progeny are constituted by the essential substances contributed by their father and mother in their act of coitus. To be sure, this would explain why for Luria a man who does not produce offspring cannot resurrect into the body that he possessed in his barren lifetime. It is as if his body never existed; it is "null and void." This is because without brood the part of his soul that was cathected into his wife in the form of the "deposited spirit" of the first intercourse remains without a physical body. This implies that for Luria, the soul remains embodied only insofar as it is being carried along a genealogical line of parentage. To say it another way, the soul's continued existence

79 See, e.g., *ShG*, ch. 39, 170: "Regarding the garments and vessels of the souls themselves that are called "lights"; from them are constructed the 248 limbs that the soul is clothed in."
80 This spirit is constituted by the two *yhvh*'s representing the two unsweetened *gevurot* (and the numerical value of the word בן which equals 52 and is also the first two letters of the name בנימין). See *ShK, Inyan Nefilat Apayim*, ch. 4; *ShP, Vayera*, 48–49.
81 This spirit that becomes the material for Joseph's soul is constituted by the three sweetened *gevurot* which compose the female waters within her as represented by the three *yhvh*'s filled with the letter ה or the name בן—52. See *ShK, Inyan Nefilat Apayim*, ch. 4.
82 See these descriptions in *ShK, Nefilat Apayim*, ch. 4. Luria's metaphysical narrative on the birth of Joseph and Benjamin is an obvious reformulation and development of motifs explicated in the Zohar. See, e.g., *Zohar* I: 155b.

is not only dependent on its self-expression in corporeal form but also on the transference of its anatomical substance from one generation to the next in an unbroken chain of progeny all the way until the time of the resurrection of the dead.

Interestingly, in the process outlined above we have Rachel giving up her physical life in order to produce a human soul (i.e. Benjamin), while in the prayer of *nefilat apayim* we have the inverse: the contemplative death of the practitioner in order to supply Rachel both with the vessels she needs to hold the female waters as well as with the substance of the female waters itself, all so that she might engage in cosmic coitus with her mate and once again receive his seminal fluids.[83]

This also explains the correlation found in many places in Vital's writings between the female waters and human souls in general, and more specifically with the souls of the righteous.[84] Since Joseph is the classic archetype of the *tzaddik* in Lurianic Kabbalah[85]—and Joseph is here associated with the female waters ejaculated into Rachel in the second intercourse—the associative jump that equates all righteous with the female waters is thus to be expected.

However, Vital weaves this associative thread one stitch further. While the souls of the righteous are equated with the female waters, it is the actual *physical bodies* of the righteous that provide the mechanism for the most ensnared sparks trapped inside the *qelipot* to ascend. This trope stands out in the various Lurianic formulations of the esoteric meaning of the death of the ten martyrs

---

83 On the transference of soul substance from the mother and father to the child in the conception process, see *ShP*, *Vayera*, 48ff. This cyclical process is one expression of the interpenetration of sex, death, and soul in the Lurianic corpus. On the theme of sex in kabbalistic texts in general, and on "barrenness" in particular, see Mopsik, *Sex of the Soul*, 42ff. On the concept of the *hahu rucha* and the differences between the first and second intercourses, see Kallus, "Theurgy," 247–248 and my discussion above, page 70 note 55. Notably, the themes of sleep, death, and sex intersect in a fascinating passage in the text *Olat Tamid* that articulates the closest thing I have seen to a kabbalistic doctrine of immaculate conception and virgin birth. See *Olat Tamid*, 117–120. On the "orgasmic" nature of the contemplative death ritual in general, see Fine's comment cited above on page 106 note 27.

84 See e.g. *ShK*, *Inyan Nefilat Apayim*, ch. 5: "The female waters of *malkhut* are the souls of the righteous." For other sources see my discussion above on pages 78–79 and the notes there.

85 Binyamin is given the symbolic moniker "lower *tzaddik*" since he is the *yesod* of *nuqvah*, constituted by the spirit deposited in the first insemination, in contradistinction to Joseph who is the *yesod* of *zeir* and thus the "upper *tzaddik*." See *ShK*, *Inyan Keriyat Shema*, ch. 6, 147. In essence, Vital explains the generative process that links the three sweetened *gevurot* with the female waters and the female waters with the soul of Joseph.

during Mishnaic times.[86] For example, concerning these ten martyrs, Vital writes:

> their *actual bodies* [emphasis mine] were in the aspect of female waters
> to *malkhut*, and they thus gathered the soul-sparks that were [trapped] in
> *asiyah*, because there was no other way to gather them [aside from physical
> death].[87]

The topic of the death of the ten martyrs seems to have particularly fascinated Luria, serving as the mythological template of some of his most esoteric teachings, particularly those related to intentional martyrdom, death, and the somatic integration of the soul at resurrection.[88] As we shall see, the notion that the physical body is offered as a sacrifice to the *sitra aḥra* (the demonic "other

---

86 The legend of the ten martyrs first appears in its mature form in a midrashic text of Geonic provenance titled *Midrash Asarah Harugei Malkhut*, or *Midrash Eleh Ezkerah*, of which there are four versions, each differing from the others in various points of detail. See Jellinek, *Bet Ha-Midrash*, i. 64, vi, 19 (Vina: n.p., 1878). Earlier instantiations of this lore appear in various sections of the Talmud and in Midrash Rabbah (See, e.g., *BT Avodah Zarah* 17b, 18a; *Ber.* 61b; *San.* 14a; *Lam. R.* ii. 2; *Mishlei. R.* i. 13). The main difference between the two renditions of the story pertains to whether or not these ten sages were executed at the same time. The earlier versions profess that there were intervals between the executions, while the *Midrash Asarah Harugei Malkhut* describes their martyrdom as occurring on the same day. The myth gained popularity largely through its inclusion in a famous liturgical poem that was incorporated into the Yom Kippur prayer service. Regarding the internal struggle that accompanied the development of this myth among the midrashists, see Ra'anan S. Boustan, "The Contested Reception of the Story of the Ten Martyrs in Medieval Midrash," in *Envisioning Judaism: Studies in Honor of Peter Schäfer on the Occasion His 70th Birthday*, ed. Ra'anan S. Boustan, Klaus Hermann, Reimund Leicht, Annette Yoshiko Reed, and Giuseppe Veltri, (Tübingen: Mohr Siebeck, 2013), 1:369–194.

The mystical interpretations that attached hidden esoteric import to the ten martyrs are developed in the Zohar, where Luria clearly found the inspiration for his more radical incorporation of the myth into his theurgic system. See, e.g., *Zohar* II: 254b.

87 *ShK, Inyan Tefilat ha-Shachar*, ch. 1:

כי הגופין עצמן דילהון נעשו בחינת מ"ן אל המלכות והם המלקטים את הנצוצות הנשמות שבעשיה
כי א"א ללוקטן בשום אופן אחר.

Also see, *EH*, gate 39, ch. 1: ואמנם העלאת מ"ן דנוקבא דז"א מתתא מן הקל' למעלה בנוקבא הנ"ל אינו אלא ע"י גופין דילהון ממש שנהרג. (And indeed the raising up of the female waters of *nuqvah* of *zeir anpin* from below in the *qelipot* to above in *nuqvah* as mentioned above, only occurs through their bodies that were actually killed.)

88 See e.g., *EH*, ch. 39; *ShG*, ch. 39; *ShMRshBi, Shir ha-Shirim shel ha-Zohar*, 304. On the relationship between the soul-garments of the ten martyrs and the ten *gevurot* of *imma* and *abba*, see Fine, *Physician of the Soul*, 310. Also see Jonathan Garb's mention of the ten martyrs

side") to enable the female waters to ascend serves as the blueprint for understanding the theurgic import of the practice of contemplative death performed
during *nefilat apayim* and the morning *shema*.[89]

According to this mystical lore, the death of the ten martyrs during the
time of the Mishnah was required in order to rectify the particularly decrepit
situation that befell the cosmos during the period of the destruction of the second temple. Sin had proliferated to an unprecedented degree and as a result
even the female waters that belong to *imma* had descended into the realm of
the *qelipot*. Such an extreme state of affairs required an equally radical method
of rectification:

> And behold during the time of the destruction of the second temple and
> the time of the ten martyrs of the kingdom, the sins had multiplied very
> much and not only did the terrestrial human beings not have sufficient
> strength to isolate these sparks and raise them up with their prayers in the
> secret of female waters, but even the female waters of *binah* descended
> below and returned to mix with the husks … and because of this the world
> was doomed until the blessed one needed to fix the world. [He did this]
> through the martyrs of the kingdom.[90]

---

and Lurianic Kabbalah in *Yearnings of the Soul: Psychological Thought in Modern Kabbalah*
(Chicago: University of Chicago Press, 2015), 38–39.

89 Vital explicitly correlates the death of the ten martyrs with the notion of human sacrifice. See
EH, gate 39, *Sha'ar Mayin Nukvin u'Dekorin*, ch. 1: והנה גופות שלהם היו מבחינת הקרבנות (And
behold their bodies were in the aspect of sacrifices). This correlation with human sacrifice
has its roots in the Zohar and even earlier midrashic literature. See, e.g., *Zohar* II: 143a and
the *Nitzotzei Zohar* there (published in the Margoliot edition by Mosad ha-Rav Kook), who
quotes a provocative passage from the *Midrash Rabbah, Naso* 12:12 that states that the angel
Metatron sacrificed the souls of the righteous.

90 *EH, Sha'ar Mayin Nukvin u'Dekorin*, gate 39, ch. 1:

והנה בזמן חורבן בית שני בזמן י' הרוגי מלוכה גברו מאוד העוונות ולא די שלא היה כח ביד בני אדם התחתונים
לברר ניצוצין אלו ע"י תפילתן להעלותן בסוד מ"נ אלא אפילו גם המ"ן דבינה ירדו למטה וחזרו להתערב בקליפות ...
וע"ז היה העולם נאבד עד שהוצרך הש"י לתקן העולם וזה היה ע"י הרוגי מלוכה

Also see later on in this section the following alternate formulation:

והנה אז בחורבן בית שני לא היה כח להעלות מ"ן הנ"ל אם לא בבחינת אחרת רביעית והוא
שהוצרכו י' חסידים ההם ליהרג ולמסור עצמם על ק"ה בפועל

(And behold during the destruction of the second temple they did not have the strength to raise
up the aforementioned female waters without a different fourth aspect. And that is that they
required those ten pious to be killed and to give themselves over on the sanctification of the name
in actuality.)

What is it about the execution of these ten sages that bears such redemptive repercussions? Firstly, for Luria these ten righteous souls are instantiations of the souls of the twelve sons of Jacob, and thus represent the source and essence of all souls in creation.[91] Since the female waters are constituted by souls, these ten martyrs—as the source of all subsequent human souls—have the power to attract the sparks of female waters trapped inside the *qelipot* in order to facilitate their redemption. Secondly, their physical death allows for a magical process of release through the pain involved with the extermination of the body:

> The bodies of the ten martyrs of the kingdom were given over to the hand of the other side and they were killed in order that they should have the power to raise up the female waters of *nuqvah* of *zeir anpin* from there by their merit. For did not their bodies receive the pain of death?[92]

The physical torture and death of the ten martyrs thus represents a theurgic sacrificial rite in which their mortified bodies served to extract the loftiest souls from the darkest regions of the netherworld.[93] But this process also betrays a hidden signification: the physical death of these ten righteous is really transmogrified by Luria into an alchemical process of what we might call *apoangelosis*:[94]

---

91 See *EH, Sha'ar Mayin Nukvin U'dekorin*, gate 39, ch. 1. While in this section Luria does not account for the discrepancy in the number of people involved (ten martyrs vs. twelve tribes), he does attempt to explain the correlation elsewhere. See, e.g., *ShMRsh, Shir ha-Shirim shel ha-Zohar*, 301–304, where Vital explains that the significance of the number ten pertains to the fact that each of the ten correlated with one of the ten sefirot of the *sitra ahra*: כן עשרה הרוגי מלכות נמסרו עשר גופין לעשר שמצד הקליפות. (So too the ten martyrs of the kingdom gave over their ten bodies to the ten [aspects] from the side of the husks.)

92 *EH*, gate 39, ch. 1:

גופם של י' הרוגי מלוכה נמסרו אז בידם דסטר"א והרגום כדו שיהיה בהם כח להעלות המ'נ דנוקבא
דז"א משם בזכותן כי הלא הגופין הם מקבלין צער דהריגה

93 The inclusion of the necessity for pain in this theurgic rite of cosmic integration is also echoed in Vital's description of the performance of the *kavvanot* of soul ascension that accompany the recitation of the bedtime *shema*, where one is encouraged to contemplatively submit themselves to the four methods of capital punishment. See, e.g., *ShK, Inyan Derushei ha-Laylah*, ch. 5, 355.

94 I am crafting this word from the Ancient Greek *apo* + *angelos*, meaning "to angelicize." The typical locution referring to the process of the transformation of the physical body into a spiritual substance that is free from the inevitability of physical death is *apotheosis*, derived from the Ancient Greek, meaning "to deify." For example, in works of scholarship that treat the metamorphosis of the biblical characters Enoch and the prophet Elijah, the

Do not be surprised by this, for behold their bodies were so purified until they were considered the same constitution as other human souls. For this is the stature of the righteous that they purify their bodies and transform them into "form." And this is the reason that death does not apply to the righteous. Proof of the matter is Elijah of blessed memory, for he ascended to heaven in body and soul … and even more so these holy ten martyrs of the kingdom who were killed on the sanctification of the name for the purpose and intention mentioned above. For certainly their bodies literally ascended in the aspect of spirit and [through this] they raise up the female waters of *nuqvah* of *zeir anpin* from now and onwards until the days of the messiah. And behold their bodies are in the aspect of sacrifices.[95]

In this account, Vital presents a somewhat paradoxical outline of the phenomenological elements involved in the death of the ten martyrs. On the one hand, their physical bodies were transformed into spirit through the righteousness of their conduct, allowing both their bodies and souls to ascend as a single unit. On the other hand, their bodies are handed over to the realm of evil, the *sitra aḥra*, as sacrificial nourishment for the demonic appetite. This latter facet of the process is underscored and developed further in another passage that explicates the death of the ten martyrs:

Their death needed to come from the hand of the *sitra aḥra* in order to acquire the kingdom of heaven, in the secret of ten from below are [so too] above in *malkhut*, in order to attach to [the aspect of] heaven in the secret of her female waters that are produced by these ten spirits of the martyrs of the kingdom that entered *malkhut*. And their bodies remained

term *apotheosis* is typically used. However, this term is not accurate, since they are not transformed into divine beings but rather their physical bodies are essentialized into the same material as the angels. In the case of Enoch, the mystical tradition explicitly assumes that he was transformed into the angel Metatron. See. e.g., Scholem, *MTJM*, 67. Therefore, I suggest the word *apoangelosis* as a more appropriate term denoting this process. On the phenomenon of *apotheosis* in Lurianic Kabbalah in general, see Magid, *Metaphysics*, 50ff.

95 *EH*, gate 39, ch. 1:

ואל תתמה מזה כי הנה גופות שלחם חזו כ"כ מזוככים עד אשר היו ראוין בערך נשמות של בני אדם אחרים כי זהו מעלת הצדיקים לזכך גופם ולעשותן צורה וזהו הטעם שאין מיתה נזכר בצדיקים וראייה לדבר מאליהו ז"ל כי עלה בשמים בגוף ונפש ... ומכ"ש גופות אלו הקדושים י' הרוגי מלוכה שנהרגו על ק"ה לתכלית ולכוונה הנ"ל כי ודאי גופם ממש עלו בבחי' רוח והם מעלין מ"נ דנוקבא דז"א מאז ואילך עד ימות המשיח והנה גופות שלהם היו מבחינת הקרבנות.

in their place in this world which is the world of *asiyah*, within which are the *qelipot*, and they take their portion from these ten bodies and they do not enter into the place of holiness and the dross is selected out from the food.[96]

In this version of the myth, the physical bodies of the ten martyrs do not seem to undergo a process of *apoangelosis* at all; rather, they are subjected to a similar fate as other mortals insofar as their souls are detached from their bodies at death. However, their journey is unique in that their flesh provides sacrificial provision for the demonic belly. This seems to be the exclusive theurgic contribution of the death of the ten martyrs: their corporeal ingredients satisfy the hunger of the *sitra aḥra* in a way that frees the most stubbornly trapped sparks of light to ascend to the higher realms.

But the fullest realization of this process suggests a more radical integration of the two paradoxical elements echoed in this text. Luria articulates this idea by linking the myth with the resurrection of the dead:

> At the resurrection of the dead the souls will return to these bodies because in the time of the resurrection of the dead the other side will be nullified and it will no longer need these ten bodies to be a part of the other side.[97]

Here we see the age of the resurrection of the dead as indicative of the dissolution of evil as an ontological reality. Such actuality, which marks the equalization of all gradation and hierarchy in the cosmos, is paradoxically both generated by physical death (of the ten martyrs and by the Lurianic *mekhaven* who contemplatively reenacts such self-sacrifice) and by the reconstitution of physical life (in the event of resurrection). This two-pronged process reveals a nondirectional bias insofar as physical life and death are concerned; indeed, they are integrated in this ultimate metaphysical vision as two sides of the same coin.

---

96 ShMRsh, *Shir ha-Shirim shel ha-Zohar*, 304:

כי הוכרח להיות מיתתם ע"י סטרא אחרא כדי לקנות מלכות שמים בסוד עשר מלמטה למעלה במלכות
להתחבר עם שמים בסוד מ"ן דילה שנעשו עם עשר רוחין אלו של הרוגי מלכות שנכנסו במלכות וגופין דלהון
ישתארו בדוכתייהו בהאי עלמא שהוא עולם העשיה שבו הקליפות והם יקחו חלקם בעשרה גופין אלו ולא
יכנסו במקום הקודש ויתברר הפסולת מתוך האוכל.

97 Ibid:

בתחית המתים יחזרו הנשמות להם בגופין אלו כי בזמן תחית המתים תתבטל סטרא אחרא ולא יצטרכו אליה
אלו העשר גופין להיות חלק לסטרא אחרא.

Ultimately it is this fundamental act of theurgic martyrdom that is reenacted during the performance of the *kavvanot* of *nefilat apayim* and the *shema*. The intention of "giving oneself over to death" thus involves a contemplative rehearsal of this ancient event of physical martyrdom on behalf of the ten martyrs of the kingdom, themselves reincarnations of the original tribes of Israel and the mythological source of all human souls.[98]

However, there is no exclusively pneumatic art that is sufficiently potent to induce a permanent condition of cosmic unification. The most these *kavvanot* can accomplish is a temporary harmonization of the supernal realms: *nefilat apayim* effecting the *zivvug* of *zeir* and *nuqvah* and *keriyat shema* that of *abba* and *imma*. A permanently enduring rectification of the comic dysfunction requires more extreme maneuvers; namely, the physical death of the practitioner. This perspective is expressed in the following passage, appearing in Vital's discussion of the *kavvanah* for *nefilat apayim*:

> And behold even though a person who gives himself over to death unifies *tiferet* and *malkhut* in the secret of kissing, and one who gives himself over to the sanctification of the name unifies *ḥokhmah* and *binah* in the secret of kissing, this is only temporary, and it does not create a permanent vehicle for this, unless he gives himself over to death on the Torah and on the commandments and on the sanctification of the name *in action* [בפועל] as did R. Akiva.[99]

---

98 Luria capitalizes on the rabbinic legend that R. Akiva, the greatest exemplar of the sagacious ten martyrs, recited the *shema* while being skinned alive. See *BT Berakhot* 61b; *ShK, Nefilat Apayim*, ch. 5 and *ShK, Keriyat Shema*, ch. 5. For other Lurianic texts that treat the topic of the ten martyrs, see *Kitzur ABY"A*, ch. 5; *Sha'ar ha-Hakdamot*, 158; *EH, Sha'ar ha-Kellalim*, ch. 1.
99 *ShMRshBi, Shir ha-Shirim shel ha-Zohar*, 314:

> והנה אעפ"י שהמוסר עצמו למיתה מייחד ת"ת ומלכות בסוד נשיקין וכן המוסר עק"ה מייחד חו"ב בסוד
> נשיקין זהו לפי שעה אבל אינו נעשה מרכבה תמיד לכך אא"כ ימסור עצמו למיתה על התורה ועל המצוות
> ועק"ה בפועל כמו שעשה ר"ע.

Compare with *ShMRshBi, Shir ha-Shirim shel ha-Zohar*, 311:

> ודע שעד זמן הי' הרוגי מלוכה היו מאירים ת"ת ומלכות והיה די באורם להעלות מ"ן לבינה ממטה
> למעלה עם קצת סיוע מהצדיקים אשר מוסרים עצמם עק"ה בכח בעת ק"ש אבל בזמן עשרה הרוגי
> מלוכה שמש וירח קדרו בעון הדור ולא היה בהם כח להעלות מ"ן עד אשר נהרגו הרוגי מלכות
> בפועל.

(Know that until the time of the ten martyrs of the kingdom, *tiferet* and *malkhut* were illuminated, and their light was sufficient to raise up female waters to *binah* from below to above with only a little help from the righteous who give themselves over on the sanctification of the name during

While the *kavvanot* of *nefilat apayim* and *keriyat shema* require the intention to dismember the soul from the body in order to ascend into the necessary ethereal loci, the body in both cases remains tangibly alive.[100] The only way to accomplish a permanent state of cosmic unification is to literally physically die in the contemplative act of "giving oneself over to death." This moribund process unifies the fragmented dimensions of these practices with their embodied potential. That is, only when inner death as dismemberment is integrated with the organic expiration of the physical body is the eschatological promise of permanent union fulfilled. This paradoxical process expresses one of the most radical and provocative doctrines in all of Kabbalah: that is, that the full realization of human embodiment occurs through the death of the body.[101]

Viewed from this angle, the entire Lurianic contemplative project gestures toward a radical erasure of the lines that typically demarcate life from death. Just like the death of Rachel provides the life potential for Benjamin, the death of the body supplies both life to the upper realms in the form of female waters and nourishment to the *sitra ahra* in the form of corporeal foodstuff. What seems like death to the conventional perspective thus turns out to be life-giving. But there is more to the story. The ultimate fulfillment of this process is only realized in the paradoxical resomatization of the soul in the revivification of the physical body. In this act, the body reconstitutes and in the process the cosmos simultaneously dissolves. This paradoxical dialectic between physical life and death constitutes the mystical heart of Lurianic metaphysics and its performative features.

---

keriyat shema. However, during the time of the ten martyrs of the kingdom, the sun and moon were darkened due to the sins of the generation and they did not have the power to raise up the female waters until the ten martyrs of the kingdom were killed in actuality.)

And see ibid., 311:

וכאשר אין איש מוסר עצמו עק"ה לא בכח בק"ש ולא בפועל כעשרה הרוגי מלוכה אז אין הזיווג שלם לצורך הבנים ת"ת ומלכות להריק בהם ברכה עד בלי די.

(When a person does not give himself over to the sanctification of the name, neither in force in *keriyat shema* nor in action like the ten martyrs of the kingdom, then the unification is not complete for the needs of the children *tiferet* and *malkhut* to supply them with ceaseless blessings.)

100 See, e.g., *ShK, Inyan Nefilat Apayim*, ch. 5, 311.

101 This provocative principle which is so fundamental to the Lurianic worldview is also a key feature of postmodern philosophy. Note, for example, the quotation from George Bataille, one of the major influences on postmodern thought, that I used as an epigraph for chapter two of this book: "In a sense, the corpse is the most complete affirmation of the spirit." See George Bataille, *Theory of Religion* (Brooklyn: Zone Books, 1989), 40.

RESURRECTION AND THE NULLIFICATION OF HIERARCHY

The relationship between the death of the physical body and the raising up of the female waters reaches its most mature eschatological expression in Vital's explanation of the function of the resurrection of the dead in the theurgic process. Not surprisingly, this interpenetration of tropes is once again evinced by Vital in his treatment of the biblical narrative of the birth of Joseph and Benjamin.[102] The context of this discussion is the injunction to "honor your father and mother" (Exodus 20:12), which according to rabbinic tradition also includes the requirement to honor one's older brother.[103]

The esoteric reason for the inclusion of the brother in this commandment pertains to the dynamics of transmission that occur when the mother gives birth: that is, the firstborn child inherits the substantive portion of the "spirit" deposited inside her in the first intercourse with her husband. The souls (or more precisely, the soul garments) of ensuing children born to the same mother are also constructed from this "deposited spirit," but their portion is less appreciable than that transmitted to the firstborn.[104] Therefore, all the younger children are required to pay homage to their eldest brother

---

102 See *ShM, Yitro,* 33–35, which presents the clearest correlation between the resurrection of the dead and the birth of Joseph and Benjamin. For more elaborate formulations of the esoteric significance of the birth of Joseph and Benjamin found in Lurianic literature, see, e.g., *EH, Shaar Mayin Nulvin u'dekorim,* chs. 7–8; *ShP, Vayera,* "ותהר ותלד שרה"; *ShK, Keriyat Shema,* ch. 6; *Talmud Eser Sefirot,* section 9 (at the beginning). Some of these passages will be explicated in the foregoing discussion.

103 See *BT Ketubot* 103a. In this section of the Talmud, the addition of the brother is exegetically derived from the presence of the apparently superfluous word את in the biblical verse.

104 The soul garments of the child are actually constructed from the soul substance of both the mother and father. See, e.g., the following passage in *ShM, Yitro,* 34:

בעת שמזדווג האדם עם בת זוגו הם ממשיכים הנשמות הנזכר ואז אביו נותן בה מבחי' החסדים אשר בו קצת חלק מהם ומתחבר עם הנשמה החדשה הזו ונעשה בחי' אביו כעין מלבוש אליה ... וכן עד"ז אמו נותנת בנשמה זו חלק מבחי' הגבורה אשר בה ונעשית לה כעין לבוש ....

(When a man has intercourse with his partner they draw down the aforementioned souls and the father thereupon bestows it with a small portion of the aspect of the *ḥasadim* that are in him, they combine with this new soul and this aspect of the father becomes like a garment for her [i.e. the child's soul] ... and so too in this manner the mother gives to this soul a portion of the aspect of *gevurah* that is in her and it becomes for her [i.e. the soul] like a garment.)

Also see *ShP, Vayera,* 49, where the construction of the soul garments is explicitly associated with the "deposited spirit" of the first intercourse: אבל מההוא רוחא דשבק בה בעלה נעשה לבושים לכל הנשמות הנוצרות בה מאז ואילך תמיד (But from that spirit that the husband deposited, the garments are made for all the souls that are formed in her from now on and always).

insofar as he inherits a greater, and more elevated, portion of soul substance from their parents.[105]

A second reason presented by Vital for the additional clause of honoring one's older sibling relates to the innovative notion that in addition to the firstborn receiving the "deposited spirit" at birth, he also leaves behind a portion of his (i.e. the child's) soul inside the mother. The implications of this thesis are significant for the firstborn's younger siblings, since upon their parturition they accrue the parts of their eldest sibling's soul that he left inside the womb of his mother. This means that all the remaining children's soul garments are constructed with constituents of the firstborn's soul, thus requiring that they pay reverence to their elder sibling as a quasi-progenitor, second only to the parents themselves.[106]

This scene, outlined most explicitly by Vital through the prototype of the birth of Joseph and Benjamin, is then projected onto (or reflected from) the cosmic stage in the theurgic drama acted out among the *partzufim*, with *imma* and *abba* starring in the role of the parents and *zeir* and *nuqvah* in the role of the firstborn child(ren). Human souls also have a part in this performance as the younger children of *imma* and *abba*, and consequently the younger siblings of *zeir* and *nuqvah*.[107]

---

105 See *ShM, Yitro*, 34: הבנים יורדים בסדר המדרגות כי הבן הבכור לוקח התמצית ושורש דכל ההוא רוחא וכל
השאר חלקים הנשארים שם הם כעין ענפים משועבדים אל הבן הבכור. (The sons descend in order of hierarchy, because the firstborn son takes the essence and root of that [deposited] spirit and the remaining parts are like branches that are subservient to the firstborn son). Luria clearly only considered a firstborn son in this equation. He is following the rabbinic tradition that did not consider firstborn daughters legitimate heirs of inheritance. See, e.g., *Sif. Deut.*, 215.
106 See *ShM, Yitro*, 34–35.
107 Thus Vital explicates the verse "Honor your father and your mother" to be an injunction for the human soul to honor the *partzufim* of *imma* and *abba*, with the extra word את indicating the requirement to also give *kavod* to one's elder siblings, namely *zeir* and *nuqvah*. See *ShM, Yitro*, 34–35:

הנה זו"ן הם הבנים הראשונים שיצאו מזווג אבא ואמא וכל שאר נשמות בני אדם התחתונים
הנמשכים מזיווג אבא ואימא כנודע הנה הם נקראים אחים קטנים של זו"ן ח"ס כבד את אביך ואת
אמך הם או"א ומלת את ואת אתא לרבויי זו"ן אחינו הגדול.

(Behold *zeir* and *nuqvah* are the first children that result from the union of *abba* and *imma*. And all subsequent terrestrial human souls that are drawn down from the union of *abba* and *imma* as is known are called [the] younger children of *zeir* and *nuqvah*. This is the secret [of the verse from Ex. 20:12] "Honor your father and your mother." כבד את אביך ואת אמך) They [refer to] *imma* and *abba*. And the words את and ואת come to include *zeir* and *nuqvah*, the older siblings.)

For the metaphysical underpinnings of the notion that human souls are the siblings of *zeir* and *nuqvah* in terms of the principle of inheritance, see *ShM, Pinchas*, 74–76.

Consequently, just as in the biblical script the firstborn son leaves behind a piece of his soul inside the womb of his mother, so too in the cosmic act some portion of *zeir* and *nuqvah* essential substance remains lodged inside *imma* and *abba*. Therefore, humans can only theurgically impact *imma* and *abba* through the intermediary channel of *zeir* and *nuqvah*, since they (i.e. human souls) are constituted by elements of *zeir* and *nuqvah* that remained embedded inside *imma*'s womb, and thus are beholden to respect *zeir* and *nuqvah* as their spiritual progenitors. In this hierarchical model of cosmic functionality, Luria is able to account for the contemplative elements of the most potent *kavvanot*:

> And through this you can understand the matter of the recitation of the *shema*. For there we explained that you must intend to raise up the female waters with the word *eḥad* to *abba* and *imma*. And we must attach to *zeir* and *nuqvah* in order to raise up the female waters. And the reason is that behold *zeir* and *nuqvah* are our older siblings and we can only ascend by means of them. For we are subservient to them for the reason stated above. And the reason they [i.e. *zeir* and *nuqvah*] are able to ascend above is because *zeir* and *nuqvah* left their roots above in the supernal *imma* as mentioned earlier. Therefore, the other younger children cannot raise up the female waters unless by means of *zeir* and *nuqvah* who left their roots there in *imma*.[108]

The premise of this passage is that human souls are ontologically linked with *imma* and *abba* both through the transmission of soul substance that is passed directly to them by their parents (i.e. *abba* and *imma*) but also through the portion of *zeir* and *nuqvah*'s soul that was imparted to them as a result of *zeir* and *nuqvah*'s soul parts that remained encapsulated within *imma*'s womb. This dynamic explains how the *kavvanah* of *kriyat shema*, a pivotal component of the daily liturgical operation, is to be properly effected. That is, the *mekhaven* must penetrate the recondite dimensions of *abba* and *imma* by consciously attaching his soul to *zeir* and *nuqvah*. Because of the partial ontological homogeneity between the human being and his "older siblings," and the substantive

---

108 ShM, Yitro, 35:

ובזה תבין ענין הק"ש כי שם ביארנו שצריך לכוין להעלות מ"נ במלת אחד לגבי או"א וצריכים אנו להתחבר
עם זו"ן להעלות מ"נ והטעם הוא כי הנה זו"ן הם אחינו הגדול ואין לנו עליה אלא על ידם כי אנו משעובדים להם לטעם
הנ"ל וטעם עליותם למעלה הוא כי זו"ן הניחתו שרשם למעלה באימא עילאה כנ"ל ולכן אין שום עליית מ"נ של בנים
אחרים הקטנים מהם אם לא ע"י זו"ן שהניחתו שרשם שם באימא.

link between *zeir* and *nuqvah* and their "parents," this mechanism of ascent is efficacious.

In our earlier discussion of the *kavvanot* for reciting the bedtime *shema* in chapter one, we noted how the adept was encouraged to "be like *zeir anpin*" in order to fulfill the theurgic function of the rite.[109] Here we see a similar but somewhat hedged version of this formulation in the expectation that the practitioner attach himself to *zeir* and *nuqvah* during the contemplative performance of the *shema* prayer. In light of this passage, which recognizes that the *mekhaven* must first traverse *zeir* and *nuqvah* in order to affect *imma* and *abba* since he is constituted by elements of *zeir* and *nuqvah*'s soul, the former injunction "to be like *zeir*" makes sense. That is, insofar as the practitioner is made up of elements of *zeir*'s soul, he is, to some ontological degree, *zeir* himself.[110]

While there are several examples in Lurianic literature where the human practitioner is explicitly identified with *zeir anpin*, in large part the duality between the human and the divine is maintained. This dialectic between a dualistic metaphysics and a unitive existence that sees no ontological separation between the different parts of the cosmos—and between the human and the cosmic—represents the very core of Lurianic mysticism. The sexual interplay of the cosmic entities in the form of *partzufim* and the human participation in this unitive dance epitomize the process of self-exhaustion that the cosmic hierarchy undergoes as the human being moves inextricably toward its teleological goal. For the human person, this process typically involves many lifetimes of reincarnation and culminates in the resurrection of the physical body.[111] For the cosmos,

---

109 See page 61 note 24.

110 This reflects the basic view in Lurianic Kabbalah that the individual person is constituted by several different souls simultaneously. In the introduction and in chapter one of this book we saw how this dynamic played out in the *gilgul* process, whereby the soul-parts of up to four individuals could simultaneously inhabit a single body. Here we see how this assumption regarding the composite nature of the soul also extends to the *partzufim*. For a rich discussion of the topic of selfhood in Kabbalah, and its complex intersection with Lurianic conceptions of rebirth, see Fishbane, "A Chariot for the Shekhinah: Identity and the Ideal Life in Sixteenth-Century Kabbalah," *Journal of Religious Ethics* 37, no. 3 (2009): 389–390.

111 On resurrection as the culmination of the human teleological journey, see *ShM, Pinchas*, 76: וכל משפטי התורה וסודותיה וסודותיה כולם בנויים עליהם למי שיש בו דעה להבין מתחלת האצילות עד תחיית המתים. (And all the laws of the Torah and its secrets are built upon them for one who has knowledge to understand from the beginning of the emanation until the resurrection of the dead, etc.) This teleological trajectory is stated even more explicitly in the Zohar, where resurrection is explicitly declared as more ultimate than even the messianic age. See, e.g., Zohar I: 139a:

אמר רב יוסף וכי ימות המשיח ותחיית המתים לאו חד הוא א"ל לא דתנן בית המקדש קודם לקבוץ גליות קבוץ גליות קודם לתחיית המתים ותחיית המתים הוא אחרון שבכלם.

it entails the maintenance of the divine family of distinct personalities while simultaneously dissolving the hierarchical structure of its patriarchal existence.

Note, for example, the following passage, where Vital relates this dialectical process to the theurgic function of the resurrection of the dead:

> And know that this attachment only applies until the time of the resurrection of the dead. Afterwards, each one takes his portion and there is no relationship between the father and son, or between the son and the father, nor with his mother, nor with his older brother. Each one goes to his root, unless their souls are all from the same root, in which case they remain attached as they were at the beginning.[112]

The performative function of attaching oneself to *zeir* and *nuqvah* in order to contemplatively penetrate *imma* and *abba* is only relevant until the time of the resurrection. With the advent of the resurrection of the dead comes the dissolution of the hierarchical framework that organizes the cosmos. The categories of upper and lower, parent and child—indeed, all the cosmic familial relationships of the *partzufim* that characterized the varied ontological strata of reality—are erased. However, while the conceptual framework that categorizes the cosmic dimensions in accordance with hierarchical rank is nullified of its reality, this eschatological vision does not nullify the ontological existence of the particular gradations themselves. This paradoxical and all-inclusive mystical vision represents the culmination of the Lurianic project, the implications of which require further elaboration.[113]

(R. Yosef said: are not the resurrection of the dead and the days of the messiah one and the same thing? He said to him: No, as it is taught, the holy temple precedes the ingathering of the exiles; the ingathering of the exiles precedes the resurrection of the dead, and the resurrection of the dead is the last of them all.)

The notion that the only distinction between the condition of resurrection and ordinary life is epistemological is already suggested by the Talmud. See, e.g., *BT Berakhot* 34b: אין בין העולם הזה לתחיית המתים אלא נקיות והשגת ידיעה. (There is no difference between this world and resurrection of the dead except for cleanliness and the apprehension of [esoteric] knowledge.)

112 *ShM, Yitro,* 35:

ודע שאין התחקשרות הזה אלא עד תחיית המתים ואחר כך כל אחד נוטל חלקו ואין יחס לאב עם הבן ובן עם האב ועם אמו ועם אחיו הגדול וכל אחד הולך לשרשו אם לא בהיות נשמותיהם כולם משורש אחד כי אז נשארין מחוברין כבראשונה.

113 A related principle is that of the soul garments, which are also constituted by both an inner (פנימיות) and outer (חיצוניות) core. The outer layer is derived from the *netzah, hod,* and *yesod*

As we above, the use of the term "death" is technical in the Lurianic contemplative system. Thus, "giving oneself over to death" points to an inner journey of descent into the realm of "death," i.e. the *qelipot*. So too, in conveying the esoteric lore pertaining to the resurrection of the dead, Luria suggests a metaphysical process that reflects this shamanic and eschatological orientation. In this manner, the resurrection of the dead points to the elevation of the realm of the dead—the *qelipot*—back to its supernal source. This expresses itself in the following passage, in which the human experience of resurrection parallels the cosmic process of the reintegration of the *qelipot* back into the upper worlds:

> And behold, just like when a human dies his body descends into the grave, and the spirit returns to God that gave it to him ... so too is the issue with these seven kings. That is, for do you not know that they consist of essence and vessels and this is the secret of body and soul? And we explained that their body which are the vessels descended into the world of *beriyah* which is the secret of the supernal dust that is beneath *atzilut*. And there was its burial, and its *ruaḥ* and *neshama* and essence within them ascend above to the God (*Elohim*) that gave, which is *imma*. ... Indeed, the bodies of the vessels that are rectified and elevated are the secret of the resurrection of the dead, towards the bodies that are sleeping the sleep of the dust. Behold through this you will understand how everything that was, is, and will be, they are all in the secret of the seven kings. That is, they are the source of everything, and everything exists from them, and all the foundations

---

of either *imma* or *abba*, while the inner core is derived from the consciousness (מוחין) that enlivens the *netzaḥ*, *hod*, and *yesod* of these *partzufim*. Both the outer and inner layers are constructed from the ten drops of semen that fell from Joseph's (or *yesod*'s) phallus onto the ground when he was nearly seduced by the wife of Potiphar. See *ShG*, ch. 39. More fundamentally, however, the body and soul are discriminated along the same categories. The physical body is the "outer" layer while the soul is the "inner." See, e.g., the statement in *EH, Heichal Nuqvah de-Zeir Anpin*, gate 40, *Shaʿar ha-Hashmal*, ch. 1: הנשמות נקראו פנימיות והכלים שהוא הגוף נקרא חיצוניות. (The souls are called "innerness" and the vessels—which are the body—are called "outerness.") The constructs of "inner" and "outer" layers of the soul also reflect the larger metaphysical design that has the same categories describing the cosmic realms. On this theme, see my review of Shaul Magid's approach above on page 22 note 48. A review of the complex Lurianic doctrine on the "inner" and "outer" aspects of reality is beyond the scope of this study, but it remains a desideratum in the academic study of Jewish mysticism. For more on this topic, see *EH, Shaʿar Penimiyut v'Chitzoniyut* and see my discussions of this theme above on page 67 note 47.

of the Torah are built on these seven kings. And the wise will fear and understand.[114]

Here we have one of the most explicit articulations of a monistic metaphysics in all of Lurianic Kabbalah. These two processes—the human movement toward resurrection and the cosmic shift toward structural dissolution—are ultimately one and the same mechanism. With the contemplative death of the human practitioner the most recondite dimensions of the cosmos are harmonized, and with the resurrection of the human body the cosmic hierarchy dissolves. The fact that cosmic dissolution occurs through the integration of all the fragmented parts of the human soul back into its corporeal body suggests a radical mystical vision at the very heart of Lurianic teaching, one that equalizes the body and soul as two sides of the same unitive reality.[115]

In this view, the epistemological categories that determine the perceptual dichotomies that separate the human and divine—and the body and soul—are

---

114 *Sefer Ta'amei ha-Mitzvot*, Pinchas, 229–230:

> והנה כמו שבמות האדם יורד גופו לקבר והרוח תשוב אל אלהים אשר נתנה לו ... כן הענין בז'
> מלכים אלו והוא כי הלא ידעת כי הם עצמות וכלים והיא סוד גוף ונשמה ובארנו כי גוף שלהם שהוא
> הכלים ירדו לעולם הבריאה שהוא סוד עפר העליון שתחת האצילות ושם היתה קבורה ורוח ונשמה
> ועצמות שבהם נסתלק למעלה אל האלהים אשר נתנה והוא אמא הנקראת אלהים ... אמנם גופות
> הכלים שנתקנו ועלו הם סוד תחיית המתים אל הגופים השוכבים שוכני עפר הרי בזה תבין איך כל
> מה שהיה הוה ויהיה הכל הוא בסוד הז' מלכים והוא כי הלא הם שרש הכל וכלם נמצאו מהם וכל
> יסודי תורה בנויה על ז' מלכים אלו והמשכיל יראה ויבין.

> Also see the alternate version of this teaching in *Sefer Sha'ar ha-Mitzvot*, Pinchas, where Vital frames the esoteric meaning of the resurrection of the dead in terms of the principle of ירושה, or inheritance. Also see ShHK, Derush RaPaCh Nitzotzim, 101–102. It seems to me that this passage from *Sefer Ta'amei ha-Mitzvot* is being alluded to by Vital in his discussion of resurrection found in ShK, Inyan Kavvanat ha-Amidah, ch. 5, 225–228.

115 In a remarkable passage that brings together the interlacing themes of this analysis, the Zohar III: 177a points out that the verse immediately following Job 34:14 ("If he puts his heart to it") alludes to the reconstitution of the physical body. The verse reads: יגוע כל בשר יחד ואדם על עפר ישוב (All flesh shall die together and man shall return upon dust). The Zohar intimates that the phrase "man shall return *upon* the dust" refers to the reconstitution of the physical body after death. Thus, the scriptural association of the phrase "If he puts his heart to it" with the resurrection of the dead further establishes the esoteric and teleological implications of the Lurianic usage of this phrase that I suggested above. To be sure, it also further demonstrates that these esoteric allusions all point to the thesis that the goal of liberation from rebirth is only the doorway to a more ultimate realization of a radical condition of cosmic/human nonduality of body and soul that is embodied at the resurrection of the dead. I believe this passage from the Zohar is the source for the unidentified textual reference made by Vital that I mention above on page 122 note 66.

erased. Paradoxically, it does this while maintaining the ontological integrity of the variegated forms of existence. In other words, Lurianic mysticism seeks to erase epistemological duality but not ontological duality. This is epitomized in the dissolution of the perception of hierarchy in the cosmic structure without doing away with the various divine personas that determine its makeup.

In this vision, it makes sense that the physical body is no longer an obstacle to spiritual evolution but rather the vehicle to transcend the categories of dual and nondual altogether. It is only by fully embodying one's physicality—that is, by integrating all the fragmented soul parts into the primary physical body at the resurrection of the dead—that the epistemological distinctions between physical and spiritual can be properly deconstructed and absorbed into the perception of reality as a nonhierarchical phenomenon.

Thus, the physical body, typically viewed as the essence of limitation, separation, and dualism, is here transformed into the organ of a nonhierarchical perception that allows for particulars without it implying a gradated cosmic structure that superimposes hierarchical categories of physical and spiritual. What results from this process is an integral expression of monism that recognizes that reality manifests particular and distinct forms (i.e. it encompasses both a real ontological duality and nonduality simultaneously) without it implying architectonic categories of hierarchical rank.

LURIANIC KABBALAH AND EASTERN MYSTICISM

In the above sections, we have explored a specific subset of Lurianic contemplative practice; namely, the *kavvanot* associated with the *nefilat apayim* prayer designed to hasten the adept's liberation from rebirth. These esoteric exercises call upon the adept to engage a process in which he first splits his soul, then traverses the boundaries of his physical body altogether through the act of intentional death, and finally reintegrates the fragmented parts of his soul into a reconstituted body at the resurrection of the dead.

This inner orientation of "intention unto death" that characterizes the *kavvanot* of *nefilat apayim* is moreover conceived by Luria as the primary method of accessing and manipulating the deepest recesses of the supernal realms. But this inner movement toward death only reaches its fullest expression in actual physical martyrdom "for the sake of the name," which induces the permanent union of the divine paramours and ushers in the eschatological event of resurrection. It is the physical death of the practitioner's body that facilitates the permanent procreative union of the cosmic bodies (i.e., the *partzufim*); and then, paradoxically, it is the reconstitution of the adept's physical body at the resurrection of the dead that facilitates the equalization of the cosmos and its "death" as a hierarchical constellation.

The embodiment of these two contra-directional movements—one toward greater fragmentation, the other towards greater integration—represents the radical dynamic at the heart of Luria's paradoxical mysticism. As demonstrated above, in formulating these contemplative techniques of simulated death, Luria is thereby putting into practice a more fundamental theoretical position that erases the distinction between the conventional categories of life and death and embraces a more inclusive, nonhierarchical vision that includes within its perspective both dual and nondual possibilities.

This dialectical relationship between life and death, dual and nondual, body and soul, human and cosmic, is thus brought into sharp relief in our investigation of the metaphysical and performative characteristics of these Lurianic *kavvanot*. Ultimately, it is this dialectical interplay between a dualistic cosmology on the one hand and a unitive vision of existence on the other that represents the heart of Lurianic metaphysics. And it is the embodiment (through the death of the practitioner) of the epistemological truth of integral nonhierarchy (through the realization of the death of the cosmos) that represents the ultimate goal of Lurianic contemplative practice.

Discriminating more precisely these radically monistic characteristics of the mystical vision in Lurianic literature opens up the door for comparison with other mystical traditions. As scholars of comparative mysticism have long been biased toward claiming a common essential core to mystical experiences across traditions, I wish to be clear that in the following discussion my suggestions of similarity are not meant to conflate these traditions through simplistic claims of sameness. Due to the epistemological limitations of language as a vehicle for communicating the nature of mystical experience, descriptive similarities across traditions cannot be relied upon as a measure of essential sameness or even, for that matter, similarity.[116] Therefore, the following reflections are meant only as gestures toward appreciating some potentially interesting lines of inquiry that may bring greater clarity both to similarities of mystical approach (without making any claims about the similarity of essential experience) as well as to their distinguishing characteristics.[117]

---

116 On the epistemological limitations of language in the study of comparative mysticism, see Katz, "Language, Epistemology, Mysticism," 22–74

117 See my overview of scholarship regarding comparative mysticism and the respective approaches of essentialism and contextualism above, page 66 note 45.

While there are many potentially fruitful areas of comparative inquiry between Lurianic Kabbalah and other traditions, I will limit the present discussion to select lineages of eastern mysticism that share certain core features with Lurianic Kabbalah: Nondual Hindu Tantra, Advaita Vedanta, and Tibetan Buddhism.[118] I began this line of inquiry above in chapter one, where we compared Lurianic conceptions of sleeping, dreaming, and the throat center of consciousness with similar expressions found in certain schools of these three lineage streams. Now, I want to turn our attention to how these eastern streams of mysticism relate to Lurianic Kabbalah more broadly in terms of their understanding of death, rebirth, nonduality, the teleological function of the physical body, and integral monism.

I will begin with the nondual Hindu tradition of Kashmir Shaivism, particularly as it is expressed in the writings of one of its most celebrated masters, the tenth-century mystic, Abhinavagupta.[119] His mystical system and the broader Kaula and Trika traditions that he drew from, not only outline a theory of cosmogenesis with interesting parallels to Luria's, but they also articulate a radical kind of inclusive monism that includes within its purview an integral relationship between dual and nondual elements.[120]

The mystical principle of monism holds that only one reality exists, and that all distinct forms that appear to our perceptual senses (individual persons, objects, etc.) are aspects of this one reality. In the nondual Shaivite lineage, the absolute reality of the relative forms of existence is emphasized; that is, all

---

118 For a deeper exploration of some of the methodological considerations in the comparative study of reincarnation traditions, see Gananath Obeyesekere, *Imagining Karma: Ethical Transformation in Ameridian, Buddhist, and Greek Rebirth* (Berkeley: University of California Press, 2002).

119 See Paul Muller-Ortega, *The Triadic Heart of Shiva: Kaula Tantricism of Abhinavagupta in the Nondual Shaivism of Kashmir* (Albany: SUNY Press, 1989). On Kashmir Shaivism in general, see Muller-Ortega, ibid.; Dyczkowski, *The Doctrine of Vibration*, Lakshman Jee, *Kashmir Shaivism: The Secret Supreme* (Albany: SUNY Press, 1988), and Christopher Wallis, *Tantra Illuminated* (Petaluma: Mattamayura Press, 2013). Several important primary texts from this tradition have been translated into English by Jaideva Singh and published by Motilal Banarsidass Press. See, e.g., his translations of the *Siva Sutras, Spanda-Karikas, Vijnanabhairavatantra* and the *Pratyabhijnahrdayam*.

120 On the nondual features of Kashmiri Shaivism, see Dyczkowski, *The Doctrine of Vibration*, 33–57. Dyczkowski prefers the term "Integral Monism" to refer to the Trika's inclusion of both dual and nondual elements in its mystical vision, a designation that I have adopted in my articulation of Lurianic metaphysics. On the Kashmiri Shaivite theory of cosmogenesis, see the traditional (i.e. nonacademic) outline by Swami Muktananda, *Introduction to Kashmir Shaivism* (South Fallsburg: S. Y. D. A. Foundation, 1977).

the dualistic details that undergo a process of change within the dimensions of time and space are seen to be as fundamentally real as the nondual ground of existence. Indeed, it is the simultaneous inclusion of both the dual and the nondual that accounts for the true mystical realization of unity. In the words of Abhinavagupta: "Where duality, unity and both unity and duality are equally manifest is said to be [true] unity."[121] This classical formulation of Shaivite monism is explicated by the Kashmir Shaivite scholar Mark S. G. Dyczkowski:

> The Saiva absolutist rejects any theory that maintains that the universe is less than real. From his point of view a doctrine of two truths, one absolute and the other relative, endangers the very foundation of monism. The Kashmiri Saiva approach is integral: everything is given a place in the economy of the whole. It is equally wrong to say that reality is either one or diverse. Those who do so fail to grasp the true nature of things which is neither as well as both.[122]

This approach parallels the Lurianic acceptance of both absolute and relative dimensions of reality as fundamentally coexistent and equally real. However, the similarities of approach between these two traditions are perhaps even clearer when we compare Luria's view of the physical body as the locus of ultimate cosmic redemption with the nondual Shaivite relationship to matter:

> Matter cannot sully the absolute, nor is it unreal. Freedom is achieved by knowing "matter-unreality" completely; ignorance of the spirit is ignorance of the true nature of matter. From this point of view ignorance is failure to experience directly the intimate connection (*sambandha*) between the infinite and the finite, thus justifying an active participation in the infinite-finite continuum. Following this New Way the transition from the finite to the infinite does not require that we postulate any ontological distinction between them. The finite is a symbol of the infinite. The infinite stamps its seal (*mudra*) onto its own nature replete with all possible forms of the finite. This is the transcendental attitude of the absolute, namely its impending manifestation as the finite. ... True knowledge (*sadvidya*) from this point of view, is to know that the apparent opposites

121 See Dyczkowski, *The Doctrine of Vibration*, 41
122 Ibid., 37.

normally contrasted with one another, such as subject and object, unity and diversity, absolute and relative, are aspects of the one reality.[123]

Here we see that Kashmir Shaivism and Lurianic Kabbalah share a radical perspective vis-à-vis the nature of reality: that ultimately matter is one with spirit. In both lineages, there is the simultaneous and paradoxical erasure of distinction between the infinite and the finite, body and soul, human and cosmos on the one hand, and the simultaneous affirmation of these realities as distinct forms on the other.

To be sure, it is also possible to adhere to a nondual perspective whilst at the same time denying the ultimate reality of the dualistic details that arise from the nondual ground of existence. This is the perspective of Advaita Vedanta, another Indic mystical lineage that holds that all temporal forms that appear in our perception are fundamentally illusory, a play of light projecting themselves upon the screen of the mind.[124] In some sense, the Advaitin view parallels the Lurianic teaching that sees the hierarchical structure of the cosmos dissolve in the final act of *tiqun*; however, unlike later formulations of acosmism such as found in the Lurianic-inspired school of Habad Hasidism, we do not have an explicit indication from Luria that the variegated and distinct expressions of form that appear to the senses lack ontological existence.[125]

---

123 Ibid., 39–40.

124 See Deutsch, *Advaita Vedanta: A Philosophical Reconstruction*.

125 See, for example, the following statement by R. Shneur Zalman of Liadi, the founder of the Habad school of Hasidism: "Even though it appears to us as that the worlds exist, this is a total lie." See S. Z. Liadi, *Torah Or* [1899], *Ki Tisa* 86b, cited in R. Elior, "Habad: The Contemplative Ascent to God," in: Green, *Jewish Spirituality from the Sixteenth Century Revival to the Present*, 161. On the acosmism of Habad Hasidism and for a deeper sense of how some of the paradoxical and dialectical expressions of mysticism that we find in Luria manifest in Habad and in Hasidism more broadly, also see R. Elior, *The Paradoxical Ascent to God* (Albany: SUNY Press, 1992), as well as her article "Between 'Yesh' and 'Ayin'; the Doctrine of the Zaddik in the Works of Jacob Isaac, the Seer of Lublin," in *Jewish History, Essays in Honor of Chimen Abramsky*, ed. A. Rapoport Albert and S. Zipperstein (London: Peter Halban, 1988), 393–455. Other works of scholarship that touch upon these themes include Seth Brody's article on nondual thought in early Hasidism, "'Open to Me the Gates of Righteousness': The Pursuit of Holiness and Non-Duality in Early Hasidic Teaching," *The Jewish Quarterly Review* 89, nos. 1/2 (1998): 3–44 and Miles Krassen's study *Uniter of Heaven and Earth: Rabbi Meshullam Feibush Heller of Zbarazh and the Rise of Hasidism in Eastern Galicia* (Albany: SUNY, 1998). The mystical principle of monism that undergirds the Lurianic project also has precursors in earlier expressions of Jewish mystical literature. See, for example, Moshe Idel, *Kabbalah: New Perspectives* (New Haven: Yale University Press, 1990) and Eitan

Mention should also be made of the schools in the Vajrayana lineages of Buddhism that have sophisticated metaphysical and contemplative systems that pertain to the journey through death and the subsequent process of rebirth. For example, in the *bardo* teachings outlined in the contemplative classic *Tibetan Book of the Dead*, the practitioner contemplatively moves through the various stages of inner dissolution in order to prepare for actual death, at which time the conceptual mind dissolves and in most cases, is reborn into another body.[126] These practices echo the themes of intentional death that we discussed above, in particular the Lurianic perspective that in the process of contemplative death and in resurrection the lines between death and life are blurred to the point of complete dissolution.

In another similarity, there are sources from the Dzogchen lineage of Tibetan Buddhism that describe the fragmentation of the practitioner's mind into multiple "emanations" in order to be reborn into several bodies simultaneously, echoing the Lurianic process of soul fragmentation and *gilgul* explored in this book. For example, according to the traditional texts, the nineteenth-century master Jamyang Khyentsei Wangpo emanated five different parts of his awareness into five separate bodies, some of which lived simultaneously.[127] This points to a striking parallel between these two traditions, both of which recognize the possibility of fragmenting the soul (or mind, in the case of Buddhism), and consciously placing individual soul-parts (or emanations, in the case of Buddhism) into distinct bodies.

Fishbane, *As Light Before Dawn: The Inner World of a Medieval Kabbalist* (Stanford: Stanford University Press, 2009).

126 See, e.g., the discussion of the *bardos* in the *Tibetan Book of the Dead*, trans. Robert Thurman (New York: Bantam Books, 1993); Sogyal Rinpoche, *The Tibetan Book of Living and Dying* (San Francisco: Harper, 1994); and Holecek, *Dream Yoga*, 255–261. For an overview of Tibetan Buddhist teachings and practices of death and rebirth, see Reginald Ray, *Secrets of the Vajra World* (Boston: Shambhala, 2001), 329–359.

127 See Nyoshul Khenpo, *A Marvelous Garland of Rare Gems: Biographies of Masters of Awareness in the Dzogchen Lineage* (Junction City: Padma Publishing, 2005), 270–318 for a review of his life and the life of his students and specifically 296 for a list of the five reincarnated parts (namely, his "enlightened form, speech, mind, qualities and activity") and the names of the recognized *tulkus* that reincarnated these aspects. Also see Dudjom Rinpoche, *The Nyingma School of Tibetan Buddhism* (Boston: Wisdom Publications, 1991), 849–858 and especially (towards the back of the book) 84n1189 and the two sources listed there. Also see Thulku Thondup, *Masters of Meditation and Miracles* (Boston: Shambhala, 1996), 215–221. This latter source lists a total of six incarnations, and states that there were actually "many incarnations" in total. Furthermore, based on the dates provided in this last source, at least five of these reincarnations lived at the same time.

Conclusion

The findings of this study call into question long-held assumptions concerning the dualistic character of Lurianic mysticism. Such suppositions, first articulated by Scholem and Tishby, were largely taken for granted by subsequent generations of scholars. Only recently, with the works of scholars such as Magid and Kallus, have some of these assumptions about the nature of Lurianic mysticism been called into question. For Magid, it is the erasure of the boundaries between self and other—refracted through the prism of biblical exegesis—that suggests a more radical stance; for Kallus, it is the inclusion of *ein sof* into the contemplative purview of the practitioner that points to a more nondual (in his words, "panentheistic") perspective.

Building upon the works of these scholars, in this book I have attempted to shine light on another expression of this mystical dynamic in Lurianic literature, emphasizing the dialectical relationship between dualism and nondualism that is implicit in Lurianic contemplative practice; specifically, in those *kavvanot* designated to expedite liberation from rebirth. In illuminating the metaphysical underpinnings and detailed performative features of these practices we can appreciate a more radical mystical dialectic at play in Luria's contemplative perspective. This dialectical interplay is embodied by the human practitioner in a surprising manner, requiring him to dismember the soul from the body and fragment it into dislocated parts. This act of *disembodiment* ironically reaches its fullest and most extreme expression of *embodiment* in the actual death of the physical body, a self-sacrifice that supplies the cosmic realms with both the nourishment and the sexual stimulation necessary for the erotic union of the cosmic paramours.

With the anatomical integration of the cosmic "interfaces" (*partzufim*) through inter/intra-divine sex, the conditions are then ripe for the final teleological fulfillment of the human journey. This is realized in the re-somatization of the physical human body in the resurrection of the dead, an event that marks both the integration of the dismembered parts of the soul (a human re-membering) and the epistemological transformation of the human consciousness on the one hand, and the erasure of all categories of cosmic hierarchy on the other (a cosmic dis-membering).

Here the most paradoxical and excessive expressions of Lurianic mysticism come to fruition: it is ultimately through the fragmentation of the human soul and the death of the physical body that the cosmos can draw procreative life, while it is through the revivification of the human anatomy that the cosmos is erased of all hierarchical rank. This dialectical interplay reveals that Lurianic Kabbalah embraces a paradoxical mystical vision of total inclusivity that ultimately seeks to erase all hierarchical dualism while simultaneously upholding the reality of an ontological dualism. That is, distinct forms of manifested existence remain (ontological dualism) even while they are realized through the transformed gaze of the contemplative as equalized and neutralized of all hierarchical rank (hierarchical nondualism).

To say it another way, the deconstruction of the human soul is in a dialectically reciprocal relationship with the reconstruction of the cosmos: as the self is deconstructed (through the *kavvanot* to expedite rebirth), the cosmos is reconstructed (that is, *zeir* and *nuqvah*'s anatomical development and sexual unification is completed), and as the self is reconstructed (through resurrection of the dead), the cosmos is deconstructed (of hierarchical rank). Therefore, ultimately it is the resuscitation of the human body at the resurrection of the dead that paradoxically institutes a cosmic dissolution; or, rather, allows for human perception to conceive and realize the cosmos as an equalized expression of ontological truth. This epistemological transformation allows the inclusion of opposites within the perceptual frame of the human mind and represents the contours of the core mystical experience in Lurianic Kabbalah. Here the internal movement towards excessive fragmentation of self on the one hand, and the eradication of all boundaries of self on the other, come together as two sides of the same polar dynamic. This integral monism—which includes within its purview the fragmented dualistic nature of self as well as the nondual nature of the cosmos—thus represents the paradoxical mystical heart of Lurianic Kabbalah.

These extreme formulations of contemplative suicide and the subsequent re-inhabiting of dead flesh in resurrection also reflect the excessive bodily perspective of this path, one that embraces the processes of sleep, death, and sex as the central pivots around which the entire cosmos both emerges and dissolves. It is this radically monistic embrace of the most excessive expressions of the physical body that serves to transgress the boundaries of physicality altogether, thus providing the contemplative with a means of integrating dualism and non-dualism as integrally embodied truths.

Before we put this book to sleep, a final word on some implications of this undertaking. Reading Lurianic Kabbalah in the excessive and paradoxical manner described above opens up new possibilities in terms of how to relate to this tradition in a contemporary, nontraditional context. In this study I have implicitly oriented to Lurianic lore as a fictive, yet true, expression of metaphysical and pneumatic speculation. I have approached it as *fictive* in the sense that I do not read these texts as necessarily accurate descriptions of ontological existence; yet, I hold them as *true* insofar as *through the process of interpretation* they become alive in a way that is perhaps more relevant and meaningful to a contemporary, nontraditional reader.

Moreover, in this study I have also implicitly held an even more radical posture vis-a-vis this methodological approach. This is reflected in my suggestion, first articulated in the introduction, that this book can be approached as a primary expression of the Lurianic literary tradition. That is, by employing a method of "embodied *Verstehen*," which seeks to embody the intertextual and qualitative features of Lurianic literature, I am not only *deconstructing* these texts through the lens of postmodern literary criticism but also *reconstructing* the anatomy of this tradition through embodying (in the body of the text of this study) the intricate structural characteristics of Vital's literary works.

Thus, in reconstructing a contemporary, nontraditional, Lurianic document in this manner, I am attempting to embody the ultimate nonhierarchical vision that this very mysticism claims. That is, reading this literature (which claims nonhierarchy as the ultimate nature of existence) as "metafiction" (which claims nonhierarchy of textual authority) allows for the more radical claim of textual *primacy* in a scholarly/literary work of this nature.

Taking this argument to its logical conclusion, perhaps this book can be seen as *simultaneously* a work of contemporary scholarship in the tradition of Western academia as well as a literal/literary extension of the mystical tradition of Isaac Luria. If there is any merit to such a claim, this study itself reflects the very principle of integral monism implied in Lurianic mysticism; that is, one that simultaneously includes within its purview both dual and nondual truths, and thus implicitly accepts a nonhierarchical view of textual authority.

In taking such a position I am suggesting one possible method that allows the contemporary scholar to both embrace the truth of these classical mystical texts even while simultaneously subverting their authority as exclusive exemplars of the tradition. Such an approach not only opens the door for future scholarship into the metaphysical and contemplative dimensions of Lurianic Kabbalah, but it also provides the possibility of resurrecting these obscure texts from the dissociated dustbins of history in a manner that is perhaps more meaningful for the nontraditional spirit of our day.

Appendix:
The Complete *Kavvanah* Required for Expediting Rebirth

[*The following is my translation of a passage from* Sha'ar ha-Kavvanot, Inyan Derushei Ha-Laylah, ch. 10. *The practices described here, in addition to those presented in chapters one and two of this book, represent the complete set of kavvanot required to fragment the soul for the sake of expediting liberation from the cycle rebirth. The original Hebrew text is provided at the end.*]

My teacher, may his memory be a blessing, also told me concerning the aforementioned matter, that when a person knows that they have completed a part of their soul as mentioned above, they must focus[1] on the following *kavvanot* as will be explained. And they are:

Behold, [the following should be performed] after one recites [the] *ana b'koaḥ* [section of the bedtime *shema*] etc., which alludes to the name of 42 of *yetzirah*, as discussed above, and through which our souls are caused to ascend from *asiyah* to *yetzirah* by way of the name of 42 which is associated with *yetzirah*. Behold, after [this] you should focus on the name אהיה אשר אהיה which is the name of 42 of *beriyah*, as explained above, since two times the numerical value of אהיה is 42 [corresponding to the two appearances of the name אהיה in the phrase אהיה אשר אהיה]. And contemplate that through this name of 42 of *beriyah* you cause your *ruaḥ* to ascend from *yetzirah* to *beriyah*.

---

1 Vital frequently uses various verbal forms of *lekhaven* (lit. "to intend"), which I have translated alternatively throughout this text as "focus" or "contemplate."

And know that there is another name of 42 in *beriyah* that is above and beyond the [name of] 42 that was mentioned. This is the name אהיה יה"ו. The first [name of] 42 is below this [name of] 42. However, both of them are in *beriyah*, and therefore it is good to focus on both of them.

Afterwards [when you recite the verse] "into your hand I deposit my *ruaḥ*" (בידך אפקיד רוחי), etc., contemplate that the first letters [of each of the words in this verse] spell out the word באר which is a fusion of the complete name of יהוה and אלהים plus the fusion of the complete name of יהוה and אדני. And all of them [combined have the same] *gematria* as [the word] באר.[2] Also focus [on the fact that the name] אלהים has the same *gematria* as [the combination of the names] אהיה and אדני.[3]

And through this you will understand why the fusion of יהוה [and] אלהים is called the "complete name," moreso than the name יהוה [and] אדני, as mentioned in [my commentary on] the [Torah] portion of ויקהל [i.e. Exodus 25:1–38:20]. And the reason is because with it is also included the name אהיה.[4] Also contemplate that יהוה and אלהים [when combined have the same *gematria* as the word] יבק.[5]

And [when reciting the] words יהוה אל אמת [from the end of the verse "into your hand, etc."], focus on the following *kavvanot*: יהוה [should be parsed as follows]: י, יה, יהו, יהוה. You should then focus on the [fact that the] four final letters, when filled with the letter *hey* (ה), has the numeric value of 52 [ידו הה וו הה = 52]. Also, focus [on the fact that the letter] י parallels *atzilut*, יה parallels *beriyah*, יהו parallels *yetzirah* and יהוה parallels *asiyah*. And then it is filled with the [multiple letters] ה as mentioned.

Then, with the word אל, focus on יהוה of 63 [יוד הי ואו הי = 63], which contain three [of the letter] י and one [of the letter] א, and which add up to [same] numeric value as [the word] אל. And [when reciting the word] אמת, focus on the name אהיה multiplied by אהיה [441 = אהיה × אהיה] and which has the same numerical value as אמת. This calculation is called the "fourfold calculation." And this verse will be the conclusion of your recitation, and you will sleep from within these *kavvanot* and thoughts.

---

2 The calculation is as follows: (באר)203 = 65(אדני) +26(יהוה) + 86(אלהים) + 26(יהוה).

3 The calculation is as follows: (אלהים)86 = 65(אדני) + 21 (אהיה).

4 I.e. since the *gematria* of the name אהיה can be added to that of the name אדני to yield the same number as the value of the name אלהים, we can say that the name אלהים is "included" in the name אהיה.

5 The calculation is as follows: (אלהים)86 + 26(יהוה) = (יבק)112.

[*In this next section, Vital adds specific contemplative elements that should be incorporated while meditating on earlier portions of the practice.*]

Furthermore, he should contemplate the first letters [of the verse] "into your hand I deposit my *ruaḥ*" (ביד אפקיד רוחי), [that spell] באר as mentioned, and they are the fusing of יהוה אלהים [and] יהוה אדני that should be combined like this: יאהדונהי and אילהההויהם. And the *kavvanah* is to raise up our *nefesh* from this pit, to the well (באר) of living, flowing water, by means of this unification that was mentioned.

Moreover [with respect to the second half of the verse] "You have redeemed me יהוה" (פדית אותי יהוה), the first letters [spell] פאי, which is one of the 72 names [from the 72 triplets formed from the three verses in Exodus 14:19–21] as mentioned. And it is the fusing of יהוה and אדני. And he should focus on these words, that the name may he be blessed [i.e. the divine] redeem me (אותי). That is to say, [the] letter י of my holy covenant [i.e. my phallus, also called the "sign" - אות][6] that was given over to the external forces [i.e. the realm of evil] on account of wasted seminal emissions, that the holy one [i.e. the divine] redeem him and take him from their hands through the power of the name יהוה which is mentioned in this very verse, that is "יהוה the אל of truth" (יהוה אל אמת) [i.e. the name יהוה appears at the end of the verse "you have redeemed me יהוה"].

And it is necessary that he focus on this יהו, which has in it three shapes of [the letters] רי"ו in this manner: First, [the] letters י"ה [form] the shape רי"ו, like this: ה"י.[7] After this, permute the letters ה"ו and they [form the] shape רי"ו like this: ו"ה.[8] And after this, permute the letters ה"ו, and they [form the] shape רי"ו like this: ה"ו.[9] And behold these are the three instances of רי"ו.

Then you should focus [on the fact] that each one of these [three forms of] רי"ו is the secret of the [divine] name אל since אל, [in its] simple and complete

---

6   The word "me" (אותי) from the verse "You have redeemed me, *yhvh*" is parsed and deconstructed into the two words אות and י and is reconstructed by Vital to mean "the י of my אות" meaning "the *yud* of my phallus" since the word אות is a common referent to the phallus in kabbalistic nomenclature.

7   That is, if we deconstruct the letter ה from the first two letters יה into its ideogrammatic subparts, we will recognize the shape of the letter *reish*, ר, formed from the horizontal and right vertical line of the ה, and a *vav*, ו, formed from the small internal segment of the ה. Then, if we rearrange these letters we have רי"ו.

8   This is formed in the same way as described in the previous note, only in this instance the letter ה is deconstructed into the ר and the י.

9   This is formed in the same way as described in the previous note.

[form], has the [same] *gematria* as רי"ו.[10] And behold, three times *el* [אל x 3 = 93] has [the same numerical value as the word] מגן [= 93, meaning "shield"]. And the simple and complete [form] is 216, which is the *gematria* [of the word] יראה (= 216, meaning "awe").

And all of these aforementioned *kavvanot* are altogether alluded to in the verse: "was there a shield (מגן) or spear (רומח) seen among forty thousand in Israel" (Judges 5:8: מגן אם יראה ורומח במ' אלף בישראל). מגן is [equal to] three times [the name] אל, and יראה has the same [numerical value as the] letters [of] רי"ו. And [the word] רומח [alludes to the *kavvanah* of the] recitation [of the bedtime] *shema* that we explained earlier. And the intention [is that] through the power of these *kavvanot* the person can battle with the demons (מזיקין), and kill them, as is explained by us in its place [in our commentary on] this verse [from Judges 5:8–11], etc. and check in *Shaar Ruaḥ Ha-kodesh*, because it talks about the aspect of the aforementioned demons.[11]

And with the word אל, focus on the name יא"י that is derived from the יהוה of 63. And with the word אמת [meaning "truth"], contemplate אהיה multiplied by אהיה, which is the same numerical value as אמת in the secret of "it is all a true seed" (כולו זרע אמת) [from Jeremiah 2:21], as it is explained by us.

After this, recite [the verse] "You will arise and have mercy on zion" (Psalms 102:14: אתה תקום תרחם ציון), and when you say the word "You will have mercy" (תרחם), focus on the three instances of רי"ו that you intended with the shape of the name יהוה as described earlier, which is the יהוה correlated with the phrase "יהוה is אל of truth" (יהוה אל אמת). These three forms of רי"ו have a numerical value of 648 [3 × 216] which is also the numerical value of תרחם ["you will have mercy"]. Also contemplate that תרחם [has the same] *gematria* as [the combination of] יהוה and אהיה and the two names of מצפ"ץ (600) and the totality.[12]

And he should contemplate that if his *nefesh*, *ruaḥ* or *neshama* has fallen into the *qelipot* because of his wasteful emission of semen, they will now depart from there and return and be raised up to the [realm of] holiness, with the

---

10 I.e. when the *gematria* of the "simple" version of the name אל (31) is added to the *gematria* of the filled out version of the name אל (i.e. למד אלף = 185) you get a total of 216, which has the same numerical value as the three letters רי"ו.

11 See *ShK, Inyan Derushei ha-Laylah*, ch. 9 and *PEH, Keriyat Shema she-Al ha-Mittah*, ch. 11.

12 The calculation is as follows: יהוה (26) + אהיה (21)+ the two names of מצפ"ץ (600) + [1 for] the "totality" principle (הכולל) = 648 = תרחם. The "inclusionary" or "totality" principle (הכולל) is a standard *gematria* calculation technique found in kabbalistic texts that adds + 1 to the final calculation that represents the totality of the word.

nefesh of the very person now ascending there in the secret of "into your hand I deposit my *ruaḥ*," etc.

After all this, focus on the name אלוה which has several *kavvanot*: First, contemplate that this name is a garment for the *neshama*, and it guards her from the hand of the external forces [i.e. the demonic], as it is written in [the section of the Zohar II: 94b–114a called] *saba demishpatim*, [in its commentary on the verse] "seeing that he has dealt deceitfully with her" [Exodus 21:8]. Therefore, when the soul ascends at night [you] must raise it up by means of this name and make it invisible to these external forces so that they cannot grab her, like someone who is wrapped in a prayer shawl. And this matter of ascent is that she ascends to *yesod* of the upper *nuqvah* [i.e. the *yesod* of *leah*] in the secret of female waters, as is known. And then she becomes a well of flowing waters. Therefore, he should focus on the aforementioned name in its filled form, like this: אלוה: אלף למד וו הא.

Furthermore, he should contemplate on what is written in *saba* [*demishpatim*] on the verse "If he takes another wife, her food, her raiment, and her conjugal rights, shall he not diminish." [Exodus 21:10]. And he says that "her raiment" is this name אלוה, and it is the name that clothes the *neshama*, in order to make her disappear from the external forces that they not capture her, as explained above. And behold the *kavvanah* that includes this name is mentioned in the Zohar in the portion of *lekh lekha* [Genesis 12:1–17:27], whose explanation is [the following]:

א"ל ו"ה: That is to say that the [first two letters of the name אלוה that spell the] name אל is the life-force that enlivens the [final] two letters [of the name אלוה which are] וה [and] which is the secret of *zeir* and *nuqvah*. And the life-fore that is drawn to them is from *imma*, who is the secret of אהיה [filled with] the letter י [i.e.: אלף הי יוד הי], consisting of three yuds [י] and an aleph [א], which is the name ייא". And from it [i.e. from this name] are formed [the letters] א"ל.[13] And this אל is drawn from *imma* to *zeir* and *nuqvah*, which are called [by the letters] ו"ה, in order to enliven them.

Moreover, contemplate that the aforementioned name אלוה has the numerical value of 42, and they are the 42 letters that constitute the simple [form], the "filled" [form], and the "filled of the filled" [form] of [the name] יהוה.[14] And

---

13 I.e. the three letters י in the name ייא" can be ideogrammatically fused and permuted into the shape of the letter ל in the name אל. Also, the two names share the gematria of 31.

14 The 42 letters in this formula are as follows:

יהוה יוד הא ואו הא ואו הא יוד ואו דלת הא אלף הא אלף ואו אלף ואו הא אלף

behold, this name אלוה that adds up to 42 is in the aspect of the scalp of *zeir anpin*'s head.

Also contemplate that [the] letter א that is in this name [אלוה] is formed [with the letter] י, like this: א. And it has a *gematria* of 20.[15] And the three remaining letters from the name אלוה have a *gematria* of 41, and [when you add] 20, it adds up to 61. And with the "totality," [it yields] 62.[16] And this is the secret of יהוה in the following manner: יוד ה"ה ויו ה"ה. And this name is in the six extremities of *zeir anpin* [i.e. the six lower sefirot].

Also contemplate that the letter ל of this name [אלוה] is [constituted by the letters] כ"ו, like this: ל.[17] This has [the same] numerical value as יהוה [i.e. 26]. And contemplate that this יהוה is the [filled in form of the name that has the *gematria*] of 63 [i.e.: יוד הי ואו הי], and that if you merge [the letters] כ"ו [that we derived] from the ל, along with the three remaining letters [of the name אלוה] which are או"ה, the total sum will be 38. And this name brings down the expansion from above; [it] brings down the consciousness into the scalp and the expansion into the six extremities.

Also contemplate on the letter ו from the aforementioned name [i.e. אלוה], that there is a [letter] י at its top, like this: ו. And it [is constituted by the two letters]: ו"י. And with the three remaining letters which are אל"ה, it all adds up to a gematria of 52, which is the יהוה of 52 [i.e. יוד הה וו הה]. And this name represents *malkhut*. Also contemplate with the letter ה of the aforementioned name [i.e. אלוה] that it is formed [by the letters] ד"ו, which has a *gematria* of 10, and with [its] three other letters which are אל"ו, it will all be a *gematria* of 47. And this name is a fusion of יהוה and אהיה which is in *keter*. And it brings down the expansion from there [down to the realms] below.

---

15 I.e. in the ideogrammatic shape of the letter א there are two *yuds* (י) that protrude from the center diagonal line, each one of which has the value of 10.

16 On the "inclusionary" or "totality" principle (הכולל) see page 156 note 12 above.

17 I.e. the shape of the letter ל can be atomized such that it can be seen as constituted by a כ at the base and a ו protruding vertically at the top.

גם א"ל מוז"ל בענין הנז' שמי שיודע בעצמו שהשלים חלק נפשו כנז' צריך שיכוין אלו הכוונות
בכל לילה כמשי"ת ואלו הם הנה אחר שאמר תפי' אנא בכח כו' שבו נרמז שם בן מ"ב דיצירה כנ"ל
אשר ע"י העלינו את נפשינו מן העשיה אל היצירה ע"י שם זה של מ"ב שביצירה הנה אח"כ עוד תכוין
בשם אחיה אשר אהיה שהוא שם מ"ב שבבריאה שם מ"ב כנ"ל כי ר"פ אהיה בגי' מ"ב ותכוין שע"י שם מ"ב
זה דבריאה אתה מעלה בחי' רוחך מן היצירה אל הבריאה

ודע כי יש שם מ"ב אחר בבריאה והוא עליון וגבוה מן המ"ב הנז' והוא שם אהיה יה"ו ומ"ב
הראשון הוא תחת זה המ"ב אבל שניהם הם בבריאה ולכן טוב לכוין בשניהם אח"כ עוד תפקיד רוחי
כו' תכוין כי ר"ת הוא באר והוא חיבור שמא שלים של יהו"ה ואלהים וחיבור שמא שלים של הויה
ואדני וכולם בגי' באר והוא גם תכוין כי אלהים הוא בגימטרי' אהיה אדני

ובזה תבין למה חיבור הויה אלהים נקרא שמא שלים יותר משם הויה אדני כנז' בפ' ויקהל והטעם
הוא כי בו נכלל ג"כ שם אהיה גם תכוין כי יהוה ואלהים בגימט' יב"ק ובתיבות יהוה אל אמת תכוין
כוונות אלו יהוה הוא כזה י' י"ה יה"ו יהו"ה ותכוין בד' אותיות אחרונות שהם ממולאו' בההוין והם
בגימט' ב"ן גם תכוין כי י' באצילות י"ה בבריאה יה"ו ביצירה יהוה בעשי' ולכן הוא במילוי ההין כנז'
ובמלת א"ל תכוין אל הויה דס"ג שיש בה תלת יודין ואלף שעולים א"ל כנידע ובמלת אמת תכוין אל
שם אהיה פעמים אהיה שעולים בגימט' אמת וחשבון זה נק' חשבון המרובע וזה הפסוק יהיה סיום כל
דבריך ותישן מתוך כוונות אלו ומחשבה זו

עוד יכוין בר"ת בידך אפקיד רוח ר"ת בא"ר כנ"ל והם חיבור הויה אלקים הויה אדני שיהיו
משולבים כזה יאהדונה"י אילההויה"ה והכונ' היא להעלות נפשותינו מבור זה אל באר מים חיים נובעים
ע"י היחוד הזה הנז' גם פדית אותי יהו"ה ר"ת פא"י שם אחד משמות ע"ב כנ"ל והוא חיבור יהוה ואדני
ותכוין בתיבות אלו שהשי"ת פודה אותי ר"ל אות י' של ברית קדש שלי שנמסר אל החיצונים ב"מ ע"י
השחתת זרעו לבטלה והקב"ה יפדהו ויקחהו מידם בכח שם יהוה הנז' בזה הפסוק עצמו שהוא יהוה
א"ל אמ"ת וצריך שיכוין בהויה זו שיש בה ג' ציורי' של רי"ו באופן זה תחלה אותיו' י"ה הם ציור רי"ו
כזה י"ה אח"כ תצרף אותיו' ה"ו הם ציור רי"ו כזה ה"ו ואח"כ תצרף אותיו' ו"ה והם ציור רי"ו כזה
ו"ה והרי הם ג"פ רי"ו

ותכוין כי כל רי"ו מאלו ה"ס שם א"ל כי א"ל פשוט ומלא הוא בגי' רי"ו והנה ג"פ א"ל הוא מ{ג}ן
ופשוט ומלא הוא רי"ו ורי"ו הוא רגי' ירזגא וכל ה{כ}ונות הנז' נרמזו יחד בפ' מגן אם יראה ורומח במ'
אלף בישר' מגן הוא ג"פ א"ל ירא"ה הוא אותיו' רי"ו ורומ"ח הוא רי"ו והכונה שבכח הנ"ל ובזה כוונת אלו
נלחם האדם עם המזיקין והורג אותם כמבואר אצלינו במקומו בפ' זה באומרו אז לחם שערים כו' אז
ירדו לשערים עם ה' כו' ועיין בש' רוח הק' כי הוא מדבר על בחי' המזיקין הנז' ובתיבת יהו"ה תכוין אל
שם יא"ו היוב' מהויה דס"ג ובתיבת אמת תכוין אל אהיה פעמים אהיה שהוא בגי' אמ"ת בסוד כולו
זרע אמת כמבו' אצלינו

אח"כ תאמר אתה תקום תרחם ציון ובתי' תרחם תכוין אל ג'פ רי"ו שנתכונ' בציור שם ההויה הנז' והיא יהוה אל אמת ושלשתם בגי' תרחם גם תכוין כי תרחם בגי' יהוה ואהיה וב' שמות מצפ"ץ מצפ"ץ והכולל ויכוין שאם נמסרו נר"ן שלו ביד הקלי' ע"י השחתת זרעו לבטלה יסתלקו עתה משם ויחזרו ויתעלו אל הקדושה אל נפש האדם עצמו העולה עתה שם בסוד ביד אפקיד רוחי כו'

אחר הכל תכוין אל שם אלוה ויש בו כמה כוונות ראשונה תכוין ששם זה הוא מלבוש הנשמה השומר אותה מיד החיצונים כמ"ש בסבא דמשפטים על פ' בבגדו בה ולכן בלילה אשר הנשמה עולה צריך להעלותה ע"י שם זה ולהעלימה מן החיצו' שלא יתאחזו בה כמי שמתכסה בטליתו וענין עליה זו הוא שעולה עד יסוד דנוק' העליונה בסו' מ"ן כנודע ואז נעשית באר מיין נבעין ולכן יכוין בשם הנזכר במלואו כזה אלוה אלף למד וו ה"א

עוד יכוין אל מ"ש בסבא על פסו' שארה כסותה ועונתה כו' ואמר כי כסותה הוא שם אלוה והוא השם המלביש את הנשמה להעלים' מן החיצוני שלא יתאחזו בה כנ"ל והנה הכוונה הכוללת בשם זה נז' בזו' פ' לך לך שביאורו הוא א"ל ו"ה ר"ל כי שם א"ל הוא חיות המחיה לשני אותיות ו"ה שה"ס זו' והחיות הנמשך להם הוא מן אימא שהיא סוד שם אהיה דידין ויש בו ג' יודין ואלף שהוא שם ייאי וממנו נעשה א"ל ואל זה נמשך מאימא לזו"ן הנק' ו"ה להחיו' אותם

עוד תכוין כי שם אלוה הנז' הוא בגי' מ"ב והם מ"ב אותיות שיש בפשוט ומלוי ומלוי המלוי דהויה והנה שם אלוה זה העולה מ"ב הוא בחינת קרקפתא דרישא דז"א גם תכוין כי אות א' שבשם זה ציורו יוד כזה א' והיא בגי' עשרים וג' אותיות הנשארו' משם אלוה הם בגי' מ"א ור' סך הכל ס"א וע"ה ס"ב וה"ס הויה באופן זה יוד ה"ה ויו ה"ה ושם זה הוא בו'ק דז"א

גם תכוין כי ל' של שם זה היא כ"ו כזה ל' בגי' הויה ותכוין כי הויה זו היא הויה דס"ג ואם תחבר כ"ו דלמד עם ג' אותיות הנשארו' שהם או"ה סך הכל יהיה ל"ח ושם זה הוא מוריד ההתפשטות מלמעלה מוריד המוח תוך הקרקפתא וההתפשטות בו"ק

גם תכוין באות ו' של שם הנז' כי יש י' בראשו כזה י' והוא י"ו ועם ג' אותיות הנשארות שהם אל"ה יהיה הכל גי' ב"ן והיא הוי"ה דב'ן ושם זה הוא כנגד המלכות. גם תכוון באות ה' של שם הנז' שציורה ד"ו שהיא בגי' י' ועם ג' אותיות האחרו' שהם אל"ה יהיה הכל גי' מ"ז ושם זה הוא חיבור יהוה אהיה בכתר אשר הוא מוריד ההתפשטות משם ולמטה ע"כ

Selected Bibliography

PRIMARY SOURCES

Cordovero, Moses. *Pardes Rimonim*. Jerusalem: Yoseph Hasid, 1998

_____. *Tefillah le-Moshe*. Premyshlan: n.p., 1892.

_____. *Ohr Yakar*. 9 vols. Jerusalem: n.p., 1970.

Sefer ha-Zohar. 3 vols. Edited by R. Margoliot. Jerusalem: Mossad ha-Rav Kook, 1964.

Tiqqunei ha-Zohar. Edited by R. Margoliot. Jerusalem: Mossad ha-Rav Kook, 1978.

Zohar Hadash. Edited by R. Margoliot. 2nd ed. Jerusalem: Mossad ha-Rav Kook, 1978.

Vital, Hayyim. *'Ets Hayyim*. Warsaw: n.p., 1891.

_____. *Sha'ar ma-Marei Rashbi*. Jerusalem: Vitebsky, 1987.

_____. *Sha'ar ma-Marei Chazal*. Jerusalem: Vitebsky, 1987.

_____. *Sha'ar ha-Gilgulim*. Jerusalem: Vitebsky, 1987.

_____. *Sha'ar ha-Haqdamot*. Jerusalem: Vitebsky, 1987.

_____. *Sha'ar ha-Mitsvot*. Jerusalem: Vitebsky, 1987.

_____. *Sha'ar ha-Pesuqim*. Jerusalem: Vitebsky, 1987.

_____. *Sha'ar ha-Yihudim*. Jerusalem: Vitebsky, 1987.

_____. *Sha'ar ha-Kavvanot*. 2 vols. Jerusalem: Vitebsky, 1987.

_____. *Sha'ar Ruaḥ ha-Kodesh*. Jerusalem: Vitebsky, 1987.

_____. *Mavo She'arim*. Jerusalem: Vitebsky, 1987.

_____. *Sefer ha-Gilgulim*. In *Torat ha-Gilgul*. Jerusalem: Ahavat Shalom, 2004.

_____. *Sefer ha-Ḥezyonot*. Jerusalem: Vitebsky, 1987.

_____. *Likkutei Torah*. Jerusalem: Vitebsky, 1987.

_____. *Ta'amei ha-Mitzvot*. Jerusalem: Vitebsky, 1987.

_____. *Pri Etz Chayyim*. 2 vols. Jerusalem: Vitebsky, 1987.

_____. *Arbah Me'ot Shekel Kesef*. Jerusalem: Vitebsky, 1987.

_____. *Olat Tamid*. Jerusalem: Vitebsky, 1987.

_____. *Sefer Ke-Tavim Ḥadashim* Jerusalem: Ahavat Shalom, 1998.

SECONDARY SOURCES

Altmann, Alexander. "Eternality of Punishment: A Theological Controversy Within the Amsterdam Rabbinate in the Thirties of the Seventeenth Century." In *Essential Papers on Kabbalah*,
edited by Lawrence Fine, 270–287. New York: New York University Press, 2000.

Amos, Avraham. *Be-gilgul Hozer: Gilgul in Kabbalah and Other Sources* [Hebrew]. Ashkelon: Pe'er
Hakodesh, 1997.

Anonymous. *Sefer Toldot ha-Ari*. Jerusalem: Ben Zvi Institute, 1967

Arikha, Yigal. *Reincarnation: Reality that Exceeds All Imagination* [Hebrew]. Kefar Saba: Aryeh Nir, 2001.

Avitsur, Shmuel. "The Batan, a Water-Powered Fulling Mill in Nahal Ammud—Relic of the Wool-Textile Industry in Safed." *Israel, Land and Nature* 7 (1981): 18–21.

_____. "Safed—Center of the Manufacture of Woven Woolens in the Fifteenth Century" [Hebrew]. *Sefunot* 6 (1962): 41–69.

Avivi, Yosef. *Binyan Ariel*. Jerusalem: Misgav Yerushalayim, 1987.

_____. "The Lurianic Writings of Rabbi Hayyim Vital" [Hebrew]. *Alei Sefer* II (1984): 91–134.

_____. *Kabbalat Ha-Ari*. 3 vols. [Hebrew]. Jerusalem: Machon Ben-Zvi, 2008.

Bataille, George. *Theory of Religion*. Brooklyn: Zone Books, 1989.

Ben Shlomo, Joseph. *Torat ha-Elohut shel R. Moshe Cordovero*. Jerusalem: Mossad Bialik, 1965.

Benayahu, Meir. "Customs of the Kabbalists of Safed at Meron" [Hebrew]. *Sefunot* 6 (1962): 9–40.

_____. "Documents from the Geniza Concerning the Business Activities of the Ari" [Hebrew]. In *Sefer Zikkaron le-ha-Rav Yitschak Nissim*, edited by Meir Benayahu, 4:225–253. Jerusalem: Yad Harav Nissim, 1985.

_____. "Rabbi Hayyim Vital in Jerusalem" [Hebrew]. *Sinai* 30 (1952): 65–75.

_____. "Rabbi Moses Yonah, the Ari's disciple, and the first to record His Teachings" [Hebrew]. In *Sefer Zikkaron le-ha-Rav Yitschak Nissim*, edited by Meir Benayahu, 4:225–253. Jerusalem: Yad Harav Nissim, 1985.

_____. "The Revival of Ordination in Safed" [Hebrew]. In *Yitzhak F. Baer Jubilee Volume on the Occasion of his Seventieth Birthday*, edited by S. W. Baron, B. Dinur, S. Ettinger, and I. Halpern, 248–269. Jerusalem: n.p., 1960.

_____. "Spirits of Harm and their Reparation" [Hebrew]. In *Sefer Zikkaron le-ha-Rav Yitschak Nissim*, edited by Meir Benayahu. Jerusalem: Yad Harav Nisim, 1985.

_____. *Sefer Toldot ha-Ari*. Jerusalem: Ben Zvi Institute, 1967.

Bos, Gerrit. "Hayyim Vital's 'Practical Kabbalah and Alchemy': A 17th Century Book of Secrets." *The Journal of Jewish Thought and Philosophy* 4 (1994): 55–112.

Boustan, Ra'anan S. "The Contested Reception of the Story of the Ten Martyrs in Medieval Midrash." In *Envisioning Judaism: Studies in Honor of Peter Schäfer on the Occasion His 70th Birthday*, edited by Ra'anan S. Boustan, Klaus Hermann, Reimund Leicht, Annette Yoshiko Reed, and Giuseppe Veltri, 1:369–394. Tübingen: Mohr Siebeck, 2013.

Brody, Seth. "Human Hands Dwell in Heavenly Heights: Contemplative Ascent and Theurgic Power in Thirteenth-Century Kabbalah." In *Mystics of the Book: Themes Topics and Typologies, edited by Robert A. Herrera*, 123–158. New York: Peter Lang, 1993, 123–158.

_____. "'Open to Me the Gates of Righteousness': The Pursuit of Holiness and Non-Duality in Early Hasidic Teaching." *The Jewish Quarterly Review* 89, nos. 1/2 (1998): 3–44.

Canaani, Y. "Economic Life in Safed and Its Environs in the Sixteenth Century and the First Half of the Seventeenth Century" [Hebrew]. *Zion*, o.s. [pre-1935], 6 (1933–1934): 195–201.

Carlebach, Elisheva. *Divided Souls: Converts from Judaism in Germany, 1500–1750*. New Haven: Yale University Press, 2001.

Chajes, J. H. *Spirit Possession and the Construction of Early Modern Jewish Religiosity*. PhD diss., Yale University, 1999.

_____. "Jewish Exorcism: Early Modern Traditions and Transformations." In *Judaism in Practice: From Middle Ages Through the Early Modern Period*, edited by Lawrence Fine, 386–398. Princeton: Princeton University Press, 2001.

Crapanzano, Victor. "Spirit Possession." In *The Encyclopedia of Religion*, vol. 14., edited by Mircea Eliade et al., New York: Macmillan, 1987.

David, Abraham. "Demographic Changes in the Safed Jewish Community in the Sixteenth Century." In *Occident and Orient: A Tribute to the Memory of A. Sheiber*, edited by R. Dan, 83–93. Leiden: E. J. Brill, 1988.

_____. *To Come to the Land: Immigration and Settlement in Sixteenth-Century Eretz Yisrael.* Translated by Dena Ordan. Tuscaloosa: University of Alabama Press, 1999.

_____. "Safed as a Center for the Re-Settlement of *Anusim*" [Hebrew]. In *Proceedings for the Second International Congress for Research of the Sefardic and Oriental Heritage 1884*, edited by Abraham Haim. Jerusalem: Misgav Yerushalayim, 1991.

_____. "The Spanish Exiles in the Holy Land." In *Moreshet Sepharad: The Sephardi Legacy*, edited by Haim Beinart. Jerusalem: Magnes, 1992.

Deutch, Elliot. *Advaita Vedanta: A Philosophical Reconstruction.* Honolulu: University of Hawaii Press, 1980.

Dcyzkowski, Mark. *The Doctrine of Vibration: An Analysis of Doctrines and Practices of Kashmir Shaivism.* Albany: SUNY Press, 1987.

Donaldson, Terrence. "Proselytes or 'Righteous Gentiles'? The Status of Gentiles in Eschatological Pilgrimage Patterns of Thought." *Journal for the Study of the Pseudepigrapha* 7 (1990): 3–27.

Dudjom Rinpoche, *The Nyingma School of Tibetan Buddhism.* Boston: Wisdom Publications, 1991.

Eilberg-Schwartz, Howard, ed. *People of the Body: Jews and Judaism from an Embodied Perspective.* Albany: SUNY Press, 1992.

Eliade, Mircea. *The Sacred and the Profane: The Nature of Religion.* Translated by Willard R. Trask. San Diego: Harcourt Brace Jovanovich, Inc., 1987.

Elior, Rachel. "The Doctrine of Transmigration in *Galya Raza*." In *Essential Papers on Kabbalah*, edited by Lawrence Fine, 243–269. New York: New York University Press, 1995.

_____. "The Kabbalists of Draa" [Hebrew]. *Pe'amim* 24 (1985): 36–73.

_____. "Lurianic Kabbalah, Sabbateanism, and Hasidism: Historical Sequence, Spiritual Affinity, and Differences of Identity" [Hebrew]. *Mehqarei Yerushalayim* 12 (1997): 379–397.

_____. "Messianic Expectations and Spiritualization of Religious Life in the Sixteenth Century." In *Essential Papers on Jewish Culture in Renaissance and Baroque Italy*, edited by David Ruderman, 283–298. New York: New York University Press, 1992.

_____. "The Metaphorical Relation Between God and Man, and the Significance of the Visionary Reality in Lurianic Kabbalah" [Hebrew]. *Mehqarei Yerushalayim* 10 (1992): 47–57.

_____. *The Paradoxical Ascent to God.* Albany: SUNY Press, 1993.

_____. "Between 'Yesh' and 'Ayin'; the Doctrine of the Zaddik in the Works of Jacob Isaac, the Seer of Lublin." In *Jewish History, Essays in Honor of Chimen Abramsky*, edited by Ada Rapoport-Albert and Steven J. Zipperstein, 393–455. London: Peter Halban, 1988.

Ermarth, Michael. *Wilhelm Dilthey: The Critique of Historical Reason.* Chicago: University of Chicago Press, 1978.

Faierstein, Morris. *Jewish Mystical Autobiographies*. New York: Paulist Press, 1999.

Faur, Jose. *In the Shadow of History: Jews and Conversos at the Dawn of Modernity*, Albany: SUNY Press, 1992.

Feher, Michel, Ramona Naddaff, and Nadia Tazi, eds. *Fragments for a History of the Human Body*. 3 vols. New York: Zone, 1989.

Fenton, Paul B. "The Influence of Sufism on Safed Kabbalah" [Hebrew]. *Mahanayim* 6 (1994): 170–179.

Fine, Lawrence. "Approaching the Study of Jewish Mystical Experience." *Association for Jewish Studies Newsletter* 19 (1977): 10–11.

_____. "Benevolent Spirit Possession in Sixteenth-Century Safed." In *Spirit Possession in Judaism*, edited by Matt Goldish, 101–123. Detroit: Wayne State University Press, 2003.

_____. "Contemplative Death in Jewish Mystical Tradition." In *Sacrificing the Self: Perspectives on Martyrdom and Religion*, edited by Margaret Cormack, 92–106. New York: Oxford University Press, 2002.

_____. "The Contemplative Practice of *Yehudim* in Lurianic Kabbalah." In *Jewish Spirituality: From the Bible through the Middle Ages*, vol. 2, edited by Arthur Green, 64–98. New York: Crossroad, 1987.

_____. "Maggidic Revelation in the Teachings of Isaac Luria." In *Mystics, Philosophers, and Politicians: Essays in Jewish Intellectual History in Honor of Alexander Altmann*, edited by Jehuda Reinharz and Daniel Swetschinski, with the collaboration of Kalman P. Bland, 141–157. Durham: Duke University Press, 1982.

_____. "Purifying the Body in the Name of the Soul: The Problem of the Body in Sixteenth-Century Kabbalah." In *People of the Body: Jews and Judaism from an Embodied Perspective*, edited by Howard Eilberg-Schwartz, 117–142. Albany: State University of New York Press, 1992.

_____. "Recitation of Mishnah as a Vehicle for Mystical Inspiration: A Contemplative Technique Taught by Hayyim Vital." *Revue des etudes juives* 141, nos. 1–2 (1982): 183–199.

_____. "The Study of Torah as a Theurgic rite in Lurianic Kabbalah." In *Approaches to Judaism in Medieval Times*, vol. 3, edited by David R. Blumenthal, 29–40. Atlanta: Scholars Press, 1988.

_____, ed. *Essential Papers on Kabbalah*. New York: New York University Press, 1995.

_____, trans. and ed. *Safed Spirituality: Rules of Mystical Piety, the Beginning of Wisdom*. New York: Paulist Press, 1984.

_____. *Physician of the Soul, Healer of the Cosmos: Isaac Luria and His Kabbalistic Fellowship*. Stanford: Stanford University Press, 2003.

Fishbane, Eitan P. "A Chariot for the Shekhinah: Identity and the Ideal Life in Sixteenth-Century Kabbalah." *Journal of Religious Ethics* 37, no. 3 (2009): 385–418.

_____. *As Light Before Dawn: The Inner World of a Medieval Kabbalist*. Stanford: Stanford University Press, 2009.

_____. "Perceptions of Greatness: Constructions of the Holy Man in *Shivḥei ha-Ari*." *Kabbalah: Journal for the Study of Jewish Mystical Texts* 27 (2012): 195–221.

Fishbane, Michael. *The Kiss of God: Spiritual and Mystical Death in Judaism*. Seattle: University of Washington Press, 1994.

Garb, Jonathan. *Shamanic Trance in Modern Kabbalah*. Chicago: University of Chicago Press, 2011.

_____. *Yearnings of the Soul: Psychological Thought in Modern Kabbalah*. Chicago: University of Chicago Press, 2015.

Gager, John G. "Body-Symbols and Social Reality: Resurrection, Incarnation, and Asceticism in Early Christianity." *Religion* 12 (1982): 345–363.

Gamlieli, Devorah bat-David. *Psychoanalysis and Kabbala: The Masculine and Feminine in Lurianic Kabbala*. Los Angeles: Cherub Press, 2006.

Geary, Patrick. *Living With the Dead in the Middle Ages*. Ithaca: Cornell University Press, 1994.

Giller, Pinhas. "The Common Religion of Safed." *Conservative Judaism* 55, no. 2 (2003): 24–37.

_____. *Reading the Zohar: The Sacred Text of the Kabbalah*. New York: Oxford University Press, 2001.

Ginsburg, Elliot K. *The Sabbath in Classical Kabbalah*. Albany: SUNY Press, 1989.

Givens, Terry L. *When the Soul Had Wings: Pre-mortal Existence in Western Thought*. New York: Oxford University Press, 2010.

Goldish, Matt, ed. *Spirit Possession in Judaism: Cases and Contexts from the Middle Ages to the Present*. Detroit: Wayne State University Press, 2003.

Green, Arthur. *Keter: The Crown of God in Early Jewish Mysticism*. Princeton: Princeton University Press, 1997.

_____. *Menachem Nachum of Chernobyl*. New York: Paulist Press, 1982.

_____. *Tormented Master: A Life of Rabbi Nahman of Bratzlav*. Tuscaloosa: University of Alabama Press, 1979.

_____. "The Zaddiq as Axis Mundi in Later Judaism." *Journal of the American Academy of Religion* 45, no. 3 (1977): 327–347. Reprinted in *Essential Papers in Kabbalah*, edited by Lawrence Fine, 291–314. New York: New York University Press, 1995.

_____. "The Zohar: Jewish Mysticism in Medieval Spain." In *Essential Papers on Kabbalah*, edited by Lawrence Fine, 27–66. New York: New York University Press, 1995.

Hallamish, Moshe. *An Introduction to the Kabbalah*. Albany: SUNY Press, 1999.

Hellner-Eshed, Melila. "Transmigration of Souls in the Kabbalistic Writings of Rabbi David Ibn Zimra" [Hebrew]. *Pe'amim* 43 (1980): 16–50.

_____. *Seekers of the Face: Secrets of the Idra Rabba (the Great Assembly) of the Zohar*. Stanford: Stanford University Press, 2021.

Holecek, Andrew. *Dream Yoga*. Boulder: Sounds True, 2016.

Hovav-Machboob, Raza Lea. "The Ari's Doctrine of Reincarnation." DHL thesis, The Jewish Theological Seminary of America, 1983.

Idel, Moshe. "On the Concept of Zimzum in Kabbalah and Its Research." [Hebrew]. *Jerusalem Studies in Jewish Thought* 10 (1992) 59–112.

_____. *Golem: Jewish Magical and Mystical Traditions on the Artificial Anthropoid*. Albany: SUNY Press, 1990.

_____. *Hasidism: Between Ecstasy and Magic*. Albany: SUNY Press, 1995.

_____. *Kabbalah: New Perspectives*. New Haven: Yale University Press, 1988.

_____. *Enchanted Chains: Techniques and Rituals in Jewish Mysticism*. Los Angeles: Cherub Press, 2005.

_____. *Kabbalah and Eros*. New Haven: Yale University Press, 2005.

_____. *Messianic Mystics*. New Haven: Yale University Press, 1998.

_____. *The Mystical Experience of Abraham Abulafia.* Translated by Jonathan Chipman. Albany: SUNY Press, 1988.

_____. "'One from a Town, Two From a Clan': The Diffusion of Lurianic Kabbala and Sabbateanism: A Re-Examination." *Jewish History* 7, no. 2 (Fall 1993): 79–104.

_____. "On Mobility, Individuals and Groups: Prolegomenon for a Sociological Approach to Sixteenth-Century Safed." *Kabbalah: Journal for the Study of Jewish Mystical Texts* 3 (1998): 145–173.

_____. "Particularism and Universalism in Kabbalah: 1480–1650." In *Essential Papers on Jewish Culture in Renaissance and Baroque Italy*, edited by David Ruderman, 324–344. New York: New York University Press, 1992.

_____. "Sexual Metaphors and Praxis in the Kabbalah." In *The Jewish Family: Metaphor and Memory*, edited by David Charles Kraemer, 197–224. Oxford: Oxford University Press, 1989.

_____. "Some Concepts of Time and History in Kabbalah." In *Jewish History and Jewish Memory: Essays in Honor of Yosef Hayim Yerushalmi*, edited by Elisheva Carlebach, John M. Efron, and David N. Meyers, 153–188. Hanover: University Press of New England for Brandeis University Press, 1998.

_____. *Studies in Ecstatic Kabbalah.* Albany: SUNY Press, 1988.

Irwin, Lee. *Reincarnation in America: An Esoteric History.* Lanham: Rowman and Littlefield, 2017.

Jacobs, Louis. *Jewish Mystical Testimonies.* New York: Schocken Books, 1977.

Jacobson, Yoram. "The Feminine Aspect in Lurianic Kabbalah." In *Major Trends: Fifty Years After*, edited by Peter Schafer and Joseph Dan. Tubingen: Mohr, 1993.

James, George. *Interpreting Religion: The Phenomenological Approaches of Pierre Daniël Chantepie de la Saussaye, W. Brede Kristensen, and Gerardus van der Leeuw.* Washington: Catholic University of America Press, 1995.

James, William. *Varieties of Mystical Experience.* New York: Penguin, 1982.

Jee, Lakshman. *Kashmir Shaivism: The Secret Supreme.* Albany: SUNY Press, 1988.

Kallus, Menachem. "Pneumatic Mystical Possession and the Eschatology of the Soul in Lurianic Kabbalah." In *Spirit Possession in Judaism*, edited by Matt Goldish, 159–185. Detroit: Wayne State University Press, 2003.

_____. "The Relationship of the Baal Shem Tov to the Practice of Lurianic Kavvanot in Light of His Comments on the *Siddur Rashkov*." *Kabbalah: Journal for the Study of Jewish Mystical Texts* 2 (1997) 151–168.

_____. *The Theurgy of Prayer in Lurianic Kabbalah.* PhD. diss., Hebrew University, 2002.

Kaplan, Aryeh. *Meditation and Kabbalah.* York Beach: Weiser, 1982.

Katz, Steven T. "Language, Epistemology, Mysticism." In *Mysticism and Philosophical Analysis*, edited by Steven Katz, 22–74. New York, Oxford University Press, 1978.

_____. "The Conservative Character of Mystical Experience." In *Mysticism and Religious Traditions*, edited by Steven Katz, 3–60. New York: Oxford University Press, 1983.

Khenpo, Nyoshul. *A Marvelous Garland of Rare Gems: Biographies of Masters of Awareness in the Dzogchen Lineage.* Junction City: Padma Publishing, 2005.

Kimelman, Reuven. *Lekha Dodi ve-Kabbalat Shabbat: Their Mystical Meaning* [Hebrew]. Jerusalem: Magnus, 2003.

Klein, Eliyahu. *The Kabbalah of Creation: The Mysticism of Isaac Luria, Founder of Modern Kabbalah.* Berkeley: North Atlantic Books, 2005.

Krassen, Miles. *Uniter of Heaven and Earth: Rabbi Meshullam Feibush Heller of Zbarazh and the Rise of Hasidism in Eastern Galicia*. Albany: SUNY Press, 1998.

Kristensen, W. Brede. *The Meaning of Religion: Lectures in the Phenomenology of Religion*. Translated by John B. Carman. The Haugue: Martinus Nijhoff, 1960.

Law, Jane Marie, ed. *Religious Reflections on the Human Body*. Bloomington: Indiana University Press, 1995.

Liebes, Yehuda. "The Messiah of the Zohar: Concerning the Messianic Image of R. Shimon bar Yohai." In *Ha-ra'ayon ha-Meshihi be-Yisrael* [The Messianic Idea in Jewish Thought: A Study Conference in Honour of the Eightieth Birthday of Gershom Scholem] [Hebrew]. Jerusalem: Israel Academy of Sciences and Humanities, 1982. English translation in idem, *Studies in the Zohar* (see below)

_____. "Myth vs. Symbol in the Zohar and in Lurianic Kabbalah." In *Essential Papers on Kabbalah*, edited by Lawrence Fine, 212–242. New York: New York University Press, 1995.

_____. "New Directions in the Study of Kabbalah" [Hebrew]. *Pe'amim* 50 (1992): 150–170.

_____. "Sabbath Meal Songs Established by the Holy Ari" [Hebrew]. *Molad* 4 (1972): 540–555.

_____. *Studies in Jewish Myth and Jewish Messianism*. Translated by Batya Stein. Albany: SUNY Press, 1993.

_____. *Studies in the Zohar*. Translated by Arnold Schwartz, Stephanie Nakache, and Penina Peli. Albany: SUNY Press, 1993.

_____. "'Two Young Roes of a Doe': The Secret Sermon of Isaac Luria Before His Death" [Hebrew]. *Mehkarei Yerushalayim* 10 (1992): 113–169.

_____. "Zohar and Eros" [Hebrew]. *'Alpayyim* 9 (1994): 67–119.

_____. *Perakim be-Milon Sefer ha-Zohar* [Hebrew]. PhD diss., Hebrew University, 1976.

Liebes, Yehudah, and Rachel Elior, eds. *Lurianic Kabbalah: Proceedings of the Fourth International Conference on the History of Jewish Mysticism*. Jerusalem Studies in Jewish Thought 10 [Hebrew]. Jerusalem: Magnes Press, 1992.

Magid, Shaul. "Conjugal Union, Mourning, and Talmud Torah in R. Isaac Luria's *Tikkun Hazot*." *Da'at* 36 (1996): xvii–xlv.

_____. "From Theosophy to Midrash: Lurianic Exegesis and the Garden of Eden." *Association for Jewish Studies Review* 22 (1997): 37–75.

_____. "The Divine/Human Messiah and Religious Deviance: Rethinking Chabad Messianism." In *Rethinking the Messianic Idea in Judaism: Historical, Philosophical and Literary Perspectives*, edited by Michael L. Morgan and Steven Weitzman, 316–351. Bloomington: Indiana University Press, 2014.

_____. "Ethics Disentangled from the Law: Incarnation, the Universal, and Hasidic Ethics." *Kabbala* 15 (2005): 31–76.

_____. *Hasidism on the Margin*. Madison: University of Wisconsin Press, 2004.

_____. "Origin and the Overcoming of the Beginning: *Zimzum* as a Trope of Reading in Post-Lurianic Kabbalah." In *Beginning/Again: Toward a Hermeneutic of Jewish Texts*, edited by Shaul Magid and Aryeh Cohen. New York: Seven Bridges, 2002.

_____. "Lurianic Kabbalah and Its Literary Form: Myth, Fiction, History." *Prooftexts* 29 (2009): 362–397.

_____. *From Metaphysics to Midrash: Myth, History, and the Interpretation of Scripture in Lurianic Kabbalah*. Bloomington: Indiana University Press, 2008.

Magli, Patrizia. "The Face and the Soul." In *Fragments for a History of the Human Body*, 3 vols., edited by Michel Feher, with Romona Naddaff and Nadia Tazi, 86–127. New York: Zone, 1989.

Matt, Daniel C. "Ayin: The Concept of Nothingness in Jewish Mysticism." In *Essential Papers on Kabbalah*, edited by Lawrence Fine, 67–108. New York: New York University Press, 1995.

_____. "'New Ancient Words': The Aura of Secrecy in the Zohar." In *Gershom Scholem's "Major Trends in Jewish Mysticism" Fifty Years After: Proceedings of the Sixth International Conference on the History of Jewish Mysticism*, edited by Peter Schafer and Joseph Dan, 181–207. Tubingen: Mohr, 1993.

_____. "The Mystic and the Mitzwot," In *Jewish Spirituality: From Biblical Times through the Middle Ages*, edited by Arthur Green, 367–404. New York: Crossroad, 1986.

Meroz, Ronit. "Early Lurianic Compositions" [Hebrew]. In *Massuot: Studies in Kabbalistic Literature and Jewish Philosophy in Memeory of Ephraim Gottlieb*, edited by Amos Goldreich and Michal Oron, 327–330. Jerusalem: Mossad Bialik, 1994.

_____. "Faithful Transmissions Versus Innovation: Luria and His Disciples." In *Gershom Scholem's "Major Trends in Jewish Mysticism" Fifty Years After: Proceedings of the Sixth International Conference on the History of Jewish Mysticism*, edited by Peter Schafer and Joseph Dan, 257–274. Tubingen: Mohr Siebeck, 1993.

_____. "Selections from Ephraim Penzieri: Luria's Sermon in Jerusalem and the Kavvanah on Eating Food" [Hebrew]. *Mehqarei Yerushalayim* 10 (1992): 211–257.

_____. "Torat ha-Ge'eulah be-Kabbalat ha-Ari" [The Teachings of Redemption in Lurianic Kabbalah] [Hebrew]. PhD. diss., Hebrew University, Jerusalem, 1988.

Mopsik, Charles. *Sex of the Soul: The Vicissitudes of Sexual Difference in Kabbalah*. Los Angeles: Cherub Press, 2005.

Mottolese, Maurizio. *Bodily Rituals in Jewish Mysticism: The Intensification of Cultic Hand Gestures by Medieval Kabbalists*. Los Angeles: Cherub Press, 2016.

Muktananda, Swami. *Play of Consciousness*. South Fallsburg: SYDA Foundation, 1978.

_____. *Introduction to Kashmir Shaivism*. Oakland: SYDA Foundation, 1975.

Muller-Ortega, Paul. *The Triadic Heart of Shiva: Kaula Tantricism of Abhinavagupta in the Nondual Shaivism of Kashmir*. Albany: SUNY Press, 1989.

Nikhilinanda, Swami. *Vedantasara or the Essence of Vedanta of Sadananda Yogindra*. Calcutta: Advaita Ashrama, 1968.

Obeyesekere, Gananath. *Imagining Karma: Ethical Transformation in Ameridian, Buddhist, and Greek Rebirth*. Berkeley: University of California Press, 2002.

Ogren, Brian. *Renaissance and Rebirth: Reincarnation in Early Modern Italian Kabbalah*. Leiden and Boston: Brill, 2009.

Olson, Carl. *Theory and Method in the Study of Religion*. Belmont: Thompson Wadsworth, 2003.

Oron, Michal. "Lines of Influence in the Doctrine of the Soul and Reincarnation in Thirteenth-Century Kabbala and the Worlds of R. Todros Abulafia" [Hebrew]. In *Studies in Jewish Thought*, edited by Sara O. Heller-Wilensky and Moshe Idel (Jerusalem, 1989), 277–290.

Pachter, Mordechai. "The Concept of Devekut in the Homiletical Ethical Writings of 16th Century Safed." In *Studies in Medieval Jewish History and Literature*, vol., 2, edited by Isadore Twersky, 171–230 Cambridge, MA.: Harvard University Press, 1984.

_____. "The Homiletic Eulogy by R. Samuel Uceda upon the Death of the Ari" [Hebrew]. In *Matsfunot Tsfat*, 39–68. Jerusalem: Merkaz Zalman Shazar, 1994.

_____. "Kabbalistic Ethical Literature in Sixteenth-Century Safed." In *Studies in Jewish History, Thought, and Culture*, vol., 3, edited by Joseph Dan, 158–178. Westport: Praeger, 1994.

_____. "Clarifying the Terms *Katnut* and *Gadlut* in the Kabbala of the Ari and a History of Its Understanding in Hasidism" [Hebrew]. *Mekharei Yerushalayim* 10 (1992): 171–210.

Pinson, Dov Ber. *Reincarnation and Judaism: The Journey of the Soul*. Northvale: Jason Aronson, 1999.

Plantinga, Theodore. *Historical Understanding in the Thought of Wilhelm Dilthey*. New York: Edwin Mellen Press, 1992.

Ray, Reginald. *Secrets of the Vajra World*. Boston: Shambhala Press, 2001.

Ripsman Eylon, Dina. *Reincarnation in Jewish Mysticism and Gnosticism*. Lewiston: Edwin Mellon, 2003.

Rinpoche, Sogyal. *The Tibetan Book of Living and Dying*. San Francisco: HarperOne, 1992.

Rothberg, Donald. "Contemporary Epistemology and the Study of Mysticism." In *On the Problem of Pure Consciousness: Mysticism and Philosophy*, edited by Robert Forman, 163–210. New York: Oxford University Press, 1997.

Ruderman, David. *Kabbalah, Magic, and Science: The Cultural Universe of a Sixteenth-Century Jewish Physician*. Cambridge, MA: Harvard University Press, 1988.

Schatz Uffenheimer, Rivka. *Hasidism as Mysticism: Quietistic Elements in Eighteenth-Century Hasidic Thought*. Translated by Jonathan Chipman. Princeton: Princeton University Press; Jerusalem: Magnes Press, Hebrew University, 1993.

Scholem, Gershom. "The Authentic Kabbalistic Writings of Isaac Luria" [Hebrew]. *Qiryat Sefer* 19 (1943): 184–199.

_____. "The Document on Solidarity of Luria's Disciples" [Hebrew]. *Zion* 5 (1940): 133–160.

_____. *Kabbalah*. Jerusalem: Keter Press, 1974.

_____. *Major Trends in Jewish Mysticism*. Jerusalem: Schocken Publishing House, 1941; 3rd rev. ed. New York: Schocken Books, 1954.

_____. *On the Kabbalah and Its Symbolism*. Translated by Ralph Manheim. New York: Schocken Books, 1965.

_____. *On the Mystical Shape of the Godhead: Basic Concepts in the Kabbalah*. Translated by Joachim Neugroschel. Edited by Jonathan Chipman. New York: Schocken Books, 1991.

_____. *Origins of the Kabbalah*. Philadelphia: Jewish Publication Society, 1987.

_____. "Physiogonomy of the Face" [Hebrew]. In *Sefer Assaf*, edited by Umberto Cassuto, 459–495. Jerusalem: Mossad ha-Rav Kook, 1952–1953.

_____. *Shabbatai Sevi: The Mystical Messiah*. Princeton: Princeton University Press, 1973.

_____. "Towards the Study of Transmigration in Thirteenth-Century Kabbalah" [Hebrew]. *Tarbiz* 16 (1944): 135–150.

Sharma, Arvind. *Sleep as a State of Consciousness in Advaita Vedanta*. Albany: SUNY Press, 2004.

Sharma, Ramesh Kumar. "Dreamless Sleep and Some Related Philosophical Issues." *Philosophy East and West* 51, no. 2 (April 2001): 210–231.

Sharot, Stephen. *Messianism, Mysticism, and Magic: A Sociological Analysis of Jewish Religious Movements*. Chapel Hill: University of North Carolina Press, 1982.

Shekalim, Rami. *Torat Ha-Nefesh ve-Ha-Gilgul be-Reshit ha-Kabbala*. Tel Aviv: Rubin Moss, 1998.

Sogyal Rinpoche. *The Tibetan Book of Living and Dying*. San Francisco: Harper, 1994.

Starr, Karen E. *Repair of the Soul: Metaphors of Transformation in Jewish Mysticism and Psychoanalysis*. New York: Routledge, 2008.

Thondup, Thulku. *Masters of Meditation and Miracles*. Boston: Shambhala, 1996.

Thurman, Robert, trans. *Tibetan Book of the Dead*. New York: Bantam Books, 1993.

Tishby, Isaiah. "Gnostic Doctrines in Sixteenth-Century Jewish Mysticism." *Journal of Jewish Studies* 6 (1955): 146–152.

_____. *Torat ha-Ra' ve-ha-Qelippah be-Kabbalat ha-Ari*. Jerusalem: Akademon, 1942; rev. ed. Jerusalem: Magnes Press, 1982.

_____. *Mishnat HaZohar* [Hebrew]. 2 vols. Jerusalem: Mosad Bialek, 1971

Twersky, Isadore. "Talmudist, Philosophers, Kabbalists: The Quest for Spirituality in the Sixteenth Century." In *Jewish Thought in the Sixteenth Century*, edited by Bernard Cooperman, 431–459. Cambridge, MA: Harvard University Press, 1983.

Van der Leeuw, Gerardus. *Religion in Essence and Manifestation: A Study in Phenomenology*. 2 vols. Translated by J. E. Turner. New York: Harper & Row, 1963.

Verman, Mark. "Reincarnation and Theodicy: Traversing Philosophy, Psychology, and Mysticism." In *Be'erot Yitzhak: Studies in Memory of Isadore Twersky*. Cambridge, MA: Harvard University Center for Jewish Studies, 2005.

Waardenburg, Jacques. *Reflections on the Study of Religion: Including an Essay on the Work of Gerardus van der Leeuw*. The Hague: Mouton Publishers, 1978.

Wallis, Christopher. *Tantra Illuminated*. Petaluma: Mattamayura Press, 2013.

Wangyal Rinpoche, Tenzin. *The Tibetan Yogas of Dream and Sleep*. Ithaca: Snow Lion, 1998.

Weber, Max. *Collected Methodological Writings*. Edited by Hans Henrik Bruun and Sam Whimster. Translated by Hans Henrik Bruun. New York: Routledge, 2012.

Werblowsky, R. J. Zwi. *Joseph Karo, Lawyer and Mystic*. Oxford: Oxford University Press, 1962.

Wiener, Aharon. *The Prophet Elijah in the Development of Judaism: A Depth-Psychology Study*. Littman Library of Jewish Civilization. Boston: Routledge & K. Paul, 1978.

Wolfson, Elliot R. *Along the Path: Studies in Kabbalistic Myth, Symbolism, and Hermeneutics*. Albany: SUNY Press, 1995.

_____. *Circle in the Square: Studies in the Use of Gender in Kabbalistic Symbolism*. Albany: SUNY Press, 1995.

_____. "Circumcision, Vision of God, and Textual Interpretation: From Midrashic Trope to Mystical Symbol." In *Circle in the Square: Studies in the Use of Gender in Kabbalistic Symbolism*, edited by Elliot Wolfson, 29–48. Albany: SUNY Press, 1995.

_____. *A Dream Interpreted Within a Dream: Oneiropoesis and the Prism of Imagination*. New York: Zone Books, 2011.

_____. "Images of God's Feet: Some Observations on the Divine Body in Judaism." In *People of the Body: Jews and Judaism from an Embodied Perspective*, edited by Howard Eilberg-Schwartz, 143–183. Albany: SUNY Press, 1992.

_____. "The Influence of Luria on the Shelah" [Hebrew]. *Mehqarei Yerushalayim* 10 (1992): 423–448.

_____. *Through a Speculum That Shines: Vision and Imagination in Medieval Jewish Mysticism*. Princeton: Princeton University Press, 1994.

_____. "Weeping, Death, and Spiritual Ascent in Sixteenth Century Jewish Mysticism." In *Death, Ecstasy and Other Worldly Journeys*, edited by John J. Collins and Michael A. Fishbane, 209–247. Albany: State University of New York Press, 1995.

_____. "The Body in the Text: A Kabbalistic Theory of Embodiment." *The Jewish Quarterly Review* 95, no. 3 (2005): 479–500.

Yisraeli, Oded. *The Interpretation of Secrets and the Secrets of Interpretation: Midrashic and Hermeneutic Strategies in Sabba de-Mishpatim of the Zohar* [Hebrew]. Los Angeles: Cherub Press, 2005.

Zack, Bracha. *Be-Sha'arei ha-Kabbalah shel R. Moshe Cordovero* [Hebrew]. Jerusalem: Ben Gurion University Press, 1995.

Index

Lightning Source UK Ltd.
Milton Keynes UK
UKHW022139160921
390714UK00001B/12